Teaching Practice Handbook

Roger Gower, Diane Phillips, Steve Walters

NEW EDITION

Heinemann English Language Teaching
A division of Heinemann Publishers (Oxford) Ltd
Halley Court, Jordan Hill, Oxford OX2 8EJ

OXFORD MADRID ATHENS PARIS FLORENCE
PRAGUE SÃO PAULO CHICAGO MELBOURNE
AUCKLAND SINGAPORE TOKYO IBADAN
GABORONE JOHANNESBURG PORTSMOUTH (NH)

ISBN 0 435 24059 5

Designed by Mike Brain

Cover photograph by Gareth Boden
Illustrations by Nick Hardcastle

Thanks to staff and students at the Bell College, Saffron Walden,
especially Pat Lodge, David Manlow, Lisa Shipp, Rosy Delia,
Alexander Dmitruk and Hajime Komaba.

The authors and publishers would like to thank the following for
permission to reproduce their material:

Heinemann ELT © Adrian Underhill 1994 for the phonemic chart
on p 158; Jill Cosh for the problem-solving activity on p 108; Nelson
ELT for the extract from *Signature Intermediate* on p 93

Printed and bound in Great Britain by The Bath Press

95 96 97 98 99 10 9 8 7 6 5 4 3 2 1

Contents

Introduction

1 What is teaching practice (or TP)?

Teaching practice can be described as a situation in which a teacher in training teaches a group of students under supervision. The aim is usually to improve the trainees' teaching skills and develop their awareness of how students learn. TP can be set up in many ways. For example, you, the trainee, may be:

- one of a group of trainees teaching 'volunteer' students in a class especially arranged for TP;
- an 'apprentice', attached to an experienced teacher, and teaching some of that teacher's lessons;
- an untrained and/or inexperienced teacher working with your own class of students and learning on the job.

A TP 'lesson' can range from informal practice of a particular technique, perhaps with other trainees acting as students, to a formally assessed lesson.

The assumptions behind this book are that TP can take place in an English-speaking country or in a country where the first language is not English. The trainees can be native speakers of English or non-native speakers and the classes can be multilingual or monolingual. Although much of the methodology outlined could be applicable to the teaching of children it is assumed that the students are adults or teenagers.

2 Assumptions about learning

Learning a language is essentially different from learning many 'school' subjects where students are required to memorize and apply factual information. Certainly there is a body of knowledge to be acquired about language – facts about grammar, vocabulary and pronunciation – and there is a place for conscious 'learning'. However, acquiring this knowledge is only part of what a successful language learner does.

Language learning is also concerned with becoming proficient in certain skills – skills which are perfected through practice. It is common to think of there being four language skills: *listening*, *reading*, *speaking* and *writing*. They are often grouped in pairs under the headings *receptive* (listening and reading) and *productive* (speaking and writing). It can be useful to divide the skills up in this way as they share features which affect the way they are approached in the classroom.

The receptive skills are concerned with the understanding of anything written or spoken – from a short greeting such as *Good morning* to long pieces of writing such as newspaper articles or extracts from novels. Listening or reading texts can be *authentic* (produced by native speakers primarily for native speakers) or constructed especially for the language classroom.

When the productive skills of speaking or writing are being practised the main focus at any one time may be on getting things right (*accuracy*), or on getting the meaning across (fluent communication or *fluency*). Often different types of activities are used, depending on the main emphasis, and it is important that both teacher and students are aware of the aim and focus of the activity.

However, although we can make the division into receptive and productive skills, to have a conversation we need to listen as well as speak; to have a correspondence we need to read as well as write. In real life we rarely use our skills separately – they are usually closely integrated.

Increasingly the importance of another set of skills is being stressed – that of study skills, or skills concerned with 'learning how to learn'. Emphasis is being put on helping learners to take responsibility for their own learning, to be less dependent on the teacher, to extend their learning beyond the classroom and beyond the course. Many students also welcome help with techniques needed to study other school and university subjects in English: listening and note-taking, writing from notes, essay writing, etc.

Another important consideration is that people can be successful language learners in a number of different ways. Some people achieve success through conscious studying: by analysing and memorizing. Others are able to 'acquire' or pick up language almost unconsciously when they are in an environment where the language is used. In the classroom different types of practice activities can help different individual students: some benefit from repetition exercises while others respond best to more creative or challenging tasks. Whatever approach is used it is important that motivation is maintained. It is obviously true that the most effective learning takes place when motivation is high and the teacher takes into account how the students like to learn.

3 The aims of this book

The *Teaching Practice Handbook* sets out:

- to increase awareness of the many aspects of the TP situation (mainly at a pre-service or an early in-service level);
- to provide some basic guidelines for TP and practical information to help you get the most out of it;
- to clarify the reasoning behind many of the skills and techniques needed and to provide activities to help and improve them.

The focus is not so much on the language and the language skills being taught but on the teaching skills and techniques where the teacher is required to direct or orchestrate the learning activities of the class, largely from 'up-front'. There are other ways of organizing language learning, for example through self-access systems, which are outside the scope of most TP situations and so outside the scope of this book.

The danger of a book of this kind, where what is talked about is *why* certain things are done and *how* they can be done most effectively, is to sound as if there are no other ways of doing them. It should be said, then, that the rationale and practices given here are the subject of constant discussion and revision in most teacher-training establishments. The principles which the *Teaching Practice Handbook* is based on form the mainstream of EFL teaching at the present time and the techniques and procedures are those to be found on many early training courses. It ought to be said, too, that because the book focuses on the teacher it runs the risk of suggesting that the EFL classroom is more teacher-centred that it need be. You should reject anything that you feel works against the best interests of the learners and a learner-centred classroom. Wherever possible try to assess what is going on in the classroom in terms of *What are the students learning?* rather than *What is the teacher teaching?*

4 How to use this book

The *Teaching Practice Handbook* is not a coursebook. After you have read this introduction and Chapter 1, *Approaching teaching practice,* there is no need to read any one section before any of the others. It is a handbook and as such it is intended to be dipped into. In order to find what you need you can refer to the contents list and to the index.

Although we aim to keep the use of jargon to a minimum there are certain words and expressions which are commonly used when talking about teaching EFL and your teaching practice supervisor may use some of them. When you come across an unfamiliar term you will find the glossary on pp209–12 helpful. Alternatively, if you want to check how familiar you are with these common terms before you start the course you can try the task at the end of this introduction.

How the book is used in relation to a course will depend very much on the overall structure of the course and on individual trainers. Your trainers may ask you to read a section before an input session or they may ask you to do some of the practice tasks (see below). Although the chapter on lesson planning comes towards the end of the book you will probably want to refer to it throughout the period of TP. As TP proceeds and you deal with the different elements that make up a lesson, and a series of lessons, so the process of planning lessons will become clearer.

One way of using the book might be as follows. When planning a TP lesson decide which areas you are going to concentrate on and read the appropriate section. After the lesson, with the help of your supervisor, try to identify areas that need improvement and see if there are any tasks at the end of the section that you can do alone or with other trainees. The *Teaching Practice Handbook* can also be used, rather like a car manual, to help you put things right when they go wrong.

There are a number of tasks at the end of each chapter/section which are linked to points in that section or chapter. Some of these are *observation tasks* that you can use when observing other teachers or other trainees. Observing a peer and giving feedback afterwards should be helpful both to the person teaching and to the person observing. Some of the exercises are designed to be used in a 'peer teaching' situation. This involves one of you teaching the other trainees who are either pretending to be students or just being themselves. It is particularly useful for the isolation and practice of particular teaching techniques (sometimes called *microteaching*). In order for these activities to be successful it is important for everyone to 'play the game'. It can be a waste of time if everyone collapses with laughter every time they pretend to be students.

The tasks are coded as follows:

 can be done by an individual

 pairwork with colleague

 groupwork

 to be used in a microteaching situation

 an observation task

Even if you don't do all the exercises it is a good idea to read them when they are referred to and think about how they might work.

Task

Aim
To become familiar with some of the jargon used in English language teaching.

Procedure
Match definitions **a–f** with the words and expressions on the right.

a to draw out students' knowledge by asking questions and guiding them towards answering questions;

b to call on an individual by name;

c to repeat what the learner has just said;

d to reduce a word, usually when it is combined with another word: for example, *I am* into *I'm*, *should have* into *should've*;

e to listen to one's own or another's performance to compare what is said or done with what was intended;

f to focus on language or topics which are of interest to individual student(s) or which are relevant to individual students' situations.

to nominate

to contract

to echo

to personalize

to elicit

to monitor

Comment
1 You may like to try this exercise in pairs.
2 If the jargon is very new to you, you can read through the glossary on pp209–12 and then use this exercise to see how much you have remembered.
3 How much jargon do you already use? When is it useful? Is it always necessary?

Further reading

Krashen, S. 1991 *Language Acquisition and Language Education* (Prentice Hall International)

Lightbown, P. and Spada, N. 1993 *How Languages are Learned* (OUP)

Littlewood, W. 1984 *Foreign and Second Language Learning* (CUP)

Medgyes, P. 1994 *The Non-Native Teacher* (Prentice Hall International)

Richards, J. and Rodgers, T. 1986 *Approaches and Methods in Language Teaching* (CUP)

Stevick, E. 1982 *Teaching and Learning Languages* (CUP)

Chapter 1 Approaching teaching practice

This chapter discusses the purpose of teaching practice (TP). It also examines the roles played in TP by you the trainee, by your supervisor, the other teachers and your fellow trainees. We also look at ways to get the maximum benefit from your own lessons and feedback sessions, and from those of your fellow trainees.

1 The role of TP on a teacher training course

Why have teaching practice on a course?

You can learn a lot *about* teaching by discussing it and talking about materials and techniques but, like most skills, including using a language effectively, you can't really learn it without doing it. It is one thing to describe what you are going to do in a lesson, when you might be allowed to talk without interruption; it is quite another to carry it out when it includes a group of people who expect to contribute to the lesson and perhaps influence its progress. Before you teach students who expect you to be able to do your job, there are obviously huge benefits in being able to try things out beforehand in a supportive atmosphere, such as TP should provide.

What does TP practise?

It normally focuses on four areas:
1 sensitivity to problems of language use for learners;
2 sensitivity to how learners learn, the skills they need, the strategies they employ and the problems they have;
3 classroom management skills;
4 teaching techniques.

What are the objectives of TP?

Depending on the overall aims of a particular course and the stage that TP has reached, its objectives would normally be one or more of the following:

- to allow you to simulate or approach the real teaching situation under sympathetic supervision;
- to provide you with an opportunity to try out techniques;
- to provide an arena for assessment;
- to provide you with an opportunity to have your teaching evaluated and constructively criticized;

- to provide an opportunity for you to get used to being observed (as observation often forms part of teacher appraisal in many teaching institutions);
- to encourage development of criteria for self-evaluation and self-awareness;
- to create a situation of gradually increased freedom so that you become increasingly more independent – able to make decisions about what you teach and how you teach;
- to help you develop your own teaching style;
- to provide you with exposure to real learners, their learning problems and the factors which influence their learning;
- to expose you to students at a range of levels and to develop an understanding of the differences of approach required;
- to develop your sense of responsibility for your students.

Of course TP should also provide genuine learning for the students involved.

How is what to do on TP decided?

Supervisors or tutors will probably give a lot of support and help initially, both with what to teach and with techniques and materials to use. This detailed guidance is often gradually withdrawn as trainees' ability increases in identifying the students' language needs and in preparing activities and materials to satisfy them.

The aim of a lesson should initially be identified for you. Some supervisors like to give out beforehand a timetable or a syllabus of what you are to teach and how your lessons fit in with the students' timetable and that of other teachers or trainees. Or you and your supervisor may discuss and decide the timetable together – especially if you are the class's main teacher. The syllabus should ideally reflect both your needs and the students' needs.

Shouldn't TP be based around the needs of the trainees?

In some ways this is so and most courses ensure that a wide range of teaching skills are worked at. But the most effective way of meeting those needs is by making TP reflect the real situation as closely as possible: this can only mean basing it, as far as possible, on what the students need to learn.

How can particular skills and techniques be practised?

In many of the following chapters there are references to a number of tasks. They don't form a complete programme and no doubt you and your supervisor will be able to think of others. Some are intended simply to provoke discussion, others are of the 'get up and do it' type and involve peer teaching – where one trainee teaches and the other trainees act as students.

Does this mean that things have to be got right before going into TP?

No. TP is a time for experiment. It is one of the few opportunities you may ever have for trying out a new idea and having one or more critical but supportive observers. When anything is tried out for the first time you are likely to make mistakes. Sometimes, more can be learned from the lessons that don't go so well than from the great successes.

How will I know if I am making progress?

Through self-awareness

Sensitivity won't really come until you have had experience and learned to relax with your students. As the basic classroom skills are mastered and different parts of a lesson are handled more confidently you should be able to stand back mentally and observe the class as it is going on, see what the students are doing well, what they are having problems with as well as how they are interacting as a group. You will gradually become more self-aware – of your particular strengths, and of areas where improvement is needed.

Feedback from observers

Other trainees (if they are available) and, of course, supervisors can help develop your awareness. They can sit back and observe what is going on in a more objective way, unhindered by the nerves and anxieties of the teacher.

Feedback from students

To help yourself it is worth getting to know the students well, both inside and outside the classroom, not only to find out about their interests but also to give them the opportunity of expressing what they feel their problems are with the language. They can provide useful feedback on your classes, both what they found useful and what they didn't.

What should be the end result of TP?

After TP you should:

- be more aware of the language you are teaching;
- be more aware of the factors that aid and impede learning in the classroom;
- be in control of basic classroom management skills;
- be able to plan a series of lessons, perhaps based around published materials (such as a coursebook), which are relevant to what the students need to learn;
- be able to present, practise and revise language;
- be able to use activities and materials that develop language skills;
- be able to help students develop their awareness of how they learn and what learning strategies suit them;
- be able to think critically and creatively about your own lessons.

2 Working with others

During your training, as in most teaching situations, you will be liaising and co-operating with other teachers: perhaps fellow trainees, TP supervisors, teachers to whom you are apprenticed, other teachers working in the institution.

Working with a supervisor and/or a teacher to whom you are attached

In most institutions this person's role is:

- to help with lesson preparation;
- to observe critically;
- to give helpful feedback.

Make the most of your tutor's experience and expertise. However, it is vital that you are not over-dependent on your tutor. Certainly ask for clarification of any point you are supposed to be teaching – you can't say to a group of students that you don't know what you are supposed to be doing – even ask for your lesson plan to be checked, provided there's enough time for changes to be made. But your attitude is all-important: it shouldn't be *I don't know how to do it* but *I wasn't sure how to do it but I thought this might work. What do you think?* Expect to get less help as the course proceeds. You should always be moving positively towards independence and eventually you should get close to the real-life situation when you may be working with little or no help. Don't blame the tutor if things go wrong; you're the one with responsibility for the class while you are teaching it. Respond positively to suggestions and criticism; by all means give your reasons for doing something, but try not to be defensive.

Co-operating with other teachers working in the institution

In addition to your supervisor or 'attached' teacher other teachers can be a great help. For example, some may be prepared to give guidance as to what materials to use or tell you what you need to know about particular students. They can also give you a good picture of what teaching is actually like. However, they are likely to be busy and preoccupied with their classes and shouldn't be pestered unnecessarily. Remember: if they are teaching the same students as you are, they can make a big difference to how those students think of you. If you are observing, participating in or teaching another teacher's class it is imperative that you do everything you can to co-operate with the group's main teacher, that you know what your role is and that you don't tread on anyone's toes by turning up late, interrupting at an inappropriate time, contradicting the teacher in front of the students, etc!

Try to behave professionally with colleagues (teachers and fellow trainees) from the start:

- Clean the board when you finish.
- If you rearrange the furniture return the room to the state you found it in.
- Return borrowed materials.
- Start and finish lessons on time.
- Make sure you know how to use the machinery. Try not to break it and if the worst does happen, report it!

It is also worth remembering that institutions have expectations as to your behaviour and personal appearance. Be guided by the teachers as to what is considered appropriate. While a certain informality may be acceptable, and indeed necessary to help the students relax, a lack of cleanliness and tidiness isn't. If you are working with students who come from different cultures from your own remember also that there are marked cultural differences as regards what is considered to be appropriate dress. Aim to gain the respect of your students, not to embarrass them.

Working with other trainees

In many TP situations you'll be expected to work together in the preparation of classes and in the sharing of views after the classes. TP isn't a competitive situation where one person's good lesson diminishes the value of someone else's.

Often in TP you're working as part of a team in which each member supports the others and you're tackling common problems.

- You may work together on some of the tasks in this book. (See Introduction Section 4: *How to use this book*.)
- As well as giving support, other trainees can be an extremely useful resource. You can give one another ideas and information about language, resources and about students.
- You can offer constructive help in preparation, and check each other's plans. TP is a good opportunity for you to talk about the students and classes with other people.
- You may be able to help in other ways: before a lesson – by being responsible for arranging the furniture and organizing equipment; during a lesson – by being a time-keeper, indicating when someone teaching has only five minutes left, etc; after a lesson – by chairing a feedback session.
- You may co-operate in providing feedback on one another's teaching. This can take a number of different forms, depending on the TP situation:
  - observing a fellow trainee's lesson with a group of 'volunteer' students and giving feedback (see Chapter 1 Section 4: *What do observers do during TP?*);
  - teaching a class with another trainee (team teaching) and evaluating the lesson together, afterwards;
  - taking part in a discussion group about lessons observed and taught with classes to which you are attached – reporting back to colleagues on what you observed or what you taught;
  - observing a video of another trainee's lesson and giving feedback.

As with other colleagues, it is important to be sensitive and professional in your relationship with fellow trainees. (See the points made under *Co-operating with other teachers working in the institution,* above.) If you're teaching the same students as other trainees it is important to work together so that the lessons interrelate. At the very least make sure you keep fellow trainees informed about what you've done and what you're planning to do with the class.

3 Your own attitude

We can't change our personalities but we can alter the impression we give in class:

- by smiling – that doesn't mean you have to walk around with a fixed grin, but showing a friendly attitude warms the students to *you;*
- by responding to what students say as communication; try to respond naturally, show interest in what they say. Don't treat every utterance as a model to be corrected or congratulated upon!
- by finding out about the students, getting to know them;
- by taking time, by showing an interest in both the learning and the personal interests of the students. Talk to them before and after the lesson. Notice if they are absent, etc;
- by trying to enjoy their company as a group;
- by showing that you are enjoying teaching them.

At first you may have difficulty in understanding what some of your students are trying to say. With experience this will get much easier. Don't panic! Apologize, say you didn't understand and be patient.

4 What do observers do during TP?

In many situations you will be observed by your supervisor, perhaps by other trainees not teaching, and possibly by a trainee supervisor. Your supervisor will usually sit apart, and will probably take no part in the lesson but observe and note what is happening.

If you are observing, let the trainee who is teaching concentrate on the students:

- Sit apart from the students.
- Be as silent and inconspicuous as possible (don't chat to other trainees!).
- Try not to make eye contact with the person teaching.
- Never interrupt.

There are obvious exceptions to this: when, for example, a trainee wants help with monitoring pairwork (perhaps in the early stages of a course), when supportive laughter might be helpful, or when you are helping the trainee with timing by indicating how much time is left.

You may be asked to observe a particular aspect of a fellow trainee's lesson, perhaps doing one of the observation tasks, such as Task 1 on p27, or Task 1 on p59. This may concern a whole general area, perhaps related to topics currently being dealt with on your course: for example, *classroom management; aims; correction; interaction between students.* Or it might be more specific, perhaps relating to a problem that you know *you* have: for example, *instruction-giving; eye contact; 'concept' checking.* Observing how others perform in these areas can be very helpful. Alternatively you may concentrate on problems that the trainee who is teaching has. Your supervisor may select an appropriate observation task or the trainees who are teaching may ask you to observe and give feedback on an aspect they are consciously working on in that particular lesson. Of course, all observers should make notes as discreetly as possible when trainees are trying to concentrate on the lesson they are giving. Otherwise this can create unwelcome pressure!

5 Feedback on lessons

The timing and format of feedback can vary, depending on the TP situation. Feedback is often given soon after you have finished teaching, though it can take place some time later – perhaps the following day. Some supervisors like to give the trainees time to reflect on their own lesson and expect them to make written notes. Even if you are not required to do so, from time to time you might like to do a critique of one of your lessons. If you need a checklist, try using the contents list of this book.

Where feedback is predominantly oral many supervisors also give out a copy of their written notes. You may be given individual feedback by your supervisor or the feedback may take the form of a group discussion. You may be asked to give your impression of the lesson first or the other trainees may be invited to contribute, perhaps by reporting back on an observation task.

The trainees who improve most quickly are those who recognize their strengths and weaknesses and are open to suggestions for improvement. They respond positively, not defensively, to criticism – seeing all feedback as an aid to improvement.

Feedback on lessons can be frustrating and even seem unfair. This is often because:

- the students' needs are rightly being considered first;
- you may be trying out new ideas, totally unpractised. This is especially true if you are on a pre-service course and doing TP at the beginning of the course;
- you don't often get the chance to have another go at something you messed up.

But your supervisors are likely to be aware of these sorts of problems and will provide support. Listen carefully to what your supervisor says; you may want to make notes on your lesson plan. After each lesson it is worth noting the skills you have used and referring back to previous criticisms. In fact if you have shown yourself to be good at some particular strategy it might be worth *avoiding* it on TP, to give yourself practice over a wide range of skills. Don't worry about always showing your good side. Try to think of TP as *practice* even if it links to a qualification.

If you are asked to give feedback on other trainees' lessons, try to do so tactfully. *Why on earth didn't you show everyone the picture?* is likely to provoke a defensive reaction, whereas *I don't think everyone could see it* is likely to be more helpful. Try to describe what you observed rather than making value judgements. Also, although you will want to be supportive, it can be just as unhelpful to overpraise a lesson as to be overly critical. Remember: being aware of the effect language can have and being able to offer non-deterring criticism are aspects of your job as a teacher.

6 Keeping track

It is worth keeping a TP file, even on courses where the tutor doesn't require one to be handed in at the end for assessment. It could include lesson plans, reflections on your own teaching, copies of supervisor's comments, examples of materials and visual aids used, students' written work. You may like to ask fellow trainees for the plans of lessons you have seen them teach and offer yours in exchange. There are further tips on how lesson plans can be stored on p182.

You might also find it valuable to keep a personal diary of TP in which you reflect on your successes and failures: what you did, how you felt, what you resolve to do in the light of these experiences. In a diary you can include your feelings about your own TP lessons, those of colleagues, your reactions to ideas discussed in input sessions on the course and to any tasks and exercises you do.

Articulating an experience can help not only to get it in perspective but to develop self-awareness generally as a teacher. As it is of essentially private value you may or may not decide to show it to others. On some courses trainees are required to keep a TP diary and may be asked to submit part of it to their supervisor.

Further reading

Parrott, M. 1993 *Tasks for English Teachers* (CUP)
Scrivener, J. 1994 *Learning Teaching* (Heinemann)
Wajnryb, R. 1992 *Classroom Observation Tasks* (CUP)
Wallace, M. 1991 *Training Foreign Language Teachers* (CUP)

Chapter 2 Managing the class

Contrary to popular belief, it is not true that you have to be an extrovert to be a good classroom teacher. Some good teachers are very low-key in the classroom, while other teachers, both lively and amusing, survive only as entertainers. Although some teachers develop a special classroom manner, in the main your style of teaching will depend on the sort of person you are. TP is your opportunity to try a variety of approaches, to become aware of what does and what doesn't suit your personality, and to develop your own style of teaching.

However, while personality is impossible to prescribe, for a class to learn effectively you must be able to inspire confidence in your students. You must know when to be firm and directive, and when to be unobtrusive and leave the students alone. In other words, you need to subtly alter your role according to the activity without going to the extremes of dominating a class or leaving it uncertain what to do.

In this chapter various techniques for organizing and managing the class are explored. These techniques aim to help you become more professional and efficient in your approach so that your students have confidence in your competence as a teacher and as a leader. In particular we consider the balance between having a friendly, relaxed relationship with a class and the maintenance of discipline.

1 Use of eye contact, gesture and the voice

Eye contact

We all know how difficult it is to talk to someone who never looks at us or someone who looks us in the eye all the time. Similarly we know how important eye contact is in signalling such messages as *I want to speak to you* or *I'm addressing this remark to you*. Now turn to the classroom. Observe, for example, how, when and why your teacher makes eye contact with you and your colleagues.

Good use of eye contact is crucial in helping to establish rapport. A teacher who never looks students in the eye seems to lack confidence and gives the students a sense of insecurity. On the other hand, having a fixed glare doesn't help either! Trainees who find it difficult to make eye contact will need to overcome this reluctance if they are to have effective control over a class.

The teacher needs to look at the students to notice their reactions and to be in touch with the mood of the class. Do they understand? Do they look puzzled? Are they enjoying the class? Are they tired? Are they bored? Would it be a good idea to change the direction or the pace of the lesson? Does anyone want to contribute or ask questions?

You, the teacher, are in a much better position to gauge the reactions and the mood of the class than observers sitting at the back of the room. Be careful, though. It's not always easy to tell what the students are thinking – particularly if you don't know them or their culture very well. The student who is laughing may be embarrassed rather than amused. The student you think is bored may in fact be paying serious attention. Different cultures have different 'rules' about eye contact. Some students may look away as a mark of respect for the teacher, not because they are uninterested or don't want to participate.

How will eye contact vary at different stages of a lesson or in different types of lesson?

As the role of the teacher varies, depending on the type and stage of a lesson, so does the degree of eye contact. The more direct eye contact the teacher maintains with all those in the class the more teacher-controlled the lesson. In activities where the students are working more independently of the teacher less teacher–student eye contact is necessary.

How can you use eye contact?

- to ensure that the students have understood what they are supposed to do and know what is going on. Puzzled expressions quickly tell you you need to try again!
- to indicate who is to speak (usually accompanied by a nod) when calling on one after the other to repeat a word or sentence, or to make a response. Using names can slow the pace of a practice activity and pointing might be offensive;
- to encourage contributions when you are trying to elicit ideas or specific language from the students. Frequently you only know students have something to say by looking at them;
- to show a student who is talking that you are taking notice;
- to hold the attention of students not being addressed and to encourage them to listen to those doing the talking. With younger students this is a way of maintaining discipline: a darting glance around the room can show that you are aware of what everyone is doing;
- to keep in touch with other students in the class or group when you are dealing with an individual, perhaps when correcting. Your eyes can say to them: *You're involved in this too*;
- to signal to a pair or group to start, to stop or to hurry up. It can be far less dominating than the voice;
- to indicate, with an accompanying gesture, that groups are on the right or wrong lines;

- together with a gesture (such as a shake of the head) to indicate that something is incorrect, or to show that the student should try again;
- to check that everyone is participating, especially when the group is working together, perhaps doing repetition practice;
- to check silently with students whether they have finished an activity – perhaps the reading of a text, or the writing of a sentence during a dictation.

When should you avoid eye contact?

During any activity that doesn't demand teacher-centred control, avoid eye contact unless you are specifically asked for help or choose to join in. This can be true, for example, of pairwork, groupwork, speaking activities such as roleplay, simulations and student-led discussions, and even individual work when the student wishes to complete the task independently. As soon as you establish eye contact, or the students establish eye contact with you, you are brought into the activity, thus making it teacher-centred.

Is there any point in encouraging the students to look at each other?

Yes. Very much so. Confidence is gained and shyness lost through eye contact. In addition, a student who has difficulty understanding is more likely to understand if his or her eyes are on the speaker's face than if they are on the ground. So, when students ask each other questions, or help and correct each other, whether in pairwork or student to student across the class, they should look at each other. You can encourage students to address their remarks to each other, not through you, by avoiding eye contact as soon as the person who is speaking starts and by looking at the person who is being addressed. It is sometimes better to get them to move their chairs to make eye contact easier.

Task 1

Aim
To learn to pace a lesson by looking at individuals in the class.

Procedure
1 Stand at the front of the group so that you can see everyone.
2 Dictate a short passage to the group, judging when to start each phrase by looking at everyone's hands. The aim is not to leave anyone behind.

Comment
Get the views of the group at the end, particularly the slowest writer, as to how effective you were.

Task 2

Aim
To encourage full eye contact and to practise spreading attention randomly round the class.

Procedure
1 Call out the names of members of the group.
2 Make eye contact with each person as their name is called.

Comment

1 This exercise needs to be brief and rapid to make the point. Aim to cover everyone in the group once only in random order. Ask the group if they were all called and where you tended to focus your attention.

2 A later variation might be for the group to be less willing to make eye contact. How do you, as a teacher, feel when this happens? How do the 'students' feel?

Task 3

Aim

To encourage evenly spread but random eye contact and to practise using eye contact in place of nomination.

Procedure

Use a pack of coloured felt-tipped pens. Hold different pens up and elicit by use of eye contact and a nod *It's blue, It's red*, etc. Get individual members of the group to say the sentence – changing the pens each time and signalling randomly to all members of the group. Ask each member how many times he or she spoke.

Comment

1 A variation on this exercise would be to use a facial expression to indicate that a second repetition is required.

2 You can use a controlled practice activity like this (sometimes referred to as a drill) from a coursebook or make up your own.

Use of gesture, facial expression and mime

Gestures and facial expressions are an integral part of any communication where people listen and speak to each other. They help us get across what we want to say. For example, when we give directions in the street to a stranger, we not only use our voice to give special emphasis to the important points, we often use our hands to make things clear as well.

If we are deprived of what the body can express, for example when we talk on the telephone or listen to the radio, we are forced to use our imagination and try and extract all the meaning from the inflexions of the voice or the words themselves. With direct contact we often look at the other's face to gauge what their real feelings or attitudes are.

How does gesture and mime affect what we do in the classroom?

You can use gesture and mime:

- to convey the meaning of language;
- to manage the class – for example, to reinforce instructions;
- to add visual interest;
- to increase pace;
- to cut down on the amount of verbal explanation. This is particularly important at lower levels where long verbal explanations in English can be difficult and confusing.

In the early days it is often better to exaggerate your gestures a little because:

- they need to be a conscious part of your repertoire, deliberately doing what they set out to do;

- the students need to understand them. If they are exaggerated they are less ambiguous;
- many teachers are more frozen than they think they are and move little more than their lips.

Excessive gesture, though, can be silly and counter-productive. Don't let gestures interfere with the language you are teaching.

Conveying meaning

If we are in a country where we don't understand the language, gesture will help us to get the gist of what is going on. Equally students, particularly beginners and elementary students, often need to rely on the gestures we use.

The meaning of vocabulary can often be quickly and efficiently indicated through gesture or mime. If a student doesn't understand the word *tall* the appropriate hand gesture is easy to make. The meaning of *stagger* is easily conveyed by mime.

If you are giving an example of spoken language it is well worth adding facial expression and gesture to bring it to life.

We can also teach the students to understand special gestures, to help us convey meaning or highlight aspects of the form of the language. For example:

- past time: *hitch-hiking gesture over the shoulder*
- present time: *pointing down to the floor*
- future time: *pointing into the distance in front*
- rhythm and stress: *indicated by beating with the hand, or clapping*

The students, however, need to learn what these gestures mean and you need to know that they understand. Pointing to the floor could mean 'here' and pointing in front could mean 'over there'. So teach them and check that the students understand them.

Managing the class

All language teachers develop a personal set of gestures to get a class to do what they want with the minimum of fuss and the minimum of language. There are some, however, that are quite common. For example:

- listen: *hand cupped behind the ear*
- repeat in chorus: *firm sweep of the arm or with both hands raised make a gesture to include everyone*
- get into pairs: *arm, hand or finger movement to show you are 'joining' the students*
- stop (pairwork, groupwork, noise!): *raised hand or clap*
- good: *thumb up and/or smile and nod*
- not right: *shake head or index finger and/or indicate by facial expression*
- nearly right: *outstretched hand rocked from side to side*
- interesting idea: *raise the eyebrows*
- repeat individually: *nod in the direction of the student and raise the eyebrows*
- eliciting a contribution: *beckon with a cupped hand rather than pointing, which is rude in many cultures*
- to show 'yes, that's one suggestion/idea/word ... anything else?': *'counting' on the fingers*

But you must be careful as gestures can have different meanings in different parts of the world; you may think you mean one thing and students may think you mean something completely different! If you are teaching a monolingual group there may well be gestures which are commonly used in their culture. If you are working in a foreign country you can ask the teachers in the institution for commonly understood gestures that can be used in the classroom. When you observe, watch which gestures other teachers or trainees use successfully.

Remember that the students in your TP classes may take time to become familiar with your gestures. The first time you use a gesture you may have to reinforce it with words but always be on the lookout for a way to focus attention and cut down on unnecessary teacher talk.

Is there anything to be avoided?

Yes, quite a lot:

- unclear, ambiguous expressions and gestures;
- gestures which are not obvious and which you haven't taught or checked with the class;
- gestures which are rude or obscene to the students. Common ones with some nationalities are: pointing, showing the sole of the foot or shoe, holding up the index and small finger of the same hand. If you are the same nationality as your students this is a problem you do not have but if you are unfamiliar with the culture of your students it is worth discussing different gestures with them or with their regular teachers to find out what to be wary of. This will prevent embarrassment or inexplicable laughter. On the other hand, don't worry to the extent that every move you make is fraught with danger. If in doubt just stick to the one basic rule: never touch your students anywhere but on the arm – although even that might be taboo in some countries;
- irritating habits such as grinning or blinking too much. They can be very off-putting; even language 'tics' such as *OK* or *All right?* can annoy students. Other trainees can tell you about such mannerisms or if you don't believe it when someone says you are repeatedly stroking your face or pulling your hair, try to watch yourself on video. Getting rid of a habit can paralyse you with self-consciousness but it's worth it in the long run.

Should students be encouraged to imitate the teacher's gestures?

Yes, they should certainly be encouraged to use those gestures that convey meaning. If the students are practising speaking skills, even in a controlled practice activity such as a 'drill' or a short dialogue, they should be encouraged to use realistic gestures and facial expressions. They will help them to 'say it as though they mean it' and make the language far more memorable.

The students will probably not use the gestures you use to manage the class unless they are doing the teaching. Also, they probably won't need the gestures to highlight aspects of the form – although they may do so unconsciously when talking about language. But you may want the students to use gestures in a checking activity: for example, you read out a number of sentences which contain a mixture of tenses. After each sentence, pause long enough for the students to make a gesture indicating whether they think the sentence refers to the past, the present or the future.

Task 1

Aim

To see how easily gestures are understood.

Procedure

Practise in front of a mirror the gestures you have decided to use for managing the class: for example, *repeat together, get into pairs, try again,* etc. Then try them out on friends, members of the family or colleagues. See if they can guess what you mean.

Comment

This will help you to see which gestures are obvious and which are more ambiguous and so need to be taught. Don't forget, though, that you and your friends probably share the same culture. Even if they understand certain gestures it doesn't necessarily mean your students will.

Task 2

Aim

To practise the use of gesture in front of an audience.

Procedure

Play 'Charades' in teams (one person mimes the name of a book or a film and the others have to guess what it is within a certain time limit). Decide beforehand which gestures are permitted, making sure they are ones you might feel comfortable about using in a classroom (eg a gesture to encourage everyone to contribute, one to invite a contribution from only one person, a 'nearly' gesture, etc).

Comment

1 One advantage of this game is that in the playing of it self-consciousness is often forgotten. The drawback is that those trying to guess the name of the film or book are willing and enthusiastic in what they give. A normal class might be less forthcoming and more eliciting gestures would be needed. This could perhaps be simulated if the members of the 'audience' don't offer anything unless called upon by gesture.
2 Another valuable but more difficult variant of this game is to replace the book or film with a sentence which has to be mimed/gestured.

Task 3

Aim

To show the value of gesture and facial expression in conveying meaning.

Procedure

1 Tell the group a short story or anecdote without any gesture, movement or facial expression.
2 Repeat the exercise using as much physical expression as possible.
3 Discuss with others in the group the gestures and expressions most helpful in getting across the meaning and mood of the storyteller.

Comment

This should help show the extent to which all of us rely on physical expression to convey and interpret meaning.

Task 4

Aim

To show the value of mime in conveying meaning.

Procedure

1 Pass a message round the group through a series of mime gestures (rather like a mimed version of Chinese Whispers). Make sure members of the group who have not yet received the message do not watch. It might be best to have everyone leave the room and come back in one at a time to receive the message.
2 Compare the final mime with the original message.

Task 5

Aim

To show the value of mime in conveying meaning.

Procedure

1 Everyone is 'at a party'. Divide into two groups. One group decides on three or four messages that they are to convey to their partners in the other group: for example, *My glass is empty. Can you bring me another drink?*
2 Pair up with someone from the other group and stand on the opposite side of the room from your partner. Those with the messages must mime to their partners, who write down what they understand by the messages. Those who are receiving the messages can show by gesture whether they understand or not, and ask for repetition, clarification, etc.

Comment

1 Those pairs whose 'receiver' writes down messages which are closest to the original messages are the most successful at communicating through mime.
2 This is an activity which can be used with a group of students.

Task 6

Aim

To practise the appropriate gestures for getting students to listen to a model, repeat in chorus and repeat individually.

Procedure

1 By gesture alone (eg hand behind ear) get some of your colleagues to listen to an utterance – a word, phrase or sentence either in a foreign language or a nonsense language.
2 Say the utterance.
3 Pause and check through eye contact that everyone has heard.
4 Repeat the utterance if necessary.
5 By gesturing alone (eg a sweeping arm or two raised hands gesture with a decisive gesture to start the utterance) get everyone to repeat, making sure they all start at the same time.
6 Get the members of the group to repeat individually, quickly and randomly, again by gesture alone (for example, eye contact, nodding, beckoning with the whole hand). Make sure everyone gets practice and that those that need most get most.

Comment

When you have mastered this you can introduce student–student correction. If one 'student' doesn't say the word or sentence very well or is having difficulty, gesture to a 'student' who has already said it well to say it again. Then come back to the 'student' who was having problems and gesture for him or her to try again.

Task 7

Aim

To help indicate word stress.

Procedure

1 Read out a list of words with two or more syllables.
2 As you say the words, indicate which syllable is stressed with a beating gesture.
3 The others in the group can write the words and mark the stress.

Comment

1 You can experiment with different gestures to show stress. One way is to stand and 'bob' with the whole body on the stressed syllable.
2 Instead of using English words you can say and beat the stress on nonsense words: for example, frubinátion. The others in the group note how many syllables and which syllable was stressed (first, second, third, etc). In this variation they are totally reliant on the information you give rather than on their knowledge of how the word is stressed.

Task 8

Aim

To practise using mime to convey meaning.

Procedure

1 Choose <u>one</u> of these lists and decide in which order you are going to mime the words. Do not tell the others about your choices.

A	B	C	D
walk	bake	shoot	scrub
stroll	fry	suffocate	brush
dash	grill	smother	wipe
jog	boil	drown	sweep

2 Mime your words to the group and ask them to write down what they think the words are.
3 Discuss which words were easiest to guess and why.

Comment

Make up your own list of words and mime the words to the group.

Using the voice

If your voice does not have sufficient range, variety and projection, you are going to be at a considerable disadvantage in the classroom. However, having said that, voice quality and the ways individuals use their voices vary enormously from one teacher to another.

In what way does the voice vary?

The voice alters fairly naturally, according to the activity, the size of the class, the room, etc. For getting the class's attention and for giving gentle, individual correction the quality of the voice should be very different. When talking to individuals, pairs or groups, we reduce the volume, lower the pitch and narrow the range. The aim is to act as you would naturally when talking to one or two people. When addressing a large class in a large room we increase the volume, widen the voice range and perhaps raise the pitch.

A class often mirrors the teacher's volume. If you speak quietly the students speak quietly; when you raise the volume so do they. You can 'energize' a class and increase the pace of a lesson by raising the volume of your voice slightly, or get pairwork off to a confident start by giving instructions and perhaps doing a model exchange in an enthusiastic, lively tone of voice. Conversely if the noise level is getting out of control try making your contributions at a markedly lower volume, almost approaching a whisper, and see if the students follow suit. Usually the greater the variation in the voice – providing it is appropriate – the greater the effectiveness.

How can you use your voice to gain attention?

For example:

- when students are standing around at the beginning of a lesson, talking;
- when you want to stop a group activity;
- when there's a lot of general noise and you want to regain control.

Rather than waiting quietly for students to finish, or clapping your hands or banging on the table, it is often more effective to exaggerate certain features of your voice, dwelling longer than usual on certain syllables – *All right, everyone, can we make a start?* A slight increase in volume and higher pitch is often all that is necessary. Shouting can convey anger, loss of control and, in some cultures, disastrous loss of face, so avoid it unless really necessary.

Can you help to hold the students' attention with the voice?

Yes, attention can easily be lost by speaking too quietly or slowly, or too monotonously, without varying the pitch of the voice.

When you are 'up front' it is as much *how* you say something as *what* you say that keeps your students' attention. If you are feeling tired or lethargic and let it show in your voice your students will quickly lose interest in what you are saying.

What about when you are announcing changes in the stages of a lesson?

It is not necessary to say *Right! This is a different part of the lesson. New activity coming up!* but you can use your voice to mark transition in a lesson. Look at the following transcript of a lesson and try reading the part of the teacher aloud:

 T: So – to make the simple past of a regular verb – what do we do?
S1: Add 'ed'.
 T: Right – and if the verb ends in 'e' – like 'live'?
S2: Just 'd'.
 T: OK. Good. Now close your books. Stand up and put all the tables against the wall.

When you reached *Now close your books* you should have paused, and your voice should have increased marginally in volume and risen in pitch considerably to highlight the change in activity.

Task 1

Aim
To develop awareness of the role of the voice.

Procedure
1 Record part of a real lesson.
2 Together with someone in your group identify the changes in pitch and volume in the teacher's voice and discuss the reasons for them.
3 If videoed, discuss how the changes relate to gesture and movement.

Task 2

Aim
To assess the effectiveness of your voice.

Procedure
1 Record yourself teaching.
2 Listen to see how effectively you get the students' attention, signal a change in activity, inject energy, etc. Or ask one of the other trainees to observe, note and give feedback on how you use your voice at different points in the lesson.

Comment
You may find that your voice is much 'flatter' than you had thought, creating a dull, uninspiring effect; or perhaps you are speaking all the time in a high-pitched voice, giving an impression of frenzy or panic.

Task 3

Aim
To improve the use of the voice.

Procedure
1 Make a genuine announcement to the group in the classroom or to a crowded common room full of students.
2 Ask someone in the group to assess your performance in getting attention, holding it and getting the message across.

Task 4

Aim
To help develop different types of voices.

Procedure
1 Identify three different types of voice that you can use fairly easily (for example, a voice to get attention in a crowded room, a voice for giving a language model, a voice for talking to an individual student while the rest of the class is involved in pairwork). Get someone to confirm that you have got them right.
2 Write down two or three appropriate phrases for each type of voice. For example, *OK, start now.*
3 Practise saying them to yourself in the 'correct' type of voice.

Using students' names

Why should you learn and use students' names?

It is important to make sure you know everyone's name and that they know both yours and each other's as quickly as possible, because:

- it is an important first step towards establishing rapport with the group: it helps create a friendly, co-operative atmosphere;
- it shows that you are interested in them as people – and by extension in their learning problems and in their interests;
- if the effort you make to learn their names is obvious they will be more forgiving when you make mistakes;
- it makes it possible for you to discuss the students with colleagues;
- without knowing names it is difficult to manage a class effectively.

Be careful to use the right name. Ask the students what they want to be called, but it is usually better if you use a similar part of the name for each student (either all first names or all family names). Be guided by the practice of the institution and the country you are in. In adult classes, some may expect you to use their family names and some their first names. Also in adult classes, many teachers prefer to be called by their first name because it implies a friendly, informal attitude and a more equal relationship between the teacher and the students. Usually, if students see everyone else is on first-name terms, they will accept it as a convention for that classroom. However, in certain cultures (for example, in Japan and China) it is a mark of disrespect for younger people to address their elders by their first name; so if you have a mixed age group, be sensitive to this fact. If you don't speak their language, get them to teach you to pronounce their names correctly. You'll be spending a lot of time correcting their pronunciation, so you should be prepared to put in the effort to pronounce things correctly too. If you are a native speaker of English, teach them your name and how to pronounce it. Make it clear which part of your name you expect them to use. (See Section 8: *Establishing rapport and maintaining discipline*.)

How can you learn their names?

You can help yourself and the students learn names by:

- getting the students to introduce each other to you and then going round the class in random order two or three times, saying the names aloud to check that you remember. If you do this at the end of the first couple of lessons as well as the beginning it can act as useful revision. This activity is most useful if the students know each other;
- keeping a register. This will probably be required of you anyway, but checking a register openly at the beginning of a class is a useful reminder for you, particularly when you only see the class once or twice a week. It also serves as a good focusing device at the beginning of a lesson;
- associating names with physical features. This is a useful trick with the occasional student whose name you find impossible to remember, eg Claudia – glasses, Stephan – braces. Say them to yourself two or three times. However, keep them to yourself as sometimes the physical feature could be one that the student doesn't want attention drawn to!
- using names consciously in the first few lessons to fix them in your mind. It is

usually better to ask a student to wait before replying for a few seconds while you recall the name rather than allow the situation to continue where you can't remember the name. There comes a point where you should have learned the names and it becomes embarrassing to ask;

- checking the names to yourself in periods of pairwork or groupwork;
- drawing up a seating plan and keeping it with the class register. Make sure you alter it if the students change their places;
- using the return of homework to help you remember. Trying to recall the student's face when you are marking it is a help too.

Finally, if you can't remember a name, admit it and ask the person openly. It is better for you to seem to be not very good at learning names than for students to be left feeling their names are not very important.

How can the students learn each other's names?

You can help yourself further and help them to learn each other's names by doing the following:

- Ask them to put their names on the desk for all to see or perhaps wear name badges. Or, in a small class, you might write their names on the board and get everyone to practise putting a face to the name:

  T: My name's Jan.
  S1: His name's Jan, and my name's Abdulla.
  S2: His name's Jan, that's Abdulla and I'm Ingrid.
  S3: Jan, Abdulla, Ingrid and I'm Thomas.

  and so on until you go round the whole class. If you have a class of more than, say, twenty, it is probably better to split it into two halves. This, and the following activity, is useful when everyone is new.
- Get the students to stand in a circle. Throw a ball or similar small object to a student as you say your name. The student then chooses another person in the circle, throws the ball and says his or her own name. After a while, when everyone has had a chance to say their name, change the activity – this time say the name of the person you are throwing the ball to.
- Ask the students to say their name and to describe themselves using an adjective beginning with the same letter as their name – eg *I'm Jan and I'm jolly. I'm Abdulla and I'm amusing. I'm Ingrid and I'm interesting. I'm Thomas and I'm terrific*, etc. As each person announces their name the others can suggest adjectives. This activity can be used with more advanced students.
- Introduce any new student to the others in the class.

When should you use students' names?

You can use students' names when you want:

- to organize an activity;
- to acknowledge a query or contribution;
- to indicate who is to answer a question;
- to indicate who is to respond to an instruction;
- to get an individual student's attention.

When asking questions you should normally say the name after the question.

Asking a question and then nominating an individual keeps the whole class on its toes. It also means that you can see who is eager to answer the question and so choose someone who wants to contribute.

Saying the name before the question can occasionally be useful – to indicate to individual students that they are to pay attention to the question because they are going to have to answer it. The disadvantage of this is that the other students may 'switch off' as they know they won't have to answer.

2 Classroom arrangement

Your position and the way you organize the positions of the students in your class is of great importance. Bear in mind that concepts of personal space vary from culture to culture. For example, Arabs when they talk to each other like to get closer than Northern Europeans. In multicultural classes, teachers and students sometimes cause unease or even offence to other students because they get too close. Or some students may think that people who like to keep a greater distance are cool and even unfriendly.

Students' seating arrangements

Where the students sit in a classroom can determine:

- their attitude to each other and to you;
- your attitude to them;
- how they interact;
- the types of activity they can do.

Should you determine who sits next to whom?

This depends on a number of factors: whether the students are adults or children, whether the group is monolingual or multilingual, the personalities of the students, etc. You may want to put a weak student with a strong, or a quieter student with one who is more outgoing. Or you may want to put weaker students together in activities where you can give them extra support. In a multilingual group you will probably not want students with the same mother tongue sitting together. On the other hand there may be occasions when it is appropriate for them to work together on common problems. It adds variety if students work with different people and generally the more intermingling the better the cohesion of the whole class. If there are students absent you will want to encourage students to move forward from the back or along the circle so that no one is cut off from the rest of the group.

So, feel that you have the authority to move them, politely but firmly. Remember, though, we all get attached to our own territory and moving can be a wrench. While shuffling up a class *for an activity* is acceptable – provided it is done in the right spirit – it can be unsettling if you do it often and for no apparent reason. You must also be sensitive to any personality clashes or cultural reasons for certain individuals not wanting to be together. If you feel that a student is deliberately trying to sit outside the area in the classroom where most of the activity is taking place, it may need good-humoured encouragement to bring him or her in. You will need to be sensitive, yet positive from the beginning.

How do you change the arrangement to fit the activity?

On TP you may be restricted by the types of chairs, tables or desks in the classroom. If you are lucky they will be freestanding but very often they are fixed or too heavy to move. Classroom furniture always affects the learning atmosphere to some extent but the choice will almost certainly be outside your control. Inevitably, then, you can only have flexible seating arrangements within the constraints of the institution. If you are one of the lucky ones, make sure you take full advantage of it. Remember, though, that moving furniture takes time. Make sure you have enough time (and help) to make the necessary changes. If you ask students to help, explain the necessity for the change and make your instructions clear – so that it can be done quickly and efficiently. Also, always return the classroom to the original arrangement unless you are certain that the person teaching in the room after you would like your arrangement to be left.

Activities where you need to direct from the front

With moveable desks, tables or seminar chairs of probably no more than sixteen students, a horseshoe arrangement will allow easy, face-to-face contact between the students and between you and the students:

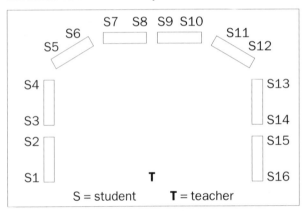

The more horseshoe shaped it is the more S16 is able to talk to S5. If the class has more than sixteen students you may be able to make a double horseshoe. If you are forced to arrange the furniture in rows it helps if the two halves are slightly at an angle:

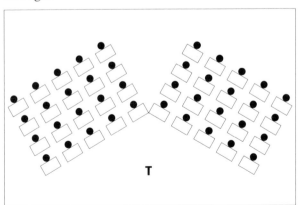

You may wish to group the students around tables, 'café style'. This works as long as they can all see what is going on at the front of the class clearly and comfortably. This arrangement ensures that, with minor adjustments, students are in a position to change to pairwork or groupwork.

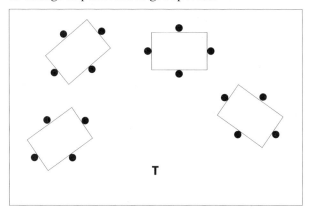

Whole class interaction

In class discussion or 'open' pairwork, when two students talk across the classroom under your control, giving other students the opportunity to hear, there is no need to change the position of the seats.

For activities where the students need to talk individually with a number of other members of the class (in a mingle activity) it is better to move furniture to the edges of the room and create a space in the centre of the room for the students to move around in.

Pairwork

When all the students are working together in 'closed' pairs, outside your direct control, then they need to be able to look at each other. So either get them to move their chairs slightly towards each other or lift their chairs and work facing someone other than their neighbour, depending on the amount of time the activity is going to take. For some activities, where it is important that the students do not see what the other student is looking at or doing, it may be worth asking the students to work back to back.

Groupwork

How the seats are arranged depends on the size of the class, the size of the groups, the types of activity and the style of the furniture. For many activities, however, say with four students per group, the ideal is probably to have the students sit round desks café style, or to remove the desks altogether.

If possible, move furniture to make good use of the corners of the room. At all costs avoid having all members of a group on one side of a table; they need to face each other. Also avoid separating the members of a group too far, making it difficult for them to talk easily.

Individual work

If there is a lot of reading or writing involved, or when you set a test, it may be worth considering turning students away from one another to give them the freedom to concentrate, and stop them cheating in a test! The isolation students can usually get in a language laboratory is a clear example of how useful this can be.

The teacher's position and movement

In the classroom, students quickly become sensitive to whether you are sitting or standing and where you are placed. It tells them:

- what type of activity it is;
- what your role is;
- what the students' role is expected to be;
- who you are attending to and not attending to;
- whether you expect a student to talk to you or not.

When should you stand and when should you sit?

If you stand your presence is more obvious, you can be seen by all students, you can easily move around to the board or to individual students. However, it is tiring for you and can make the class seem very teacher-centred. If you sit behind a desk the traditional role of the teacher is reinforced; your authority is clearly stated but the desk cuts you off from the class. Also it is easy to have your materials well laid out and ready to hand before you. If you sit with the students, perhaps in a circle or horseshoe, you make the atmosphere more intimate and some of the attention is transferred from the teacher to the group.

It is often convenient to arrange the teacher's desk or table at right angles to the board with the teacher's chair close by and facing the class. Materials are then close at hand (sideward glances at the lesson plan can be easily made), and you can stand, sit or move around, as appropriate. Moving can usefully signal transition in a lesson. For example, you may sit when creating interest in a text the students are going to read, and then stand before you give a set of instructions for the next stage.

Activities with the teacher in front of the class

Some activities (for example, introducing new language, controlled practice, giving instructions) often demand that you are 'directing' what is going on. You need to stand at the front so that:

- you can see what everyone is doing;
- you can maintain control through gesture and eye contact;
- the students can see any visual aids or mime actions you use;
- you are mobile enough to help and correct individuals;
- the students can focus on you. They need to see your facial expressions and gestures, as well as your mouth, since these all reinforce what is being said. It is essential that students see your mouth to see how words are pronounced. If you stand with your back or side to the class you are depriving them of the best conditions for hearing and understanding.

Be careful, though, not to be totally frozen out there in front, or move around too much, distracting students by constantly pacing the floor, or develop habits like rocking backwards and forwards from one foot to the other.

Find the optimum position: not so close that you are on top of the students, nor so far away that they can't see or hear you; not blocking any essential visuals or writing on the board; not blocking students from communicating either with you or each other.

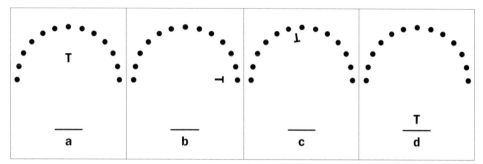

For example, position **a** excludes students at the sides. Position **b** focuses exclusively on a few students; position **c** removes control over part of the class and stops them from seeing the board. However, position **d** is ideal for a small group seated in a horseshoe shape, unless you are helping an individual or trying to make the board visible.

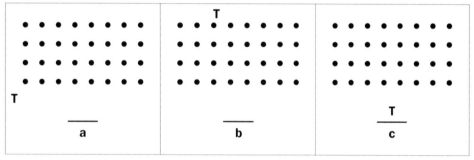

In a large class with the seats arranged in rows, position **a** weakens your control over the far side of the class, **b** can be rather menacing if you are talking to the class (unless you are reading from the board or showing slides) and, since there can be no eye contact or gestural control, ineffective if you're directing language practice; whereas **c** is ideal for most 'up-front' teaching.

How can you help an individual student during these activities?

If the layout of the class allows it, move forward. Be careful, though. Unless you retain involvement, say by eye contact, you may well exclude the other students, which is all right only if they have got something else to do. When correcting one student involve the others by inviting them to provide the required language. If you are focusing on the correction of pronunciation involve the other students by getting them to repeat the sounds as well.

Don't loom over a student or sit on the student's desk; it is intimidating. If it is really individual help you are giving, you can try leaning forwards or crouching in front.

How can you write on the board without turning your back on the students?

You can't, and for that reason many teachers now prefer to use an overhead projector (OHP). However, there are a number of ways of cutting down time spent with your back to the students:

- Prepare cards with key vocabulary or sentences written on them. They can be attached quickly to the board by tape or a product such as 'Blu-Tack'.
- If you have a revolving board, prepare your board work before the lesson begins and reveal it at the appropriate time.
- When you do write on the board you can involve the students by asking them what comes next, how to spell new words, etc, provided you don't overdo it and slow the lesson down too much.
- Invite the students to write on the board while you monitor.
- Write on the board while they are doing a task – perhaps reading.
- If you have a lot to write up, do it in small chunks and turn round and face the class from time to time, perhaps to ask the students some questions.
  (See also Chapter 3 Section 1: *The board*.)

Pairwork and groupwork

For this, either sit down on a chair, outside the communication circuits you have set up, and listen; or move around unobtrusively. The more you impose yourself the more students will look to you for help. If you make contributions, crouch next to the group or lean over at a tactful distance. Be brief and move on. If you are asked to give your ideas to a group's discussion you can participate as 'a student', not as 'an authority'.

Listening to a recording, watching a video or reading a text

When students are engaged in such activities they do not need to see you. In fact, moving around may be distracting. Don't feel that not showing yourself is not teaching. Use the time profitably: going over their names, filling in the register, getting ready for the next stage. If you do not think it will distract the students you can tidy up the board or add anything necessary for the next stage. If your students are reading a text you can read it too – only do so quite slowly, twice. You can use this as a rough yardstick to how long it will take them to read the text.

Task 1

Aim

To highlight the importance of where you stand in the classroom in relation to the class's activity. This task can be done during TP, during a real lesson, or using a video tape of a lesson, specially filmed to concentrate on the teacher.

Procedure

1 Make a rough grid of the classroom. For example:

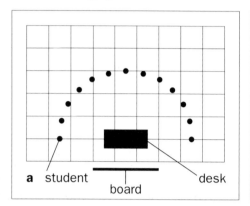

a student   board   desk

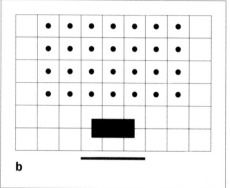

b

2 Every two minutes, or more frequently if the lesson is a short one, make an entry in the appropriate square to show the approximate position of the teacher. The first entry is number 1, the second 2, and so on. The grid ends up looking something like this:

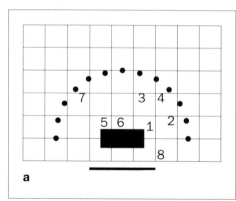

a

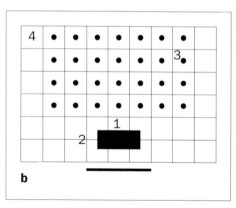

b

3 Indicate whether the position is appropriate by making a separate list of the numbers and marking them at the same time ✓ (OK), ✗ (wrong) or ? (not sure).

Comment

1 Like many observation tasks this can become tedious if it goes on too long, so it is probably better to limit it to twenty minutes.
2 Discussion should focus on how static or how mobile the teacher is and the effect this has on the students.

Task 2

Aim

To help modify patterns of movement during class.

Procedure

1 Write your TP lesson plan leaving a broad margin down the right-hand side of the page.
2 In the margin, mark the approximate teaching position most appropriate to the activity, eg:

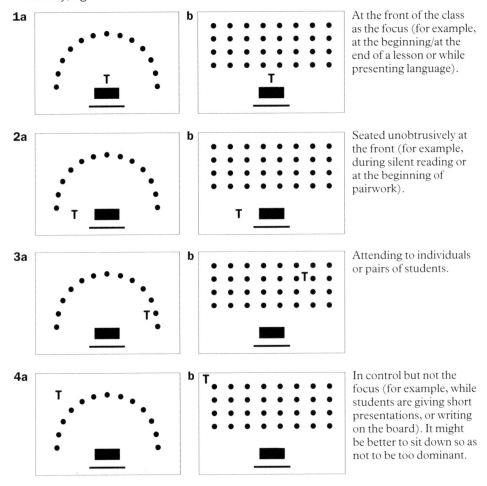

At the front of the class as the focus (for example, at the beginning/at the end of a lesson or while presenting language).

Seated unobtrusively at the front (for example, during silent reading or at the beginning of pairwork).

Attending to individuals or pairs of students.

In control but not the focus (for example, while students are giving short presentations, or writing on the board). It might be better to sit down so as not to be too dominant.

3 Ask an observer to note your pattern of movement and compare predicted positions with reality after TP.

Comment

1 Don't be unnecessarily exact. Restrict the positions to four or five typical positions and use simple symbols to indicate them.
2 The technique of using a right-hand margin as above can also be employed to concentrate on such areas as gesture, the relative amounts you and the students are expected to talk in the class, and types of activity. Symbols are much more striking and more easily read than words.

Task 3 👥👥

Aim

To consider the value of different classroom seating arrangements.

Procedure

1 With a partner, consider the advantages and disadvantages of the various seating arrangements shown below:

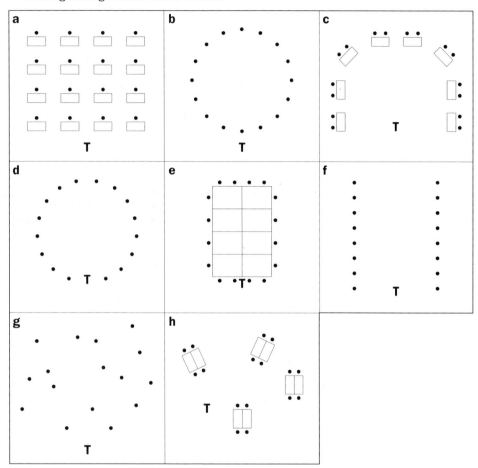

2 In particular, consider the following questions:

a How is the relationship between the teacher and the students likely to vary in each case? How will it affect the classroom atmosphere?

b Which arrangements are the most conducive to the teacher maintaining effective control over the class?

c In which situation will the teacher dominate most? What will the teacher's role be in each case?

d Which arrangement is most suitable for the students to be able to talk to each other?

e Which arrangements allow the students to communicate without interference from the teacher?

f How will the size of the group affect the arrangement?

g What activities might be suitable for each arrangement?

Task 4

Aim
To help bring out some of the differences seating arrangements can make.

Procedure
1 Work out three or four different seating arrangements for a class you know.
2 Discuss these with someone else who knows the class, going into detail about individual students and the activities you can do with them.
3 Try them out with the class, explaining beforehand what you are doing.
4 Ask the class to rank the different arrangements on scales of 1–5 (so 1 = easy to talk to partner, 5 = difficult to talk to partner; 1= easy to see teacher and board, 5 = difficult to see teacher and board). Other considerations include: ease with which written work, class discussion, open pairwork can be conducted.

Comment
You should ensure you choose a class whose English is good enough, although in a monolingual group any discussion could be in the mother tongue.

Task 5

Aim
To discover first-hand the effect of different seating arrangements.

Procedure
1 Make a note of and discuss with a partner the different seating arrangements on your training course for different types of sessions.
2 Choose at least one and give grades from 1–5 on a chart like the following:

Title of session	*Groupwork*		
Approach	*Discovery in groups*		
Seating arrangement used	*Random groups of four around desks*		

I found it easy to

a)	talk to the group	5	e) work silently	1
b)	relax	3	f) concentrate on the activity	4
c)	see the board	1	g) learn what was intended	3
d)	see the teacher	1		

3 Discuss how such sessions might have been improved by different seating arrangements.

Comment
The trainer can help such discussions by arranging the seating in a variety of ways. Some trainers may wish to do this systematically over a number of sessions.

3 Attention spread

A class, no matter how big it is, is made up of individuals, most of whom want to be listened to or addressed by the teacher directly. Ideally all students should:

- be given the opportunity to repeat any new language;
- have their errors corrected;
- have individualized tasks if necessary;
- feel that they have contributed to the class in more or less equal amounts, even though what they contribute will inevitably be different.

Obviously the larger the class the more difficult the ideal is to achieve. Sometimes in large classes it might be only possible to give the briefest acknowledgement: a smile, a gesture, a word of encouragement. Even that, though, is worth it. In smaller classes you should be able to give more individual attention to everyone. Use eye contact to draw in all the students when you are directing them together as a class. (See Section 1: *Use of eye contact, gesture and the voice.*) Also use chorus repetition work, particularly in large classes. Chorus work ensures that at least everyone repeats new language and everyone is getting equal though not individual attention.

How can you give individual attention?

There are a number of occasions when you give individual attention, depending on the stage of the lesson or on the activity: when you are asking questions, eliciting contributions, getting them to repeat, monitoring, correcting, giving help, etc.

When giving individual attention:

- Make sure you know all the students' names so you don't just call on those whose names you know.
- Dot about. Don't go round in a line. It's too predictable; students switch off until it's their turn to contribute. It doesn't matter sometimes if the same student is called on twice. It keeps the class on its toes.
- Involve students who are not being dealt with directly as much as possible. For example, encourage peer correction. (See Chapter 7 Section 2: *Correction techniques.*)
- Don't teach exclusively to either the good or the weak students. Give the good students difficult questions and tasks and the others easier ones, if possible without it being obvious. If you are giving controlled oral practice go to the weaker students after the stronger so they have more opportunities to hear the target language.
- Spend longer with students who don't understand or can't do what is expected if necessary, but try to keep the others occupied while you do so by setting them a task to be getting on with.
- Don't let individual students 'hog' your attention. If you are eliciting from the class use the students' names to let them know who you want to speak. If students persistently shout out, quieten them firmly with a word or gesture, and make it clear that it is someone else's turn.
- Remember to step back and include students at the edge of any seating arrangement. They're easy to forget, particularly those in the front, and to the side.

The sixth sense of knowing who has said what when and knowing when you have given enough individual attention without either dissatisfying the individuals concerned or boring the group, only really comes with experience. You should, though, be conscious of the need to develop it.

What about students who don't want 'public' attention?

During activities that don't involve controlled language practice or depend on the involvement of everyone, it may be better to let students who don't wish to contribute remain silent. Listening and reflection play an important part in the way many students learn a language. If students feel they are likely to be 'picked on' at random they will quickly learn not to make eye contact. By lowering their heads or looking away they may miss useful information. It may be easier for them and you if students who wish to contribute indicate (perhaps by raising their hands).

Attention during pairwork and groupwork

During pairwork and groupwork students cannot expect and often do not need constant attention from the teacher. Provided the activity has been set up well, the teacher is freed to monitor students' performance in order to give individual feedback later. Groupwork can also provide an opportunity for teachers to take individuals aside and give them specific (perhaps remedial) help.

Task 1

Aim
To increase awareness of the extent to which attention is being spread around the class.

Procedure
1 Before TP ask someone observing you to make a chart like the one on p27, allowing one box per student.
2 Ask the person to make a mark in each box when a student is addressed or invited to contribute.
3 After the lesson, say where you feel attention was focused and who you thought the weak and the strong students were.
4 Ask the person who observed to show you the chart and discuss the results.

Comment
A variation of this activity is to ask an observer to make a list of the students' names and to put a mark next to each name every time it is used by the teacher.

Task 2

Aim
To help spread attention randomly between individual students and yet evenly round the class.

Procedure
1 Before TP write out a list of the students' names in random order (not the order they sit in).
2 During one predetermined part of the lesson, go down the list and make sure everyone is included. If necessary, go through it more than once, backwards as well as forwards.

4 Teacher talk and student talk

Teacher talk

To a large extent the balance between TTT (teacher talking time) and STT (student talking time) depends on the type of lesson and activities involved, and on the level of the students. In the classroom you will usually speak more when:

- presenting, clarifying, checking, modelling new or revised language;
- setting up activities or giving instructions and feedback;
- providing language input: for example, when telling a story;
- establishing rapport by chatting: for example, about what the students did at the weekend, what you are planning to do in the evening, etc.

What are the advantages of teacher talk?

1 The teacher (whether English is his/her first or second language) is a very valuable source of language used in an authentic situation, particularly if the students are studying in a country in which English is not the first language. That is one reason for trying to avoid using the students' mother tongue if possible. (However, see Section 9: *The monolingual and the multilingual class.*) Language in the classroom is genuinely communicative. You can react naturally to the students and they will often pick up the everyday words and expressions that you use.

2 Teacher talk is needed for good classroom management – to give clear instructions, to tell the students what to expect, to call on students by name, etc. There is nothing artificial about a situation that involves you praising a student or asking another to try again.

3 You can provide authentic listening texts for your students. It is not always necessary to play a recording of an account, an anecdote or a joke if you can provide the real thing.

4 You can often provide the best model for new language. The students can both hear and see you clearly. It is often better for you to model the language than use a recording. This is particularly true when the focus is on pronunciation, providing you are consistent.

5 You can explain something about the language that is being learned in a helpful and reassuring way, and check the students' understanding.

What are the disadvantages of teacher talk?

1 The aim of most language classes is usually to get the students using the language. When you talk too much then the chances are the students aren't being given maximum opportunity to talk.

2 It is also likely that you won't be listening to the students closely enough, thinking too much about what you're going to say next.

3 If you talk 'for' the students they will think you don't appreciate their efforts and will become demotivated.

4 There is a danger, especially at lower levels, that the language you use for explanation is more difficult to understand than the language being learned.

How can you help the students understand what you say?

With experience you will automatically 'grade' your language – adapt the way you speak, your vocabulary and use of structures to the level of the students you are teaching.

Think about your speed of delivery, especially if you are providing a model of the target language. Don't gabble, but don't allow a class to get used to an unnaturally slow delivery – for example, saying *I am* instead of *I'm*, or pronouncing *an* as /æn/ rather than with the weak form /ən/. It may help them in the short run but not in the long run, as native speakers don't speak like that! Use pauses more, if necessary, but keep the contractions and the natural linking of words.

Try to choose your language carefully. Consider your students' backgrounds. The word *advertisement*, at least in writing, will be understood by French students even before they have learned it. Not so by Japanese students. Neither group, however, may understand the abbreviation *ad*. Short words are not necessarily easier – often the opposite is true. (See Chapter 6 Section 2: *Vocabulary.*) There are many international words such as *hotel, Coca-Cola, disc* that nearly all students understand. These can be a great help sometimes when practising a new structure: they give a comfortable feeling of familiarity.

Find out what your students find easy and difficult to understand and adapt your language to them. If you are teaching a class of doctors, you will soon discover that their professional knowledge will contribute considerably to their understanding of certain specialized words and phrases.

If necessary, simplify your language. For example:

T: What have you got for number six, Eric?
S: (Silence)
T: Number six, what did you write, Eric?
S: (Silence)
T: Number six, Eric?

Give the students time to do what you ask them. Often the students do understand and need a bit of time. In some cultures it is normal to allow a noticeable pause before a response. If you are nervous and concerned not to let the pace of the lesson flag, it is not always easy to remember to hold yourself back.

It may be helpful at first for you to plan the language you are going to use in the classroom. With low-level students it may be worth writing down the exact words you are going to use for such things as instructions, explanation or 'concept' checking questions (see the glossary).

How can you avoid unnecessary and unhelpful TTT?

- Choose language the students already know to give instructions and explanation. The words and structures should generally be *below* the level of the language being 'taught'.
- Avoid jargon such as 'concept checking', 'eliciting' and other 'teacher language'.
- Don't describe your every intention. Indicating a major change of activity for the students is acceptable: *All right, now we're going to write a letter together* is fine; whereas revealing all your strategies isn't – *Now I'm going to check your*

comprehension is information the students don't need to know. It sounds heavy and pedantic and may worry some students who don't know what you mean.

- Avoid running commentaries on your lesson, both to yourself and your students: *I didn't explain that very well, did I?* It's distracting and makes you seem more interested in your 'performance' than in the students.
- Don't use ten words where one will do. You may feel it is more polite to say *I wonder if you'd mind repeating this,* but *Repeat* with an appropriate gesture, using a friendly tone of voice, is much quicker, more efficient and less confusing for students. When presenting new language a clear context is usually a much better way of conveying meaning than a long explanation. (See Chapter 6 Section 1: *Structures: grammar and functions.*)
- Don't use words at all where a gesture, mime, an object or a picture can convey the meaning quickly and unambiguously. (See Chapter 6 Section 2: *Vocabulary.*)
- Don't repeat yourself unless you have to – asking questions twice can be a nervous habit. Don't panic at the silence, wait; students may need time to process the question.
- Don't automatically repeat or 'echo' what the students say – as in this exchange:

    S1: What's Susan doing?
    S2: She's having lunch.
     T: Yes, she's having lunch.

If the teacher repeats Student 2's response the other students will make no effort to understand Student 2 – they'll wait until the teacher 'interprets' it. This devalues Student 2's efforts and decreases student/student interaction. Echoing increases TTT, slows down the pace of a lesson and gives the impression of a teacher-dominated class.

Task 1

Aim
To help identify different degrees of complexity in language.

Procedure
1 Rank the following instructions according to how easy they are to understand.
What's his name?
Could you tell me what his name is?
His name. Please.
Ask him what his name is.
Ask 'What's your name?'
2 Compare your ranking with someone else's in the group and discuss why one instruction is more difficult than the other.

Task 2

Aim
To help simplify language for classroom use.

Procedure
Look at the following questions:
What do you think this object's called?
What might he be getting up to?
I wonder if you can remember where it was she was going?
What do you imagine's going to happen next?

Write down simpler ways of saying the same thing and compare your questions with someone else's.

Task 3

Aim

To simplify language for classroom use and to recognize the value of gesture and mime.

Procedure

1 Work with two others in your group. One should pretend to have almost no English. If possible, record the exercise.
2 Tell the proficient user of English how to do something, eg change a tyre, make an omelette.
3 Tell the 'elementary' speaker how to do the same thing in simpler language.
4 Compare the language used for both, possibly referring to the recording.

Comment

Try giving the instructions without using your hands. Then think about how you could use gesture and mime to make the instructions clearer.

Task 4

Aim

To create an awareness of how everyday language that is easily understood by the proficient speaker can be difficult for the low-level learner.

Procedure

1 Get hold of a set of instructions for something relatively simple like an everyday electrical appliance.
2 With another member of your group, discuss the likely difficulties that low-level students might have.
3 Write the instructions again, trying to eliminate the difficulties.
4 Compare your results with others in the group.
5 If you can, try out the instructions on an elementary student.

Comment

You can go through the same procedure with the instructions in a textbook aimed at high-level students. Then look at the instructions used in a book aimed at low-level students. Do you think the authors have managed to grade the language?

5 Eliciting, giving instructions and setting up activities

Eliciting

Eliciting is when the teacher brings out student knowledge, suggestions and ideas. You can do this by asking questions and by encouraging and guiding contributions. By eliciting you can use a little 'teacher talking time' to increase 'student talking time'. Finding out what the students already know and getting a few ideas from the students about a context or some vocabulary related to it is a useful way of setting up an activity, whether it be a roleplay, a game, a listening task, the introduction of a new language structure, etc.

What are the advantages of eliciting?

By eliciting you:

- get the students involved and interested;
- bring relevant information to the front of their minds;
- increase the amount they talk;
- help them take responsibility for their own learning. Eliciting gives members of a class the necessary and motivating feeling of being encouraged to invest part of themselves, give some of their opinions and contribute some of their knowledge so that what happens seems to depend partly on the students themselves;
- get crucial information about what the students already know and can use in relation to the language you are focusing on. This helps you to avoid teaching what they already know and helps you to assess how far students are with you as you go through the lesson.

What are the disadvantages?

- Eliciting can take time and if time is short you may want to *tell* the students and quickly check they understand.
- You can't elicit something the students don't know in the first place. You can spend ages trying to elicit language which is just not there – this leads to frustration on your part and confusion and feelings of inadequacy on the part of the students.
- There is a danger that if you elicit what you're looking for from one student you assume (perhaps mistakenly) that all the students in the group understand.

So, eliciting is quite a difficult skill. It needs practice and experience if it is not to be time-wasting and embarrassing. The most important qualities you need are the ability to really listen to the students and the ability to respond quickly and flexibly, using the techniques outlined earlier in this chapter under these headings: *eye contact, use of gesture, using students' names* and *attention spread*. For example, if a number of students are calling out at the same time you need to be able to ignore what you don't want and pick up on the contributions you are looking for.

Techniques for eliciting

Usually eliciting consists of giving clues and prompts in order to get the students to make an appropriate contribution. Eliciting should never be simply guessing what's in the teacher's head!

At higher levels eliciting might consist of something like: *What do you know about the life of Gandhi?* or *Look at this picture and describe the man as fully as you can.*

At lower levels, however, the eliciting needs to be more guided by the teacher, particularly if it serves a specific aim, as it would when you are building up a context for the introduction of a new language item. For example:

Aim
To introduce and practise the structure *need + -ing* as in *the roof needs mending.*

Context
Diana and Charlie Roberts are looking at a house they want to buy. It's in a very bad state at the moment.

Visuals
A picture of Diana and Charlie. A picture of a dilapidated house.

Instead of saying to the students *This is Diana and Charlie Roberts. They are newly married. They are looking at a house for sale. It's not in good condition. There's a hole in the roof …* you might approach the task of building up the context something like this:

Teacher:	Right. Now, do you remember Diana and Charlie? *(showing picture)*
Students:	Yes.
Alberto:	Yes, last lesson. They married.
	(Gesturing towards Alberto)
Teacher:	Married? Is that right, Alberto? They g …
Alberto:	Got married.
	(Looking at Alberto)
Teacher:	Yes, again.
Alberto:	They got married.
Teacher:	Fine. When? Ten years ago? *(Looking round the group)*
Students:	No.
Beatrice:	No, no. Two days ago.
Teacher:	Beatrice?
Beatrice:	No. Two days ago.
Teacher:	Yes, where are they here? *(showing picture)*
Students:	A house. An old house. They look at house, etc.
Teacher:	Yes. Is it theirs, Catrina?
Catrina:	No. Maybe they want to buy it.
	(Looking round the group)
Teacher:	Yes. Do you think that's a good idea – to buy the house?
Students:	No.
Teacher:	Why not, Tami?
Tami:	It's old. No good.
Teacher:	Tell me more, anyone.
Students:	Dirty. It's old. The door's broken, etc.
Matias:	Roof no good.
Teacher:	Yes, Matias, the roof's no good. There's a …….. in the roof.
Emiko:	Hole.
Teacher:	Yes, good.

Now look back at the extract and note the following points.

- The teacher makes use of characters and information about them from a previous lesson, thus reducing what has to be done in this lesson.
- The use of pictures to prompt suggestions.
- The teacher picks out the contribution he or she is looking for from a number of responses.
- The use of students' names and gesture to get contributions from individual students and the word *anyone* when eliciting from the whole group.
- By using a first-sound prompt (/g/ to elicit *got*) the teacher helps the students remember a word they know. It gives an important clue to what the teacher wants.
- An obviously incorrect suggestion (*Ten years ago?*) can sometimes provoke the

right response from the students. Use this technique sparingly and only when you are sure the students know the answer. Otherwise it might sound as though you are mocking them.

- Giving a sentence with a blank in it, filled in perhaps by humming the word (the hummed word having the same number of syllables and the same stress pattern) or by the first letter of a word allows the students to hear where the word is expected to come in a whole sentence.
- In this exchange both individual language items (*got married, hole*) were elicited as well as ideas and opinions (*Do you think that's a good idea – to buy the house?*) With specific language items you might, if necessary, provide correction and pronunciation practice, but when the students offer ideas and opinions you probably won't correct what they say since it's the *idea* rather than the *language* that's important. Before the lesson, decide where you are going to correct and where you want to focus on eliciting ideas and suggestions. (See Chapter 7: *Giving feedback to students.*)

Task 1

Aim
To establish which types of questions are most suitable for eliciting information.

Procedure
1 Choose a picture which could be interpreted in different ways.
2 Decide on your interpretation.
3 Write a list of five or six salient facts about the picture as you see it.
4 Write a number of different questions which might elicit those facts.
5 Work with a partner and try to elicit your interpretation. Discuss which questions were most effective and why.

Task 2

Aim
To give practice in asking questions to elicit information.

Procedure
1 Work with a partner.
2 Select a topic, for example 'school days'.
3 In two minutes, ask your partner as many questions as possible about his or her memories. Your partner should answer with one-word answers wherever possible.
4 At the end write down as many facts as you can remember.
5 Reverse roles and go through the same procedure.
6 Compare both sets for completeness and discuss each other's question techniques.

Task 3

Aim
To practise relating the students personally to a topic before eliciting facts about it.

Procedure A
1 Choose an unlikely topic (like 'filling in holes in the road' or 'toothpick manufacturing').

2 Try to get a group of your fellow trainees to relate personally to the topic by asking suitable questions.

Procedure B

1 Ask the group to think up a topic they have no interest in.

2 Get them to relate to it by asking interesting questions.

Task 4

Aim

To evaluate the effectiveness of eliciting techniques.

Procedure

1 Observe a teacher or another trainee and make notes on some or all of the following:
  – Did the teacher use a variety of techniques?
  – Did the students understand the questions?
  – Were the questions concise?
  – Did the teacher use visual clues?
  – Were all the students participating?
  – How many were called on to contribute?
  (You may like to add some points of your own.)

2 Compare your observations with another trainee and/or with the teacher you observed.

Giving instructions

How can you make your instructions effective?

First attract the students' attention

Make sure everyone is listening and watching. Don't give out any handouts which may distract the students' attention before you need to.

Use simple language and short expressions

Use language at a lower level than the language being 'taught'. Long, more 'polite' language is time-wasting, slows the lesson down and involves you in more complicated language than the students can easily understand. Remember, as mentioned in Section 4: *Teacher talk and student talk*, impoliteness partly comes from an inappropriate use of language. Short instructions are entirely appropriate to this situation where the students accept your authority. Also, they usually realize that a firm directive manner is necessary in order to make language practice efficient and to avoid confusion and uncertainty.

Be consistent

This is especially important with low-level classes; use the same set of words for the same instruction. Common instructions are: *Everybody; All together; Again; Try again; Look (at the picture); Listen; Repeat; Say (X); Tell me; Look at the board; Stand up; Turn to page ...* . With beginners, spend time teaching them the language they need to follow instructions. (See Chapter 5 Section 6: *Learner development and study skills*.)

Use visual or written clues

Support instructions with visual clues wherever possible: real objects, pictures, gesture and mime (see Section 1: *Use of gesture, eye contact and the voice*). It is often easier to give instructions written on cards or pieces of paper that you have prepared, especially if you want the students to do different things (as in a roleplay) or if it is important that the students don't know the instructions given to their partner.

Demonstrate

If possible, show them what to do – give a demonstration or an example. Frequently, showing what to do is more effective than telling what to do. You can demonstrate a speaking activity by playing both parts yourself (moving position to show that you are two people), by playing one part and choosing a strong student to play the other part, or by asking two strong students to do (part of) the activity in front of the class. With written work an example on the board is often useful.

Break the instructions down

If the activity requires a series of steps, each requiring instructions, give simple instructions in segments and check understanding as you go along, rather than giving out all the instructions in one go. Or you can give only some of the instructions and allow time for them to be carried out before moving on to the next step. For example, where a change of seating arrangement is required before a roleplay, it is better to give the instructions and make the change before going on to assign roles and give further instructions about what they are going to do and say. Especially with any complicated series of instructions, write down what *you* need to do and say, in your lesson plan.

Target your instructions

Sometimes, instead of giving complete instructions to the whole class when the instructions don't concern everyone, you might give each student a number, a letter, or some kind of symbol. In which case it might be the number fives, or the Cs *only* who listen for what they should do:

Teacher:	Right, listen to your number. One, two three, four, five (*pointing as the numbers are called*), one, two, three, four, five (etc). Hands up all the ones! Hands up all the twos! (etc). Monica, what's your number?
Monica:	Two.
Teacher:	Right. Listen. All the fours are going to ... . All the threes ...

Be decisive

Use a signal, like the words *Right* or *Listen,* which students will learn to recognize as a cue for an instruction. Make sure the students know when to begin an activity; for example, say something like *Everyone. Start!* – perhaps accompanied by a downward hand gesture or a clap of the hands.

How do you know that the instructions have been understood?

After you give instructions *check* that they understand them – especially complicated ones.

Examples
1 Before a roleplay, after you have assigned roles:
   Teacher: Shop assistants, hands up. Now, customers, hands up.

2 Before an information gap activity in which one student in a pair has information which the other student has to find out:
   Teacher: Juan, are you going to show Jens your picture?
   Juan: No.

3 Before a dictation:
   Teacher: Do you write after the first reading or after the second reading?
   Students: The second.

Teach the students expressions which tell you they don't understand and encourage them to use them:

Examples
Sorry. I don't understand.
Can you say that again, please?

When the activity has started, monitor to see if the students are following the instructions correctly. (See Section 6: *Monitoring.*)

Task 1

Aim
To show how clear, simple instructions accompanied by gestures are both easily understood and learned rapidly by a class.

Procedure
1 Make up a short dialogue in a fictitious or unknown language.
2 Make up some simple practice instructions to go with it: the equivalents of *listen, repeat, everybody, again* and *write.*
3 Drill the dialogue line by line (the 'students' – fellow trainees – listen and repeat) and then dictate the lines so those in the group can write it down as best they can.
4 Discuss the lesson (if possible some time later) and see how far the instructions have been remembered.

Comment
It is probable that the instructions will be remembered better than the dialogue. The discussion can then most usefully focus on the reasons for this.

Task 2

Aim
To give practice in keeping instructions to a minimum and yet making them clear.

Procedure
1 Take a coursebook and choose a page which has a variety of exercises on it.

2 Work with a partner. Discuss whether the written instructions are clear and sufficient for the students to understand without a teacher. If they are not, write out a set of instructions.

3 Discuss these written instructions and decide whether they are the same words you would say if you were giving instructions to a class. If they are not, write out the instructions you would give and say how you would check that the students understood.

4 Discuss where demonstration of the instructions might be more appropriate and how it might be done.

Task 3

Aim

To develop the ability to grade instructions to the level of the group, organize them, segment them and check the students' comprehension.

Procedure

1 Look at these role cards for a guided roleplay:

STUDENT A	STUDENT B
AT THE GREENGROCER'S	AT THE GREENGROCER'S
You are the greengrocer.	You are the customer.
Your prices: apples 90p per kilo	You want: 2 kilos apples
oranges 20p each	6 oranges
bananas £1.10 per kilo	1 kilo grapes
grapefruit 50p each	a melon if they're not
pears 95p per kilo	more than £1.50 each
melons £1.60 each	something else
You have no grapes.	You have a £10 note.
You have no small change.	You don't want to spend more than £4.

2 Read the following transcription of how the activity might be set up with proficient speakers:

Well, we're going to do this roleplay, see, and we're in the greengrocer's. Now there's a slight problem. The greengrocer hasn't got all the fruit the customer wants and hasn't got any change. Not for a £10 note anyway. Now, the customer's got a £10 note but doesn't want to spend more than £4. OK? Look, I'll give out these cards. I want you to carry out this roleplay in pairs. Right? Now, you know who you are? Right? Now, you'll see if you're the greengrocer and a set of prices and, if you're the customer, you'll see a shopping list. I want you to stick to what's on those cards. All right. Are you ready? OK. Get on with it.

3 Underline the information students need to know in order to carry out the activity.

4 Simplify the vocabulary for an elementary class and cut out any unnecessary language. Add instructions where it would clarify what the students have to do.

5 Number the instructions and arrange them in logical order.

6 Write down how you would check that the students have understood the instructions.

7 Try the activity on a group, checking understanding at each step, or compare and discuss your instructions with another trainee.

Comment

Similar instruction-giving can be done for such activities as making models from Lego, operating simple machinery (eg tape recorders), giving directions, etc. It is often worth recording and transcribing the instructions as they would be given to a) a proficient speaker, and b) a low-level class. You might find you need to give very little contextual information in your instructions, but make sure your students know all they need to know.

Setting up activities

What are the different types of activities?

For convenience, activities can be divided into the following categories, although there is often an overlap.

Controlled activities

Where *you* decide on the exact language to be used and control it accordingly, perhaps by the use of prompts, maybe spoken or written on cards.

Many drills (listen and repeat, or listen and change the language in a prescribed way) are examples of controlled practice activities. Drills can be choral (when the whole class speak together); you can cue in a part of the class at a time, or you can indicate for individual students to speak.

Other teacher-controlled activities include those in which students take part in short dialogues supplied by the teacher, or when one student asks a set question and another student has a prompt to indicate the appropriate reply. Many written exercises are controlled in that only one answer is 'correct'.

Guided activities

Where *you* decide on the language areas to be practised (eg giving directions) but give the *students* a certain amount of freedom. The materials you choose should allow the students to make different language choices, although these choices may be fairly limited. Both controlled and guided activities are often used when the focus is on the practice of particular language structures or vocabulary.

Creative or free communication

Where *you* supply the motivation and maybe the materials but the *students* are free within the constraints of the situation to use any language they have to communicate and complete the task set. These activities are often used when the focus is on the development of speaking and writing skills.

Ways to set up interactive activities

Students interact when they are doing pairwork or groupwork activities – they talk and listen to each other, rather than to the teacher. Where there is an *information gap* or *opinion gap* (when one student has some information or ideas that the other student has to find out about) these can also be referred to as *communicative activities*.

Pairwork is sometimes referred to as *open* or *closed* depending on whether just one pair is speaking, usually across the class, to provide some sort of model for the others (*open*) or whether the whole class is divided into pairs and working simultaneously (*closed*). Frequently a closed pair activity is preceded by a small amount of open pair practice to get it going.

Another type of interactive activity is the mingle activity in which all the students stand up and move around talking in turn to the other students – so that pairs and small groups are being continually formed and re-formed.

Why are pairwork and groupwork useful?

Doing these interactive activities:

- gives the students more valuable talking time. It gives them more of the time they require to practise the language than is possible when you are dealing with the class as a whole;
- allows you to withdraw and monitor individual performances;
- encourages rapport between students;
- provides an opportunity for the students to co-operate with one another and learn to become independent of the teacher;
- enables the students to invest much more of themselves in the lesson;
- gives an opportunity for shy or unconfident students to participate whereas they would be reticent about contributing in front of the whole class;
- provides a change in pace;
- adds variety to a lesson.

Special considerations for pairwork and groupwork

The way you approach pairwork and groupwork can depend on such factors as the experience and expectations of the students, their level, and whether they are in a monolingual or multilingual group.

It is important to remember that not all students are used to interactive activities in class. You may have to introduce pairwork and groupwork activities gradually, making sure the tasks are clearly defined, and pointing out the rationale and advantages of the approach. In a monolingual group it may be useful to discuss the purpose of such activities and to set up the first one or two in the mother tongue. For further considerations for pairwork and groupwork with a monolingual group, see Section 9: *The monolingual and the multilingual class.*

At lower levels tasks need to be limited, more structured and generally shorter than at higher levels. However, although lower levels will need more controlled practice than advanced students they will still need opportunities to express themselves freely, just as advanced levels will need some controlled practice.

When do you do pairwork and groupwork?

This type of activity has a place in most types of lesson. Every opportunity should be taken for the students to talk to each other – when asking about unknown words, comparing their answers to tasks, correcting each other's work as well as in activities set up especially with pairs and groups in mind – practice dialogues, information gap activities, roleplays, discussions and games, etc. (See also *How can you encourage good group dynamics and interdependence between students?* on p57, and Chapter 5 Section 4: *Productive skills: speaking.*)

The stage at which pairwork and groupwork takes place depends on the particular lesson.

Example 1

The focus is on the teacher as he or she introduces a topic or language area. The teacher elicits from the whole class and then they do some repetition practice together, followed by some 'open' pairwork. Later the students are divided into pairs or groups for some guided practice.

Example 2

The lesson starts with the students in pairs or small groups brainstorming a topic, analysing some language or doing a problem-solving activity before they come together to pool their ideas. The teacher picks out some items of language the students have been having problems with and conducts a controlled activity (listen and repeat) with the whole group for a few minutes.

Planning the activity

Make sure that:

- you have a clear idea of the purpose of the activity and how it fits in with the rest of the lesson. You may also want to make the purpose clear to the students, especially if this type of activity is new to them (see also Chapter 5 Section 6: *Learner development and study skills*);
- the activity lends itself easily to pairwork or groupwork;
- the seating can be organized to make the activity possible (see also Section 2: *Classroom arrangement*);
- the time the students spend doing the activity justifies the time you need to set it up. Often groupwork takes a long time to set up; pairwork is usually more suitable for short activities;
- all the students are occupied for most of the time, ie that some are not having to wait until another pair or group has finished;
- where different pairs or groups have different tasks these tasks will either take approximately the same time to complete or more capable groups are given the longer tasks;
- you have enough materials for each group or pair;
- you decide how you want the pairs or groups to be constituted (see below);
- you decide whether a chairperson or secretary is needed for each group;
- you think carefully about your instructions.

Organizing the class: putting the students into pairs/groups

You will need to plan how you will organize the students and perhaps indicate this on your lesson plan. You need to decide whether you want the groups to be random, 'streamed' according to level, or a mixture of weak and strong, talkative and quiet. Will they be grouped according to nationality, sex or age? Do you want friends to work together or are there some students you want to keep apart? Do you want to let the students choose who to work with? Do you want them to work in the same groups every day or in different groups each time?

Random pairing or grouping

Common techniques for doing this are:

- going round the class and giving each student a number – 1, 2, 3, 4, 5; 1, 2, 3, 4, 5, etc – and then asking all the 'number ones' to sit together;

- asking the students to line up in order of the initial of their first name or second name, birthday or height and then dividing into the appropriate sized groups;
- having as many long pieces of string in the hand as there are to be pairs. Students take an end and find their partner at the other end of the piece of string;
- blindfolding as many people as there are groups who then in turn touch the people that are to be in their group (popular with children);
- giving out to each student at random a card with a word on it. The students have to mingle and find their partner. For example – *salt* would find *pepper, fish* would find *chips, Romeo* would find *Juliet*, etc. If you want to form groups you can put words on the same topic on the cards – eg *traffic light, road, car* would sit together and *apple, banana, pear* would form a group. To make this activity more difficult you can attach the words on the students' backs so they have to find out what their word is by asking one *yes/no* question of each of the other students before going on to find their partner. In this way you are using one type of interactive activity (a mingle activity) to set up pairs or groups for another interactive activity. This is a rather time-consuming way of pairing or grouping the students. Make sure you allow enough time for it and that, if possible, it links in (perhaps by topic or theme) with the following activity.

You choose the grouping

You can do this:

- by indicating by gesture and with the words *Get into pairs* that the students pair up with the person next to them (see also Section 1: *Use of eye contact, gesture and the voice*);
- by simply saying *Petra, Ali, Paula and Georg – I'd like you to work together over here;*
- by allocating numbers or letters as above, but to particular students, rather than at random. It is a good idea to have a list drawn up beforehand that you can refer to;
- by giving out cards as above but to particular people, according to a list you have drawn up.

In large classes you can quickly divide the class into three or four large groups and then do the grouping activities with cards. You have three or four identical packs of cards and the grouping takes place within the large groups.

You let the students choose who to work with

This is usually a good idea if you want the students to work on a longer activity or project, especially if it involves them co-operating outside class hours.

For longer activities such as a roleplay or discussion you may want to group twice. For example, in a class of twenty you want to have four groups of five students each playing a part in a roleplay. The situation is that parents of a teenager come home a day early from holiday to find a party in their house. A neighbour has called the police because of the noise. The characters are the *teenager, mother, father, police officer, neighbour*. In the preparation stage you can allocate roles and put the four students playing the same part together to prepare their part – ie all the mothers together, the neighbours together, etc (five groups of four students). After they have had time to pool ideas, go to each group and allocate numbers 1, 2, 3, 4 and say *All the ones in this corner, all the twos in that corner,* etc. In this way each group should have a complete set of characters (four groups of five students) and the roleplays can go ahead.

Sometimes there are uneven numbers or the person you had planned to take a particular role is absent. You have to be quite flexible and be prepared to change your plans at times. In a quick pairwork activity you can play one half of one of the pairs, although doing this prevents you from monitoring the other students, of course. You can often make one group of three instead of a pair, especially if the activity involves pooling ideas or comparing answers. In a roleplay one group can make do without one of the characters. Or if there are one or two 'spare' people ask them to take the role of evaluators and get them to feed back on how they thought the activity went.

Organizing an information gap activity

Often in communicative activities there is an information gap which has to be bridged. One student has information that the other student has to find out. It is usually important that each student does not see the material of their partner so you have to organize the class so that pairs can sit opposite each other, with the material they are using between them. The material (perhaps a picture, a chart, a short text, etc) is often in a textbook. If you create the material it is sometimes best stuck onto stiff card or concealed in a folder. In large classes, pairs sitting opposite each other may look at the facing wall where the material may be hanging or projected. Or you could use the video (with the sound turned down) as the source of information to be conveyed to the students with their backs to it.

Managing an interactive activity

Make sure you give very clear instructions (for complicated arrangements it is a good idea to write instructions down so you can refer to them). In particular, students must know when to start and finish. Be very decisive at these points, saying something like *Right everyone, are you ready? Start.* Some teachers clap their hands, tap on a table or even blow a whistle to signal the end of an activity!

Get the timing right. If the activity lasts too long it will drag. If it doesn't last long enough it won't give any sense of satisfaction. Sometimes students need a little time before they get going while others get on with the task immediately. If one group finishes early give it a further activity, related to the task. Or you may wish to stop all the groups at that point. Generally it is better to stop an activity when it is going well, provided it has achieved its main aim, than to let it peter out. If there is a definite goal, like writing a story, the students might be encouraged to finish it later.

After the activity it is often worth asking the students whether the activity was useful, what they learned, etc. If you have asked them to do something like write an article, then do something with it, like pin it up, exchange it with other students or collate the information onto a graph. If the practice itself was the goal there may be no need. (See also Chapter 7: *Giving feedback to students*.)

See also Section 9: *The monolingual and the multilingual class* for suggestions about how to avoid the use of the mother tongue during pairwork and groupwork in monolingual classes.

Task

Aim

To promote discussion of the uses and organization of pairwork or groupwork.

Procedure

This exercise consists of a number of discussion points and should be carried out in pairs or groups. You may not want to discuss all the points.

1 Draw up a list of classroom activities (eg interviews, repetition practice, two- or three-line dialogues, roleplay, writing a letter, etc).
2 Discuss which are suitable for pairwork and which are better with larger groups.
3 Discuss ways in which those which seem best suited to pairwork could be adapted to larger groups and vice versa.
4 Write down the organizational roles that students might be assigned within a group (eg chairperson, reporter, etc).
5 Discuss which of the activities from the first list might require the assignment of roles like these.
6 Discuss which of the activities from the list might need students to be grouped and then re-grouped. How would you do this?
7 Select an activity from a coursebook and discuss how it could be dealt with in pairs, threes and larger groups. Discuss organizational roles that students might need to be assigned for each of these possibilities.
8 Discuss how you would cope if there were an odd number of students for the activity.
9 Discuss which size of group you prefer to work in for the different activities that you may do with other trainees.

6 Monitoring

When students are engaged in an activity, especially if it is independent of you, you will need to keep an ear on what they are saying or glance at what they are doing. Your aims will be to see if they have understood your instructions, to assess how well they are performing the task and to evaluate particular language strengths and weaknesses. Whether you help or correct will depend on the task and what effect it will have.

Monitoring what the students are doing is just as important a skill as teaching. Because the focus isn't on you, there's a temptation to believe that you aren't doing your job. However, giving the students appropriate tasks, knowing how and when to leave them alone and providing suitable follow-up requires sensitivity, intelligence and confidence. It is the nervous or inexperienced teachers who don't have a clear idea of why they have set up the task, who find themselves unsure of their appropriate role at different stages of the lesson and who feel the need to interfere and take control of activities.

An important aspect of monitoring is the discipline often necessary for less well-motivated students, younger students and sometimes monolingual classes, where the temptation might be to abandon the task or to talk away unnecessarily in the mother tongue. Often just being in the room and giving the students the feeling that they are being supervised is enough. See Section 9: *The monolingual and the multilingual class* for further suggestions.

Monitoring the class

Whenever the class is working with you as a whole group (for example, in a choral repetition practice or when you are illustrating a language point) part of your attention must be taken up with monitoring how well the group as a whole is getting on and how individual students within the group are reacting. This monitoring process will tell you whether you are going too slowly or quickly, whether most of the students are with you, which students need a little more time or further help, etc. Monitoring helps you make decisions about whether correction is needed, when it is time to go on to the next stage of the lesson, whether further examples are needed, etc. So try not to be so involved in your plan and your materials that you have no time to watch and listen to your students. (See also Chapter 7: *Giving feedback to students*.)

Monitoring groupwork

An aim of pairwork and groupwork is often to encourage fluent, uninterrupted communication, even at times when the students' aim is more 'product-oriented' – to decide on the answers to a set of questions, to write a story, etc. So:

1 Stand back

Once you have set up the activity, allow a short time for the students to get on with it. This will give you a chance to see which groups seem to be working satisfactorily and which are having problems. It will also give all the students a chance to get into the activity before you offer help to any one group. Don't be too concerned if a group doesn't seem to be too sure of itself at first; some groups take time to get going.

2 Quickly check

Go round, listening in briefly to each group in order to satisfy yourself that they understand what they are supposed to be doing. If one or two groups are unclear about what they should be doing, or are not doing what you intended, stop them and give the instructions again. If you find that most students are confused it is better to stop, get the whole class's attention and give the instructions again.

3 Don't interrupt unless:

- the group has misunderstood what it is supposed to be doing (see above);
- some of the groups seem to be on the verge of finishing (so either give them something else to do or get ready to stop the whole activity);
- the group you are with seems to be a long way behind (so indicate anything that can be omitted and encourage them to hurry up);
- you are asked by the group (they may properly need some advice or information, but don't let them get too dependent on you).

4 Spread your attention

If you concentrate on one particular group, they will feel cramped by your presence and you won't get a very clear idea of how well the rest of the class is doing; the rest of the class, apart from feeling neglected, may well start drifting away from the task without you realizing.

5 Be easily accessible

All the groups should feel they have equal access to you and are being supervised equally.

6 If you need to feed in ideas

It is often better to talk quietly to one member of the group and suggest a possible change of direction, rather than interrupt the flow of the whole group.

7 Provide encouragement

At the beginning, groups often need encouragement to get them going; sometimes a group may start to lose interest. Always be positive. Your enthusiasm will motivate them and give them confidence. Never suggest that the activity could be less than totally useful.

8 Give correction and/or gather data for feedback

Whether you give correction during groupwork depends on the nature of the activity. For example, you will need to correct if the activity is controlled language practice and the students are making mistakes with the target language. Or you may choose to correct if a student asks you to. Occasionally students will want you to help them say something correctly, but don't hover so close to any one group that they get self-conscious and afraid of making mistakes. If you do have to correct, do it discreetly, perhaps by crouching at the level of the group and allowing individuals to turn away from the rest of the group and talk to you. If the students need a lot of help and correction then the chances are that the task is inappropriate and/or beyond their capabilities.

Although in groupwork you are often concerned to show students that you are interested in *what* they are doing, you should always be looking at *how* they are doing the task – evaluating the performance of the group and of individuals within the group. You do this in order to:

- help you decide what to do next (go on to the next stage, give further practice, skip an activity, etc);
- plan future lessons;
- give the students feedback.

Gathering data so that you can give helpful feedback is one of the main purposes of monitoring. (For when and how to give feedback, see Chapter 7: *Giving feedback to students*. Other sections to look at for help with monitoring include Chapter 2 Section 1: *Use of eye contact, gesture and the voice;* Section 2: *Classroom arrangement;* Section 3: *Attention spread.*)

Monitoring pairwork

Most of what you need to consider when monitoring groupwork also applies to pairwork. Remember that controlled practice which calls for immediate correction is more often done in pairs than in groups. Differences between monitoring pairs and groups are that a pair is more likely to stop work when you approach than a group, and in pairwork it is easier for you to take one half of the activity for a part of the time to show the students what it is about.

Monitoring individuals

Since students are individuals with different capabilities, different speeds and different work rates, some activities set (particularly reading and writing tasks) have to be individual. It follows that giving feedback (providing encouragement, feeding in ideas, correcting) will usually be on an individual basis too, so:

- make sure everyone has enough to do before you go round;
- be discreet in your approach (not too loud or disruptive). You can do a lot from your chair, especially in small classes. You don't have to loom;
- try to be encouraging;
- consider whether you will dot around the class unpredictably or move from one student to the next down the row or round the circle (consider what the effect will be of either approach);
- make sure everyone has some attention (even if it's only *Well done. Carry on*).

If all individuals are doing the same task you can monitor to see how quickly individuals are getting on and whether you need to feed in supplementary tasks to the quicker students.

7 Starting and finishing the lesson

What should you do before the class starts?

Wherever you are teaching, if possible, be in the classroom before the students to set up aids, put things on the board, try out the tape recorder or OHP, and to check or adjust the seating arrangements. Aim to begin the class at the appointed time and not just to be present in the classroom. This will:

- show the students that you have a positive attitude towards the lesson; it will make you look professional and inspire confidence;
- encourage them to arrive on time; they won't want to miss anything valuable;
- give you a chance to greet and have a few words with individual students as they arrive, an important way of establishing rapport. Depending on their level you can talk to them about their interests, what they did the night before, about events in the news, etc. Don't forget to talk about yourself and your opinions too;
- provide an opportunity to discuss individual problems and the way individual students are approaching their studies.

Punctuality

Punctuality and its importance is viewed differently by people depending on their individual personalities and on their cultural background. In many countries it is usual for events to begin ten minutes after the scheduled time. If you are teaching children, punctuality should be less of a problem, but asking anything from half a dozen to thirty adults to be on time, in their seats and ready for a lesson to begin, is usually more difficult, especially if they are coming to the lessons voluntarily. Just as we have to wait for buses or for a conversation with a colleague to end, so do they. The major difference between us and most adults is that we have to be there for the lesson to begin, they often don't. The students will take their habits from you. If you start late, the students will arrive late.

How should you deal with late arrivals when they are adults and perhaps paying for their classes?

Some such students are bound to arrive late, no matter how positive your attitude. Your options are:

1 *To exclude them*

This is a bit extreme and rather authoritarian. If they are paying for the classes it is better to try to motivate them to want to come on time. The latecomers should be as genuinely upset as you that they are arriving late. If a student is disrupting the group by coming late and the group is unable to apply pressure of its own to remedy the situation, ask the student why he or she was late and take a 'worried you're missing so much' approach. If this doesn't solve the problem then it might be best to give a private warning with a time limit attached (for example: *If you arrive more than ten minutes late next time, you won't be allowed in*). Be sensitive and flexible, though, if the lateness is unavoidable.

2 *To stop the class and explain to the latecomer what is going on*

This, however, involves holding up the rest of the class for one student, can irritate the others and may encourage persistent late arrival. This strategy would be appropriate if the lateness was unusual and especially if the student had given you prior notice.

3 *To allow them to creep in and sit down quietly*

This is probably the best solution for most adults. Acknowledge their arrival, if only with a nod, and when there is a break in the lesson for a change of activity, either briefly explain, or ask another student to briefly explain, what they have missed.

Some teachers prefer to state their policy on late arrivals at the beginning of a course. If you do that, you have to be consistent and stick to it. In general, if you have a persistent problem you will need to increase the students' motivation if you are to get them to the classes earlier. One way which might be worth trying is to have, say, a five-minute vocabulary slot or a pronunciation exercise at the beginning of the lesson – in fact, any self-contained activity which you know the latecomers will be sorry to miss. If you launch immediately into an activity on which most of the lesson depends, then it will cause problems if they are not all there. Equally, if you simply spend the first five minutes giving back homework or dealing with individual problems then there won't be any real compulsion to turn up on time – the students will know they will get their homework back anyway, and the lesson won't seem to start until that is over. On the other hand, if your late arrivals are genuine and large in number then it might in fact be best to spend time doing something like that.

What if there are new arrivals to the class?

If there are new students, introduce them to the rest of the group or get the others to introduce themselves to the new arrivals, perhaps asking a few informal questions to find out something about them. Don't make too much of it or pressurize the students unnecessarily. Equally, don't expect too much in terms of the amount of language work you can give the new arrivals until they have had time to settle down.

How can you make the starting point of a lesson clear?

The students need to know that they are to come together as a group and start work. You usually need to supply a signal such as tapping chalk or pen on the desk audibly, or clapping your hands. Other options are to close the door or to say *Right, OK* or something similar. Scanning the whole class will also help to focus everyone's attention on you.

Should you announce what the class is about?

Some lessons can be started straight away without explanation. Perhaps the students know what to do and they can get on with it. Or you may want to keep a surprise element and encourage the students to work towards finding out what the topic or the language focus of the lesson is. For other lessons it is often useful for the students to have a clear idea as to the aim of the lesson and what they are going to do. For example, you might say *Today we're going to practise listening to two people talking about their wedding plans; then we're going to the lab to practise saying those phrases we learned last week;* or alternatively you might write the topic on the board: *Writing letters of enquiry.* Such explanations need to be brief and easily understood by the students. It is often useful to link work to be done today with work done earlier, so that the students see how the lessons are connected.

Finishing the lesson

The last activity is the one that suffers if the timing of the other activities has gone awry. This can obviously be a problem if it is to be the highlight of the lesson, if homework is to be based on it, or if another teacher's lesson is to follow on from what you've done. So good timing of all stages of a lesson is important if the students are not to go away with the feeling that the lesson finished badly. What's more, it's no good finishing exactly at lunchtime when the lunch queues are beginning to build up and then expect the students to wait attentively while you set homework or make announcements. You must allow time for these in class.

How can you make the finishing point clear?

As when you start a lesson, the students need a signal to indicate when they are to finish the final activity: for example, *Well done. Close your books, please.* or *Fine, we'll finish now.* Maintain the students' attention by looking at them and speaking in a firm voice.

Summarizing and evaluating

It is often useful to summarize the lesson. If the timing of the lesson is wrong it may be usefully lengthened to fill out these final moments, for example by eliciting the language that has been practised in the lesson. Adults often appreciate being reminded of the aims of the lesson and an assessment of what has been achieved.

Telling the students what will happen next puts the lesson into context within their course of work and may also help them to look forward to and maybe prepare for their next lesson.

Asking them for their opinion of the lesson – whether they found the topic interesting or not, whether the language practice was useful, easy, difficult, whether they enjoyed the activities, whether they would like more or less of anything – not only fills the gaps; it also provides vital feedback on your lessons.

Homework can reinforce what has been done in the lesson and/or help students prepare for the next. Make sure the students have any homework task written down before they leave, to act as a reminder. (See Chapter 5 Section 7: *Students working outside the classroom.*)

Making announcements

Administrative announcements are frequently best made at the end of a lesson since the students will take the information away fresh in their minds. However, if you can't be sure of leaving enough time it might be better to give the announcements at the beginning. They can be written in the corner of the board and the students' attention drawn to them again at the end of the lesson.

Again, before making them, make sure you have all the students' attention; make the announcements clearly and check the students have understood. Don't forget to fully exploit, through questions and comments, any notices you may wish to put up in English.

Farewells and socializing

Farewells are the final signal that the students can pack up and go. Make sure you say goodbye naturally – it's a good opportunity for the students to learn how to do it.

As they and you are packing up and leaving, it is well worth chatting to individuals in the same way you do when they are arriving. This makes your relationship with them much more natural. It prevents the lesson being viewed as a performance divorced from everyday communication.

Task

Aim
To highlight the structure of the beginnings and ends of lessons.

Procedure
1 Observe as many lessons as possible for their beginnings and ends (say the first five and last ten minutes of lessons).
2 Categorize each beginning and end in terms of the following activities:
   a greeting the group
   b greeting individuals
   c socializing with the group
   d socializing with individuals
   e setting homework
   f returning homework
   g announcements
   h summarizing, evaluating, revising
   i time-filling.
   You may need to add other categories.
3 Compare the beginnings and ends in terms of their appropriateness and success.

8   Establishing rapport and maintaining discipline

Establishing rapport and motivating students

Rapport is such an important factor in determining whether a class is a success or not. Students are prepared to contribute and learn to use the language more when the atmosphere is relaxed and you and the students all get on well together, and when they have confidence in you. While the students play a large part in determining the atmosphere in the classroom, it can nevertheless be encouraged or deterred by your general attitude.

How can you establish a good working relationship with your students?

Have the right manner

During TP you will learn to establish a style of teaching which suits your personality. Aim to treat students in a manner which is natural to you; don't put on a 'performance'. Most teachers try to balance directive control over a class with a relaxed, helpful manner. Try to see the relationship from the students' point of view. As you get to know them, and as they get to know you, you will be able to judge better what you can and cannot do. Teachers who get away with teasing or even being 'rude' to their students are only effective because the students recognize underlying sympathy and humour. This approach is only possible when rapport has been established and is not to be recommended for the early days of TP!

Don't prejudge a class

Other teachers' opinions are worth listening to but relationships with teachers vary and it is as well to assume that a 'bad' class need not necessarily be bad with you, and a 'good' class, even if initially well-motivated, can become demotivated if the students lose confidence in their teacher.

Look as if you enjoy your job

A lack of enthusiasm and interest can only be a deterrent. Don't assume that students share your low times. If you teach in the evening *you* may be feeling tired at the end of the day but students may be eager to work hard, particularly if they only come to school for two hours per week and want to get the most out of their class time.

Be positive about the activities and materials you are using

If you feel that the material you are using is boring you are likely to end up with a bored class. You are probably more critical than the class anyway. If the appearance of a text is not quite up to standard (even though, of course, you should always aim for it to be), don't apologize for it. Emphasize how interesting it is or how good it is for language practice or skills development.

Show personal interest in the students

Both inside and outside the classroom, find out about their opinions, their attitudes and their day-to-day life when they're not learning English. In monolingual classes, if you are the 'foreigner' abroad, let them tell you things about their way of life. In multinational classes, find out about their countries and cultures. Apart from anything else, knowing what interests them and what offends them can help determine topic areas for your class. Also, being able to refer occasionally to something you know about individual students in the class is, if done with tact, a good way of building up a relationship with the group as a whole.

Personalize materials and activities

Wherever possible, elicit real experiences and opinions from your students rather than relying on fictional situations and characters to illustrate and practise language. Tell the students about yourself, your friends and your family. They are more interested in you and in each other than in characters from books.

Respond and react to what students say

As you become less nervous you'll be better at hearing what the students are saying and responding in a natural and interested way. Wherever possible, respond naturally and honestly to students' questions or comments – even during controlled practice activities. It is sometimes not easy to know whether to comment on the accuracy of what has been said or whether to respond naturally. Compare these two exchanges, taking place during a break:

1 **Helmut:** You come to party tonight?
  Teacher: Are you coming!
2 **Helmut:** You come to party tonight?
  Teacher: Yes, what time is it?

In the first exchange Helmut might be confused, thinking he is being asked if *he's* coming – in fact his English is being corrected. While there's a time and place for correction (See Chapter 7: *Giving feedback to students*), it is often inappropriate to discourage genuine interaction by responding as a 'teacher' rather than as a 'friend'. You could try combining the two roles by responding: *You mean 'Are you coming to the party?' – Yes, I am. What time is it?*

Be interested in their progress

Talking to the students informally can tell you what they think they need to learn, what they think their good and weak points are. It also gives you the opportunity to judge their language needs for yourself, in normal relaxed circumstances outside the conventions of the classroom. Students can also tell you their difficulties and why they think they're having them. Such information should help you decide what to do in the classroom when you work out what the group as a whole needs.

Ask for comments on the classes

It is well worth asking your students individually and occasionally as a group, if possible, what they find useful and not so useful about your classes. Many students like to be consulted about their course, though some may be reluctant to make critical comments. See also Chapter 5 Section 6: *Learner development and study skills*, and Chapter 7 Section 3: *Evaluation and testing*.

How can you encourage good group dynamics and interdependence between students?

Obviously the larger the class and the fewer number of weeks you teach it, the more difficult it is to be concerned with, or influence, how the students feel about each other. However, you should at least try to develop a co-operative atmosphere, with students taking each other into account as much as possible and learning to share language and ideas. It is one of the teacher's tasks to manage the learning situation so that students interact. When students learn to learn from each other, the group as a whole benefits. A group which is co-operating, sharing ideas, providing help and evaluating the success of activities is likely to be taking more overall responsibility for what it learns and how it learns than a group that is used to filtering everything through the teacher. Such responsibility usually aids the success with which students learn a language. Their dependence on you is reduced and yet their motivation increases. The group develops its own positive dynamic.

Here are some practical ways to help you encourage this spirit of interdependence. They are not in order of importance, and the list could certainly be added to.

- When making seating arrangements, be aware of which students are friends and which do not get on so well.
- Make sure the students know each other's names. (See *Using students' names* on p19.)
- At the beginning of a course of lessons have a 'getting to know you activity' to break the ice and get everyone talking to one another. (See *How can the students learn each other's names?* on p20.)
- Choose activities and materials that involve the students talking to each other about their personal experiences, ideas and opinions (see above).
- Have plenty of pairwork and groupwork, especially at the beginning of a course of lessons.
- When doing pairwork, change the pairs frequently so students get to work with a variety of people. An activity in which students circulate or mingle can break down barriers.
- Encourage the students to talk directly to one another, not 'through' you in whole class activities.
- Redirect students' enquiries to other students and only answer them yourself as a last resort. If it is done regularly a simple gesture should be enough to encourage it. In time the students should by-pass you altogether.
- Get the students to help each other. If a student doesn't know the answer to something or know how to do something like pronounce a word or complete a written exercise, get another student to help. In oral work, a simple gesture may be enough to indicate that you expect this to happen.
- If a student can't correct him- or herself get another student to correct; don't jump in yourself unless you have to. (See Chapter 7 Section 2: *Correction techniques.*)
- Get students to evaluate each other's work. So if a student offers you some language for approval, turn to the others and say *Is that all right?* or *Do you agree?* Equally, get the students to look over each other's written work. Even at lower levels, where perhaps they have just copied something from the board, this can be a useful exercise. If, at higher levels, they have individually jotted down a few ideas on a topic, ask them to look at their neighbour's ideas and talk about them while they are waiting for the rest to finish.
- Get the students to prepare and ask questions to check the comprehension of a text rather than asking all the questions yourself. Before they ask the questions, go round quickly to make sure the questions are understandable and answerable. Questions can be prepared individually, in pairs or in groups.

- Give the students responsibility for other members of the group. If a new student arrives you could ask one of the students to introduce the other students and encourage them to ask the newcomer friendly questions. If a student is late, you might get the other students to find out why.
- Make sure that you discreetly acknowledge the abilities of the stronger students; disallow any impatience with weaker students; generally show that everyone has something to contribute.
- Don't let individual students dominate the group or work against the interests of the group. (See *Maintaining discipline* on p60.)
- Don't supply everything yourself. Get them to lend each other pens, to share books, to open windows, etc.
- Don't dominate a class yourself. Give the students opportunities to interact and create a positive and supportive atmosphere.

In the final analysis it is generally the teacher who creates the working atmosphere of a class. If you over-dominate, the students tend to invest little of themselves in the class and you may even have discipline problems. On the other hand, if you fail to direct the students when necessary, and give firm guidance, they are likely to make an ineffective working group and suffer feelings of frustration and insecurity.

Task 1

Aim
To show how different teachers can view the same group in different ways.

Procedure
1 Observe a class which is unfamiliar to you, if possible one doing a fairly 'free' activity.
2 Make notes on the prominent students and the least prominent students in relation to their personalities, their approach to the class, their learning habits, their relationship with the other students, and so on.
3 Show your student profiles to the class teacher and discuss the extent to which he or she agrees.

Comment
This comparison can yield very fruitful discussion, particularly if your comments are committed to paper and, in the case of a discrepancy of views, both sides are fully argued.

Task 2

Aim
To develop an understanding of the value of interaction between colleagues and mutual evaluation.

Procedure
1 Ask each member of the group to write a report on one aspect of the others' contributions to the course (for example, TP, the social atmosphere, discussion groups, etc). The report should be framed positively, noting good points first, and making criticism in the manner of *I'd like it if he or she did … more* rather than *He or she doesn't …*
2 Discuss the results.

Comment
Seriously conducted, this exercise can vastly improve the working relationship of a group and develop the habit of being able to comment critically without being destructive or making people feel threatened. For this reason it is essential that no teacher trainer should approve or disapprove of the contents of the reports.

Task 3

Aim
To discover the value of interaction activities.

Procedure
1 In pairs or as a whole group, do a selection of interaction activities. Ideally they are best done in a foreign language. For example: Find someone in your group with whom you have three things in common.
2 Discuss how you felt doing the activities, discuss language areas that arose and, if done in a foreign language, discuss language problems you had.

Comment
This exercise is best done at the beginning of a course when everyone is getting to know one another.

Maintaining discipline

The extent to which you will have to maintain discipline over and above general classroom management depends on a number of factors:

- the age of the students. Obviously children need to be more overtly disciplined than adults. Generally young teenagers are considered to be the most difficult;
- the reasons for learning and the motivation of the students – whether they are obliged to be in class or whether they are 'volunteers';
- the size of the class. It is more difficult to keep an orderly atmosphere in a large class than a small one;
- the atmosphere and ethos of the institution. Some institutions are much stricter than others in their attitude to student behaviour;
- the respect the members of the class have for teachers in general and you in particular.

Some of these factors you can influence and others you cannot. We have already mentioned the balance to be achieved between exercising control and encouraging a relaxed, friendly atmosphere in which the students can interact with each other. If in doubt, err on the side of control initially, especially with children. It is always easier to relax control as the lessons progress than to try to tighten up when the class seems to be getting unruly. Sometimes you may feel that you have to sacrifice popularity for respect but in the long run teachers who are not respected are not generally popular either.

You will gain respect if:

- you are punctual;
- you are well prepared for the lesson;
- you return homework promptly;
- you do what you say you are going to do;
- you treat people consistently and fairly;

- you try not to let your personal feelings about individual students influence the way you treat them as members of the group;
- you don't ignore problems;
- you never make threats you are not able or prepared to carry out;
- you never lose your temper.

How can you deal with problem students?

Students may cause problems in a number of ways. They may be unwilling to take part in activities, show obvious signs of boredom or disaffection, talk (in their own language) when you don't want them to, or even openly question the usefulness or the interest of the activities and materials you are using. There may be some who don't want to work with certain students or who behave badly when paired up with particular people. Some students may be persistently late or never do any homework.

With a small group of adults, dealing with students like this need not be a heavy-handed affair. Often hinting that you recognize the trouble in front of everyone is enough, but be tactful or humorous and try to win the problem student round. Sometimes a friendly chat helps, particularly when the real problem is that the student feels he or she is not being acknowledged enough by you. Listen. They may have a genuine complaint. Another tactic is to put the student into a position of responsibility – chairing a group discussion or reporting back on groupwork. Often the problem is that students don't feel responsible enough for the progress of the class.

If there are younger students who are working against the interests of the group, spend some time talking to them in private; tell them how you see the situation and how you feel about it. Listen to the student but insist on improvement. You may be able to take certain steps – such as not pairing up certain people. Try to sort out the problem but be careful not to let them command too much of your attention, especially at the expense of other students. You might easily provide the wrong sort of encouragement and lose the rest of the group.

Often there are students who are not a real problem for you but who are a problem for other students. Perhaps there is a student who is very shy and never contributes in pairwork or groupwork – in this case it can be helpful if you change the pairs frequently, put the person into a three rather than a pair, give the person more support in pairwork (a more concrete task perhaps), or even take the person's partners aside and enlist their support and understanding. A very different type of problem student is the one who is over-enthusiastic, who always shouts out the answers and is very demanding of your attention. If you have a student like this in your class, make sure you nominate well – don't acknowledge the student unless you specifically name him or her and if need be say *No, Anita, I want Ricardo to answer.*

If in doubt, ask for advice from a more experienced teacher. The problem may be a common one for which a simple solution exists. Although students frequently sort out problems for each other, don't ignore them or hope they'll go away. This is particularly the case with classes of children. It will only get worse and make you look weak and ineffectual. If control over a class is lacking it is essential that you seek advice and support from someone else in the school. (See also *Punctuality* on p52.)

How do you control noise levels in the class?

Although this is not really a discipline problem it can appear so in institutions where classes are generally conducted in silence with only the voice of the teacher to be heard. One of the inevitable consequences of trying to teach the spoken language through maximizing student talking time is that there will often be more than one person talking in the room at any one time. Using pairwork in a class of forty means that there could easily be twenty talking at once and the noise level may disturb the person using the room next door. There are ways of keeping the noise level down at times:

- Give each group a different task. If your groupwork involves a quiet reading activity as well as a discussion stage, then one group may be talking while the other is reading.
- Make sure the students are close enough to each other. A spread-out group is noisier than a huddle.
- Appoint a chairperson for groups. The chairperson can have several functions, one of which can be to make sure that only one person talks at any one time.
- Tell the students to talk quietly. This is an obvious piece of advice but often ignored. The students usually appreciate the problem as much as anyone else and if they are reminded they should do as you say.
- With repetition work you can ask the students to say the words to themselves or to whisper, or organize it so only part of the class speaks at one time.
- Prevent the activity from going on too long. Groupwork with a task which expects the students to express themselves will tend to get noisier the longer it goes on. Break it up with fresh instructions and a reminder about the noise level.
- Check with other teachers beforehand. If you anticipate a noisy lesson it is best to check that the class next door is not doing an exam at that time.

9 The monolingual and the multilingual class

Monolingual and multilingual classes both have advantages and disadvantages.

What are the advantages of teaching a multilingual group?

- All communication in the class is authentic – English is the only common language. The students are motivated to make themselves understood in English as there are no possible short cuts. Interaction is natural and the students are usually not so self-conscious.
- A multilingual class is a multicultural class. As a result a lot of interest is generated by comparing the way of life of the different students. They are usually very interested in finding out about each other and each other's cultures.
- Multilingual classes usually take place in an English-speaking country. As a result the students have more opportunities to pick up the language from the environment – when shopping, on social occasions, from the media, at their accommodation, etc. These students usually make much quicker progress than those learning in their own country.

What are the disadvantages?

- The main difficulty is being sure that all the students have understood. You often have to spend more time illustrating and checking meaning.

- The students will have different language problems depending on how different their language is from English in, for example, aspects of pronunciation, vocabulary and grammar.
- Because students come from different countries, their general educational background, their approach to learning and their study skills may be very different.

You may be familiar with one or more of the languages represented in the class and so it is inevitable that your understanding of these students' problems will be better than those whose language and culture is unfamiliar to you. Don't be tempted to translate words into those languages you know as this is not only confusing but also very unfair to those students whose languages you don't speak. It may even be better to pretend ignorance so that students can't say, for example, *It's 'jouet', isn't it?*

What are the advantages of teaching a monolingual group?

- As your students have the same mother tongue they will usually have the same problems with particular aspects of pronunciation or grammar. You can use your knowledge of their difficulties to concentrate on and give further practice in these areas.
- They may have very similar learning backgrounds and styles.
- They will probably be more homogeneous in outlook and more accepting of one another.
- There are occasions where short cuts can be made by translating a word or two.
- You can choose whether to give instructions and explanations in the mother tongue.
- It may be useful to discuss how to tackle a task in the mother tongue, or to talk about a lesson – whether students found it useful or enjoyable. This can be particularly useful at beginner level before the students have gained confidence in the language.
- You can do study skills activities which include the use of translation dictionaries.
- Translation of texts by the students can be an effective way of learning and is particularly useful at higher levels where students are having to get to grips with subtle nuances in English.
- If you are a 'foreigner' in their country there is an authentic information gap which can be exploited.

What are the disadvantages?

- The main disadvantage is that because they speak the same language your students may feel self-conscious about speaking in English to one another.
- Because they probably make similar mistakes it is not as easy for them to correct each other and you sometimes stop noticing them.
- Sometimes, especially with large classes, it is difficult to stop students chatting in their own language when they should be practising English.

For these reasons, consider carefully how much you want to use the students' mother tongue. Remember that one of the best sources of language input is the teacher. You can help provide the exposure to the language so valuable for acquisition. If you speak English in class your students get valuable listening practice, they are not so self-conscious about speaking themselves and operating in the language seems much more natural. You can make a habit of answering in English even if students ask you questions in their own language. You can even make an 'English only' rule for your classroom.

Avoiding the use of the mother tongue in pairwork and groupwork

You can make it easier for your students to use English by:

- describing your rationale clearly and getting their support from the beginning;
- deciding where you place yourself in the classroom. The groups nearest you are more likely to use English than those further away. So take an interest in what each group is doing and move around so that groups have less chance of switching back to their own language;
- monitoring more overtly: for example, by having a pen and paper in your hand;
- making the work task-oriented. If the final product has to be in English, whether it is a story, a film review or just answering comprehension questions, a greater use of English is ensured;
- keeping speaking activities short until the students have more confidence and increased fluency. It is better to have a shorter time than is strictly necessary for full practice of the language. Nothing is more likely to send students into their mother tongue than having time to spare at the end of groupwork;
- making sure that the students have the English to do what you ask. You might find it helpful to start off with very structured activities after you have taught some essential words and expressions so students are not at a loss for words;
- starting with 'open' pairwork as a model for the 'closed' pairwork;
- assigning roles. If everyone knows what they must do they are more likely to do it in English. You might consider giving someone the role of 'language monitor' – someone to make sure English is used in the group – or 'evaluator' – someone who will report back on the performance of the group overall, including their use of English and of their mother tongue.

Finally, don't be too concerned if your students resort to their mother tongue in groupwork or pairwork activities. Sometimes it saves time in the long run, as when they are clarifying instructions before they begin the task. It is worth remembering that if you are doing groupwork as an alternative to whole class work then even if only two people are using English simultaneously you have doubled the amount of student talk for that time.

Further reading

Atkinson, D. 1993 *Teaching Monolingual Classes* (Longman)
Hadfield, J. 1992 *Classroom Dynamics* (OUP)
Nolasco, R. and Arthur, L. 1988 *Large Classes* (Prentice Hall/Macmillan)
Tomalin, B. and Stempleski, S. 1992 *Cultural Awareness* (OUP)
Underwood, M. 1987 *Effective Classroom Management* (Longman)
Wright, T. 1987 *The Roles of Teachers and Learners* (OUP)

Chapter 3 Managing resources: equipment and teaching aids

In this chapter we look at how the teacher can use different resources to make lessons more interesting and effective. Teaching institutions vary enormously in the number and type of resources available to teachers. If you are doing TP in a well-resourced centre you should take the opportunity to try out the full range of resources. However, even in a relatively poorly-resourced school there are many ways that simple and 'home-made' resources can be used to good effect in lessons.

1 The board

It is unusual to find classrooms without a board of some kind, whether it is white, black or green. It is essential, then, to organize your use of it in order to obtain the maximum effect.

Four basic prerequisites:

1 Start with a clean board or with a board that only has on it what you have just put on. Don't start your lesson with the remains of someone else's still up.
2 Write legibly and neatly. If necessary, get some practice outside class time. (This includes writing in a straight line!) Try to print or at least be consistent in the letters you use – this will make your writing easier to read and is helpful for beginners and/or people who are having to learn a new script. Don't write in capitals. Learners need to know when capitals are necessary and when they are not. Even with European languages the rules that govern the use of capital letters vary.
3 Use the right implement. This doesn't apply so much to chalk boards (although some chalk is better than others) as it does to white boards. Don't make the mistake of using a pen which can't be wiped off!
4 Generally, try to keep the board as clear, as straightforward and as easy to read as possible. Clean it periodically to keep it neat and consider other ways of displaying more permanent information – a cork board or the walls of the classroom – in order to keep the board looking uncluttered.

What sort of things will be put on the board?

What you will want to put on your board will probably fall into one of the following categories:

Permanent or reference material

This may not go on the board at the beginning of the lesson but once it is up it will probably stay until the end. In low-level classes you may wish to put up the day and the date at the beginning of the lesson; it is a good way of helping the students learn the days of the week and the dates. It also encourages good study habits. You can put up reminders of items that students need constantly or persistently get wrong: for example, *What does ... mean?* The expression can then be pointed to when needed until all the students are familiar with it.

Other things that might come into this category are the main language items of the lesson: new vocabulary items and model sentences. You would expect most, if not all, the words in this section to be copied into the students' notebooks at some stage in the lesson. By putting such words into this section you are signifying their importance.

Material for the development of the lesson

This will be the material that relates to the stage of the lesson you have reached at any one moment. It could be pictures you are using to illustrate a story, an expression the students are practising saying, an outline of a grammar rule or even the score for a team game you are playing. Some of it may be transferred to the permanent section of the board.

Impromptu work

This is the work you use to illustrate or exemplify the answer to an unpredicted question or to back up an alternative explanation when the planned one doesn't work. It may be a drawing or it may be a written word. Space must always be left on the board for such work. You will usually want to erase work in this section as soon as the point has been understood and noted.

Notes and reminders

You may want to put daily class notices and announcements in this section. (See *Making announcements* on p55.) Also, questions you answer with *Ask me later* and things that you don't want to or can't answer on the spot are well worth noting in a corner. It shows that you are not just fobbing off the student and when you clean the board at the end of the lesson it will act as a reminder to you to prepare something for the next lesson.

It is essential that you plan the board and decide which part you are going to allocate to which use. Include a plan of the board in your lesson plan and refer to use of the board in specific stages of the lesson. The 'development' area is likely to be the largest so that will probably command the central part. The 'permanent' area is the most predictable and should be easy to plan for. It might be helpful to separate the different parts of the board by drawing lines: it reduces confusion.

The three stages on p67 show one possible development of a board through a lesson

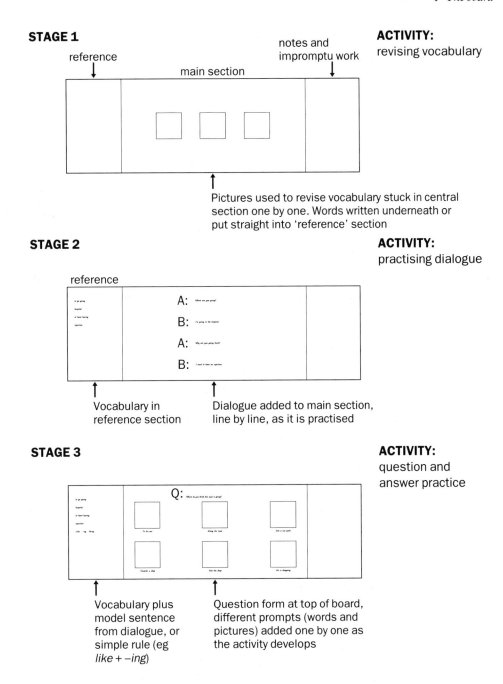

STAGE 1

reference

main section

notes and impromptu work

ACTIVITY: revising vocabulary

Pictures used to revise vocabulary stuck in central section one by one. Words written underneath or put straight into 'reference' section

STAGE 2

reference

A:
B:
A:
B:

ACTIVITY: practising dialogue

Vocabulary in reference section

Dialogue added to main section, line by line, as it is practised

STAGE 3

Q:

ACTIVITY: question and answer practice

Vocabulary plus model sentence from dialogue, or simple rule (eg *like + –ing*)

Question form at top of board, different prompts (words and pictures) added one by one as the activity develops

At what stage in the lesson should the board be used?

Exactly when the writing up is done depends on the type of lesson and your students' normal styles of learning. If you are specifically developing the writing skill, written work on the board can constitute a major part of the lesson. Often the writing stage is consolidation of oral work and comes after listening to and saying the language. If the students are impatient for you to write things down during oral practice it is sometimes better to write the words on the board for the students to copy them, rub the board clean and then tell them to close their books before returning to the oral practice.

How can you make the best use of the board?

- Use colour to make the board look attractive and its contents memorable. For example, you can reserve one colour for phonemic symbols so the students don't get confused between the spelling and the pronunciation of words. (See Chapter 6 Section 3: *Pronunciation.*)
- Use your board as a temporary display area. You can attach pictures, diagrams, etc with a product like 'Blu-Tack'. If you want to save the time it takes to write during the lesson you can write key words or sentences on card and stick them to the board at the appropriate time. Another advantage of using cards is that they can be quickly moved around on the board.
- Adjust the size of your writing to the size of the room and the size of the board.
- Don't put everything on the board – only the essential – and immediately rub off anything which is no longer needed.
- When writing up vocabulary include an indication of the part of speech, eg (*v*) after verbs, (*adj*) after adjectives, etc. Include the article *a* or *an* before nouns. Mark the word stress. (See Chapter 6 Section 3: *Pronunciation.*)
- Try and build up board work bit by bit after each activity rather than put it up in one go.
- Involve the students in the writing process by eliciting what you are going to put up, the spelling of difficult words, and so on. This will keep up their level of attention and concentration.
- Make it clear to students when they need to copy something from the board and when it isn't necessary. If you want them to write something down, allow enough time to do the job properly: write it up neatly, give the students time to read it (perhaps aloud) and then copy it down. You may wish to go round and check they have copied it correctly, particularly at the lower levels.
- When you transfer work from the main part of the board to the permanent part you provide students with a useful summary of the main stages of the lesson.
- Always clean the board at the end of a lesson.

For further ideas on this topic, see Chapter 2 Section 2: *Classroom arrangement.*

Task 1

Aim
To highlight stages in the use of the board as a lesson progresses.

Procedure
1 Look at the lesson plan on pp146–7.
2 Decide what you would need to put on the board and when.
3 Draw a diagram of each stage of the board.
4 Compare it with a colleague's diagram.

Task 2

Aim
To observe a colleague's use of the board and to give feedback.

Procedure
1 Observe a fellow trainee teaching a lesson and make a note of his or her use of the board. You can consider the following points: overall tidiness and attractiveness; legibility; helpfulness to the students.

2 Give feedback to your colleague. Try to find a number of positive points and make some suggestions for improvement.

2 The overhead projector

The overhead projector (OHP), while not replacing the board, is becoming increasingly popular.

What are the advantages?

- You can write on an OHP without turning your back on the class.
- You can prepare overhead transparencies (OHTs) in advance. This saves time during the lesson and ensures that the writing is neatly presented and the pictures clearly drawn.
- Students can write on OHTs and the results can be shown to the whole class. The results of groupwork can easily be shared using this technique.
- You can photocopy onto some special OHTs. In this way you can present complicated pictures or diagrams, pages from coursebooks, examples of students' work, etc.
- You can mask parts of OHTs, so revealing information step by step. This technique can be used to great effect when guessing the next line of a text, or the contents of a partly hidden picture.
- OHTs can be laid one over the other so that information is built up. An OHT containing the missing words can be laid over an OHT containing a gapped text, or pictures of characters in a story can be laid over the background scene, for example.

What are the disadvantages?

- OHPs are cumbersome and can be difficult to move around. As with all electrical equipment they can go wrong – in OHPs there is a tendency for the bulbs to blow.
- There may be too much light in the room, no screen or no suitable wall space.
- OHTs are relatively expensive, especially those that can be used in a photocopier. However, if you use erasable or washable pens the OHTs can be washed and re-used.
- Quite a lot of practice is needed to ensure efficient use of the OHP.
- OHTs can only be used one after the other: one OHT cannot be kept on permanent display while the next OHT is being shown; nor can they be used effectively afterwards as part of a wall display.

How can you make the best use of the OHP?

- Practise using the machine before trying it out with a class.
- Make sure you are using the correct OHTs (if you put an ordinary OHT through a photocopier it will melt), and the correct pens (some OHP pens are indelible and some are washable).
- Before the class make sure the OHP is working, try out your OHTs and check that they are focused and can be clearly seen at the back of the room. You may need to change the distance of the machine from the screen or wall and/or adjust the focus.

3   Visuals

Visuals can take many forms but the most common are real objects (sometimes called *realia*) and pictures or photographs. A number of teachers also make very effective use of Cuisenaire rods – small blocks of wood, initially designed to teach children mathematics. They have a variety of uses: for example, the illustration of colours; placed *in, on, under, behind* an object such as a box they can demonstrate the meaning of prepositions; they can be used to show word stress – one rod for each syllable in the word with a taller, different coloured rod to mark the stressed syllable.

Using visuals has a number of advantages:

- They often illustrate meaning more directly and quickly than through verbal explanation – they cut down unnecessary teacher talking time.
- They attract the students' attention and aid concentration.
- They add variety and interest to a lesson.
- They help make the associated language memorable.
- On permanent display (posters, charts, etc) they can help make a classroom a stimulating and attractive place in which to work.

What are visuals used for?

Among other things visuals are used to:

- arouse interest and concentrate attention at the beginning of a lesson;
- elicit already known language;
- illustrate a new language item, often a vocabulary item;
- create a need for new language which the teacher then satisfies;
- set the scene for a story or roleplay;
- stimulate discussion.

Finding and storing visuals

It is never too early to start collecting material that you think might be useful to show in class. The best source is magazines, but pictures and posters can also be obtained from holiday brochures, tourist information offices, catalogues, etc. If you have something particular in mind it is often easier to draw your own picture than spend a long time looking for one. You can spend some time preparing visuals to keep and use again and you can also make effective use of quick board sketches. You can ask the students to find visuals as part of their homework. They can be asked to bring in a photo of themselves when little or a member of their family, an advertisement they find interesting, even a favourite object. You can often provide visuals from objects commonly found in the classroom or on your person – examples of colours, materials, clothes, etc.

Work out a system for storing visuals you want to keep and organize them so that they become a resource you can keep re-using and adding to. Pictures simply ripped out of magazines look scrappy and unprofessional so it is worth making the visuals as attractive and durable as possible by mounting them on card and perhaps keeping each one in a plastic envelope. It might be useful to put a note on the back of each picture after you have used it to show what you have used it for. Don't forget that many pictures can be used for more than one purpose, in different lessons.

Showing visuals

When showing a visual make sure that:

- it is big enough to be seen. Before the lesson prop it up on a table where you would normally stand and look at it from the back of the room to check that it can be seen in sufficient detail;
- it is unambiguous (ie as simple as it can be for the purpose it has to fulfil) unless the ambiguity is deliberate and productive;
- you are holding it steady; when you first show the visual make sure that everyone can see it;
- if necessary you show the visual to each student in turn;
- you display a visual by sticking it to the board, on the wall or on a notice board. This makes it easier to refer to later in the lesson, particularly when you are summarizing what has been done. You may be able to make the visual into a permanent wall display, with the associated language printed on labels. This will serve as a constant reminder to the students of the work done and help make the classroom attractive.

Task 1

Aim
To assess how easily quick board drawings can be used.

Procedure
1 In a group of two or three, take it in turns to make a board drawing to represent the following: a car accident; a court room; your house or flat; a simple process such as making a cup of tea; two people falling in love; Paris.
2 Make sure that each drawing takes no more than 15 seconds to draw.
3 Discuss how effective the drawings were. Which elements conveyed the meaning most clearly and efficiently?

Task 2

Aim
To discover the ideal viewing distance for visuals.

Procedure
1 Select a picture about 20 cm x 15 cm with some bold figure in the foreground but a considerable amount of detail in the background.
2 Write a list of five or six questions which first elicit the image as a whole and then elicit some of the detail.
3 Stand a number of your colleagues at distances of 1m, 2m, 3m and 4m from you and hold up the picture.
4 Ask the questions and notice the cut-off point in terms of the detail they can perceive.

Task 3

Aim
To practise showing visuals to a group.

Procedure
1 Select one large (20 cm x 20 cm), one medium-sized (15 cm x 15 cm) and one small (10 cm x 6 cm) picture.

2 Stand in front of your group of colleagues and display each in turn, asking them to look carefully. Then put them on the board.

3 Discuss the different types of activities in which you could use the pictures.

Comment

1 It should be noticed how many different uses there are for the pictures.

2 You may be able to stand back and all the group will see the large picture, but you will have to go round and show the small one individually before any oral work can be done. It might be felt that the small one is more suitable for pairwork and groupwork only.

4 Worksheets and workcards

Although there are many excellent published materials available for the EFL classroom there are times when you will want to make your own worksheets to give to students to use in class or out of class for homework. These can take a number of forms: sheets of paper photocopied from a master you have produced, cue cards or role cards to use in pairwork and groupwork, or even home-made games.

Why should you want to make your own worksheets?

- to photocopy a text or exercise from a book which the students would not be able to keep or write in (but see the note below on copyright);
- to adapt published materials: perhaps change some of the questions to suit your students better, or introduce a new activity (by changing a straightforward text into a paragraph-sorting activity, for example);
- to write your own exercises to go with a piece of authentic material;
- to make cards for communication activities.

Making a worksheet or workcard

Many teachers have ready access to photocopiers so worksheets can be easily produced. Take care to make the worksheet as professional looking and as attractive as possible:

- If you write by hand make sure the writing is legible and neat.
- If you use a typewriter or word-processor check for typing errors.
- If you photocopy from published material it is often better to photocopy the whole page, cut out the part you want, glue it to a blank piece of paper and use that as your master.
- Don't make the writing too dense: leave space around the edge of the sheet and spread the work out.
- Include illustrations in the form of simple line drawings or pictures cut out of magazines to add interest (line drawings photocopy well but photographs don't).
- If you can, add colour – by hand to individual sheets and cards or by using a variety of coloured cards or photocopy paper.
- If you want to re-use cards, perhaps as part of a home-made game, it may be worth covering them in plastic or putting them in plastic wallets.

Other points to remember:

- It is often useful to keep a master of worksheets you make so you can use them again. Write on the back of the master details of when and why you used it, and make any changes you need before filing it away.
- As with visuals it is worth organizing and classifying your worksheets so you can lay your hands on them when you need them again.
- Don't waste time or money producing worksheets if you could achieve the same results with the board or the OHP.

Note on copyright

Unless it is explicitly stated that photocopying is allowed (this is sometimes the case with worksheets or tests in teachers' manuals, for example), it is against the law to make a photocopy of any part of a book, assuming the book is in copyright (copyright lasts for fifty years from the author's death). However, a system does exist whereby institutions can apply for a licence to photocopy a limited amount of material from published works; records are kept of copies made and the licence fee collected is distributed to those authors and publishers whose works are copied. Full details are available from The Copyright Licensing Agency Ltd, 90 Tottenham Court Road, London W1P PHE. Alternatively, the publisher can be approached directly for permission.

Always include a reference to any published material you photocopy at the bottom of the worksheet.

Task

Aim
To evaluate 'home-made' worksheets.

Procedure
1 Get together with a few of your colleagues. Each of you bring a worksheet you have made, preferably one you have used or that you plan to use with a class.
2 Give each other feedback on the worksheets. You could evaluate them in terms of their clarity, attractiveness, interest and effectiveness. Try to make one positive suggestion for improvement for each worksheet.

5 The cassette recorder

The cassette recorder is one of the language teacher's most useful tools. Nearly all coursebooks and many other published EFL materials are accompanied by cassettes. In addition, many teachers have access to authentic audio material that can be brought into the classroom – most notably recordings made from the radio, and songs. Most teachers have access to a cassette recorder for use in the classroom and if you can borrow additional machines you can set up communicative groupwork activities.

You may also have access to a language laboratory, or audioactive machines, where the students can record and listen to their own voices. As there are a number of different types of language lab you must get help in the use of the one in the institution you are doing TP in if you want to take your students there. For ideas on using this technology see Chapter 5 Section 2: *Receptive skills: listening*, and Section 4: *Productive skills: speaking*.

Using the cassette recorder

The more complex the machinery the more need there is to be efficient in operating it. Practice and preparation are essential. So:

- Before you prepare your lesson make sure you know how to use the machine you'll be using. Practise inserting the cassette; make sure you know which way round to insert the side you want; try winding and rewinding to see how fast the machine performs; practise using such buttons as 'cue', 'fast forward', 'pause' or 'recap', etc. Can you use the counter button efficiently to find your place on the tape? Does the machine need a separate speaker? Is the sound quality good? (Perhaps the heads need cleaning.) What effect do volume and tone have on the sound quality – especially as heard from the back of the room?
- Check the availability of the cassette you plan to use and give yourself plenty of time to find the excerpt you want.
- Listen to the whole of the excerpt you want to use to make sure that it is complete and clear throughout.
- Before the lesson, put the cassette on, find the beginning of the piece you want to use and 'zero' the counter.
- Make sure you rewind to the right place. You can plan to do this while the students are discussing what they heard during the first listening. However, a moment's silence while you concentrate is better than losing your place. Don't forget to set the counter button again if you use a second cassette in the lesson.

Recording your own tapes

If professionally produced tapes do not suit your needs or are not available when you want them, you may have to make your own. It is fairly straightforward to record something off-air – perhaps a topical news item – if you have the right equipment. Do check any copyright conditions that might apply, though.

It is much more difficult and very time-consuming to make your own tape from scratch. The results are often of such poor quality that it is not worth the effort. However, if you are determined to have a go:

- Find a quiet room (drawing the curtains will help), although some background noise can add authenticity.
- Use a separate microphone (built-in microphones tend to pick up a lot of noise from the machine).
- Stand the machine on a soft surface to reduce the amount of noise it makes.
- Try to use other speakers (not just yourself) to add authenticity.
- If you have a script, rehearse your piece before recording it.
- For an authentic-sounding conversation, don't give your speakers a script, but give them an outline of the sorts of thing you want them to say.

Task

Aim
To develop familiarity with the controls of a tape recorder.

Procedure
1 Select a short dialogue (about six lines) spoken at fairly normal speed.
2 Find the beginning and 'zero' the counter.
3 Play the dialogue through several times, each time using the counter to return to the beginning.

4 Play the dialogue again, stopping after one line.
5 With one finger on the 'rewind' and one on the 'stop', rewind the tape by one line of the dialogue only.
6 When you can do this successfully, move on to the next line.
7 After two or three lines, look at the further corner of the room and repeat steps 5 and 6!

6 Video

Although video cassettes are not quite as common as audio cassettes in the classroom they are generally very popular with students and can add variety and a welcome change of focus in a lesson.

Video cassettes have several advantages over audio cassettes:

- Because the students can see as well as hear what is being said the recording is much closer to 'real life'.
- Video is much easier to understand; the facial expressions, the gestures and the physical background all give additional information.
- The visual element is attractive and commands the attention better than audio alone.
- Videos are often intrinsically more interesting, as many people are more familiar with watching television and video than listening to audio material other than music and songs.

Using a video machine

When using a video playback machine (VCR), exactly the same rules apply as with an audio cassette recorder. Follow the same steps outlined in *Using the cassette recorder* on p74. However, the leads connecting the parts of a video system are slightly more complex so it is essential that these are checked beforehand. Also you need to know which channel is used for playback on the particular machine you are using.

Another point to note is that the 'pause' facility, if it exists on the VCR, is often not as refined as on an audio cassette player. It is difficult to do intensive listening work if there is a delayed pause.

Producing your own videos

You may have access to video-making equipment – anything from a hand-held camera to a fully equipped studio. As with language laboratories you need to become fully familiar with the equipment in the institution where you are doing TP before you can use video-making equipment with students. Although you can make your own videos for viewing in class it is a very time-consuming business. It is often more appropriate to use video-making equipment in lessons which aim to develop the students' speaking skills. Video is an excellent method of providing feedback on student performance. See also Chapter 7: *Giving feedback to students.*

For more information on video materials see Chapter 4 Section 1: *Published materials.* For ideas on how to use video playback facilities and video-making equipment in skills work, see Chapter 5 Section 2: *Receptive skills: listening,* and Section 4: *Productive skills: speaking.*

Task

Aim
To practise recording off-air and creating an accompanying worksheet.

Procedure
1 Record a five-minute extract off-air (from either the radio or the television) – perhaps a short news bulletin.
2 Write some questions that focus on the main points of the news item(s). (Try to have a particular class of students in mind when you write the questions – perhaps the one you are teaching on TP.)
3 Play the extract to some colleagues and ask the questions.
4 Ask for their feedback on the choice of extract and on the questions.

Comment
You may have an opportunity to incorporate the extract in one of your TP lessons.

7 Computers

If the use of computers is included in your TP you will need to be shown how the particular machines used by the institution work: how to switch on and off and how you can find your way around the programmes, using the menus; whether they are stand-alone or networked with other machines; whether the programmes are on discs and, if so, how they are stored and accessed. For information about the kind of materials and activities you can use with EFL students, see Chapter 4 Section 1: *Published materials.*

8 The photocopier

Finally, a piece of equipment which most EFL teachers have come to depend on is the photocopier. Use of the photocopier may be an area of tension in some institutions and teachers may be limited to a certain number of copies. Make sure you know the 'house rules' about use. If there is no photocopier (or when it has broken down!) you may have to use your ingenuity to compensate. Creative use of the board, flipcharts, large pieces of card or paper, and of dictation can be just as effective and the lack of individual photocopies can be turned to your advantage: the students' attention can be focused as a group and extra writing practice can be included.

Further reading

Hill, D. 1990 *Visual Impact* (Longman)
Wright, A. 1993 *1000+ Pictures for Teachers to Copy* (Nelson)
Wright, A. 1989 *Pictures for Language Learning* (CUP)
Wright, A. and Haleem, S. 1991 *Visuals for the Language Classroom* (Longman)

Chapter 4 Using materials

During your course you will probably be introduced to a great variety of materials specially designed for EFL. You will also become aware of how much authentic material there is that can be used in the language classroom. TP is a time when you can begin to explore these materials and build up knowledge of what is available. This chapter gives an overview of the most commonly used types of materials in the English language classroom under two headings: published materials and authentic materials.

1   Published materials

Coursebooks

In fact the coursebook often comprises a set of materials: student's or pupil's book (to be used in class), student's or pupil's workbook (often useful for supplementary classwork, individual work or homework), cassettes (for use in class or at home), teacher's book and sometimes even a video.

What are the advantages of using a coursebook?

Using a *good* coursebook has a number of advantages:

- It is what the majority of teachers do and what many students expect.
- It provides security for teachers and students and although time may be needed to evaluate and adapt a book it is less time-consuming than designing a syllabus and creating materials from scratch. So it takes some of the preparation load off teachers.
- It provides a syllabus which is graded roughly to the level suitable for the students.
- It normally provides variety and a balanced diet of language work: grammar, vocabulary, pronunciation, skills work; it may contain study skills and learner development activities.
- It gives continuity and progression.
- It provides a ready-made source of tried and tested activities.
- It has a teacher's book which is usually helpful in stating aims and objectives, giving guidelines for lessons and mentioning possible difficulties to be aware of.
- It is professionally produced with visuals, cassettes, etc.

What are the disadvantages?

When using a coursebook there are a number of pitfalls to be wary of:

- It is not always easy to find a coursebook that will suit the needs and interests of all the students in your group both in terms of the language syllabus and the topics of the texts. You may have to compromise and use a coursebook that suits *most* of your students most of the time.

- You may be forced to use a coursebook which is for different students, in terms of age and background, from the ones you are teaching.
- The students may not like the book and be reluctant to use it. Perhaps a student who considers himself to be 'intermediate' doesn't want to use a book labelled 'elementary'. This may seem a fairly trivial reason but to the student it may be really important.
- Exclusive use of a coursebook can become a straitjacket; it can be very predictable and boring for the students.
- It can stop you from being creative in your search for texts and activities that will interest and motivate your students.
- If you are an inexperienced teacher, following a coursebook may prevent you from exploring in depth the language you are teaching: you may find yourself 'going through the motions' without really understanding what you are doing or why.
- A coursebook is nearly always a compromise. There are too many things to be fitted into too small a pot.

So the coursebook is an invaluable resource but it may need adapting to meet the class needs. These needs will vary according to the age, language background, culture and ability of the students. Every class is different and the success of a coursebook depends to a large extent on how well it is used by the teacher.

How can you make the best use of a coursebook?

There are a number of decisions you can make and actions you can take to make the best use of a coursebook:

- Look at a range of coursebooks that could be used with the group. Your TP supervisor should give you some idea of suitable books. If a coursebook has been chosen for use in TP, spend time getting to know it – look at all the components carefully.
- If possible, don't use a coursebook immediately for the whole lesson. Spend time in the first few lessons getting to know about the students and their needs.
- When planning your lessons, think about which parts of the coursebook could be omitted, which could be used and which need supplementing with activities and materials from other sources.
- You may want to do the activities in a different order from in the book. However, this can be dangerous. When omitting, supplementing or changing the order of activities make sure that this does not cause problems – that one activity doesn't depend on doing another one first.
- Think about how long your group will take to complete tasks – you must decide how long to give an activity before going on to the next, or when to extend a task.
- Explore ways in which the book could be 'personalized' to suit the needs and interests of the students.
- Think about how activities and texts could be 'brought to life' through mime, actions, visuals and other aids.
- Above all, approach the coursebook *critically*: read the teacher's book carefully but also do your own research into the language; examine the exercises and texts for difficulties not highlighted by the book's authors.

Skills books

Skills books, as their name suggests, focus primarily on the language skills rather than specific areas of language. Many publishers produce a series of skills books (one on reading, one on listening, one on speaking and one on writing) at two or more levels. The 'listening' and 'speaking' books are often accompanied by cassettes, and tapescripts are usually included in the back of the student's books. The teacher's books that go with the skills books often include lesson aims, guidelines as to how to use the material and activities, and a key. Increasingly, however, as publishers respond to the demand for 'self-access' materials, the student's book also contains a key.

Although the skills books go under the heading of an individual skill they nearly all link and integrate some of the skills. For example, a 'speaking' book can contain short listening or reading texts and can include tasks which practise writing. Also, in addition to books devoted to one skill (listening, reading, etc), 'integrated' skills books are available. These aim to integrate skills practice within each lesson.

Why are skills books useful?

Usually skills books are organized according to topic and so provide a clear vocabulary focus. Often, particularly at higher levels, they contain authentic materials which have been specially chosen for their accessibility and interest to learners. The accompanying tasks can be extremely useful for developing particular skills and strategies (see also Chapter 5: *Developing skills and strategies*), and many teachers use them to supplement the class's coursebook. Because they don't usually follow a syllabus based on grammar structures, it is possible to 'dip into' different skills books – choosing units that fit in well with the class's programme of work. It is important to develop students' confidence in the receptive skills of listening and reading texts in which they will not understand everything, and skills books can provide materials and activities that are a 'halfway house' between a very carefully graded coursebook and ungraded authentic material.

Are there any problems?

It is not always easy to assess the level of skills books: the labels attached (elementary, upper intermediate, etc) are often only a rough guide. Often they contain authentic materials and it is the tasks which are graded according to level. As most skills books do not follow a particular structural syllabus they may have texts which contain structures unfamiliar to your students. However, if you anticipate these difficulties and choose carefully, this should not prevent you from taking advantage of these materials and tasks.

Readers

Another type of book commonly used in the EFL classroom is the simplified or graded reader. These books are designed for the foreign language learner and are either specially written or adaptations of well-known novels and stories. The language content is graded according to specified levels by restricting the vocabulary and grammatical structures used. Readers are particularly useful for practising extensive reading skills. See also Chapter 5 Section 3: *Receptive skills: reading*.

Other supplementary books

In addition to skills books and readers there are a number of books which aim to provide practice in language and skills work and which are very useful in providing materials and activities which can be used to supplement the coursebook. They include books of language games and songs, roleplays and simulations, chants and drills. Many include communicative activities which students can do in pairs or groups. Carefully selected activities from these books can add variety and enjoyment to your lessons. However, try to make sure that activities taken from different sources link together to make a cohesive whole, and that they serve to fulfil the aims and objectives of your lesson. There's a danger that you might be tempted to give the students a series of unrelated 'fun' activities.

Reference books

With the increasing emphasis on helping learners to become more independent, the use of reference books, both in and outside the classroom, is becoming more popular. The most commonly used reference books are dictionaries and grammar books. There are many excellent dictionaries specially designed with the English language learner in mind. They not only give the meanings of words but also give information about grammatical rules, pronunciation and use. They often contain useful reference sections on such things as irregular verbs, spelling rules, the difference between British and American English, etc. Some even give cultural information about the countries where English is spoken.

There is also a wide choice of grammar reference books. Again they are designed with particular learners in mind. Grammar reference books are available for students at different levels. They often have integrated exercises or are accompanied by workbooks or exercise books. Most have a key so that the answers can be checked by the students themselves.

Other reference books that can be used in the ELT classroom include specialized reference books on particular aspects of the language such as prepositions, phrasal verbs, idioms, slang, etc. Also, authentic English language reference works can be used, such as a thesaurus or an encyclopaedia. Of course, in addition to reference books designed for the learner, there are those that you as a teacher will find useful when you are researching the language you plan to teach. (See also Chapter 8 Section 2: *Researching the language*.)

How can you use reference books in the classroom?

Before the students can use reference works to help them in their studies they need to be taught how to use them. You may want to plan one or more lessons, particularly at the beginning of a course, to help the students make the best use of any reference books they have access to – in particular their dictionary and grammar book. For ideas on how to do this, see Chapter 5 Section 6: *Learner development and study skills*. Once the students have good reference skills you can integrate the use of reference books into lessons dealing with grammar, vocabulary, pronunciation and skills practice and set homework which involves student use of reference books.

Resource books

In addition to books that you can take into class for use with students there are a number of books written for teachers that combine sections on a particular aspect of teaching methodology (teaching speaking, using drama techniques, using video, etc) with sections containing practical ideas for activities you can do in the classroom. Many even have specific lesson guidelines and plans. For example, a resource book on 'conversation' might discuss ways of promoting speaking, particularly speaking in an informal style, and then go on to give examples of lessons you can do to help the students practise the art of conversation.

As with skills and other supplementary books these 'ideas' books are an excellent source of practical activities and are well worth exploring. You will probably be able to pick up ideas for lessons that you can use many times with different classes or adapt to suit particular groups. As noted above, you have to be careful to make sure that the activity justifies its inclusion – that it fits in with the other activities and helps to fulfil the aims and objectives of the lesson.

Video

Using video in the classroom is becoming quite commonplace and videos especially produced for the EFL classroom are improving in quality and variety all the time. Videos can be used to introduce grammatical and functional structures and they are particularly useful if you want to practise listening and speaking (including pronunciation) with a class. See also Chapter 5: *Developing skills and strategies.*

There are video courses which can be used instead of a more conventional coursebook and videos which are designed to supplement coursebooks in the same way that skills books and other supplementary books do; the approach you take, therefore, depends on many of the factors discussed above in relation to the more usual coursebooks and supplementary materials. However, videos are relatively expensive and so there's a more limited choice than for books. The big advantage of videos specifically published for the language learner is that they are accompanied by materials – usually students' workbooks and teachers' books. The activities and tasks are designed for students at a particular level and sometimes those with particular needs (for example, those who need English for specific purposes such as business). There are also a few interactive video packages which enable the viewer to listen to and then reply to a stimulus from the screen. These are primarily for use by individuals in self-access and so are not relevant to the TP situation.

If you are using video for the first time it is a good idea to stick fairly closely to the material prepared by professionals. However, many videos are designed to be used as a course over several lessons and you will probably not want to spend that much time on one type of lesson during TP. If you are using EFL video material only occasionally you will have to make sure, as with all supplementary materials, that you select carefully so that the video is well-integrated with the other elements of your lesson.

In addition, you may want to use television material recorded off-air, or commercially-produced videos which are not designed for the EFL classroom – most notably films. In this way you have authentic viewing materials. (Before you do, check carefully the relevant copyright laws.) Again, you have to be very careful when selecting relevant extracts and creating and grading the accompanying tasks and materials. The same rule applies to non-EFL videos as to those specifically designed for the English classroom: don't play any tape unless it serves to fulfil the learning objectives of the lesson – the provision of entertainment is not enough. As with any type of material, used judiciously video can add variety and interest; used too often and with no clear purpose it becomes boring and demotivating.

For more information on using video, see Chapter 3 Section 6: *Video*.

CALL

CALL, or Computer Assisted Language Learning, is popular in some institutions and there are a number of software packages designed for the English language classroom. One of the most popular and widely used requires the student to reconstruct a text. Other tasks ask the user to fill gaps with the correct word or match words and sentences. Much of this software can be 'authored' – the teacher can create the text – so the students can be working on a text they have already met, perhaps in their coursebook, or completing sentences with words they have learned for homework. Other programs are based on games and simulations: for example, the students have to find their way round London or compete on the stockmarket.

Teachers can also make good use of word-processing programs to encourage writing activities. Students who find handwriting in English difficult often welcome the opportunity to create attractively presented written work.

Many of the specially designed programs have feedback built in (in the form of answers or the successful completion of the task). For this reason they are very suitable for individual work in self-access. However, by asking two or three students to share one computer you can increase interaction and communication. The whole class can be set the same task if the computers are networked or if you have time in advance to set up the same program in each machine. In this way time spent using computers can be a useful integrated stage of a longer lesson or a series of lessons.

As with all materials you will have to spend time familiarizing yourself with the software available in the institution where you are doing TP and you will need to discuss the possible use of computers in your lessons with your supervisor. In addition, don't assume that all the students are familiar with computers; they may need some help in word-processing skills and familiarization with an English keyboard.

2 Authentic materials

What are authentic materials?

Anything a native speaker of English would hear or read or use can be described as authentic: theatre programmes, newspapers, magazines, poems, songs, brochures, information leaflets, menus, news broadcasts, films on video – the list is endless. Because authentic materials are not designed for the EFL student they are not graded for level, although some are obviously more difficult to understand than others. (As they would be for native speakers.)

The teacher should select the material carefully, with the needs and interests of the students in mind, and also decide what the students are to do with the material. So the same piece of authentic material can be used at different levels; an easier task can be set for lower level students and a more difficult task set for higher level students. For example, an entertainment guide from a newspaper: students at elementary level could find the price of tickets and times of performances for different shows while students at a higher level could select a show they want to see and telephone to book tickets. The first, though it may usefully practise reading skills, is not an authentic task – normally we do not write down the answers to a series of questions about theatre performances and ticket prices. The second, if the students are planning a theatre visit, is a 'real-life' situation. We should distinguish, then, between authentic *material* and authentic *tasks*.

Why do we use authentic materials in the classroom?

- For most students authentic materials, because they are 'real', are intrinsically more interesting and motivating and they give students confidence when they understand them.
- They provide examples of language as it is really used. By being exposed to authentic materials students have the opportunity to acquire or 'pick up' language.
- The real cultural content of many authentic materials encourages involvement and comparisons (especially in a multicultural group).
- Authentic materials lend themselves to authentic tasks: for example, getting information students may really need if they are planning a trip; listening to songs for pleasure; reading the menu of a restaurant they are going to eat in; etc.
- The use of authentic materials can be effectively linked with ways of helping students be more independent learners: making predictions and guesses, using reference books (grammar and vocabulary books, dictionaries).

Are there any drawbacks?

It is generally not enough to take a piece of authentic material into the classroom and let them get on with it! It takes time to find something that fits in with the class's programme of work and which is both interesting and accessible. You will have to make sure that the material is exploited well, that you have thought through the purpose of using the materials and that they are accompanied by suitable tasks.

Exposure to ungraded language needs confidence-building – so you will probably need to start off with easy tasks and convince the students that it is not always essential that they understand every word they read or hear. You may have to shorten authentic texts, or add a glossary in order to make them more accessible.

You will have to consider carefully how to grade the task to suit your students. For example, you may use the same authentic material with different level students, but ask them to do different things with it. Be careful, though, that at lower levels the task is not so simple as to be meaningless!

For more ideas on how to use materials – both published and authentic – see also Chapter 5: *Developing skills and strategies*, and Chapter 6: *Presenting and practising language*.

Task 1

Aim
To evaluate one or more coursebooks.

Procedure
1 Evaluate one or more coursebooks by considering them under these headings:
Layout and presentation (paragraphing, headings, density on the page, use of colour, illustrations and photographs, etc)
Ease of access (contents page/map, index, reference sections, etc)
Topics (interest, variety, cultural balance?)
Language content (grammar and functions included, vocabulary, pronunciation, balance of skills, ordering of language items)
2 Choose one unit and decide what you would include, omit and supplement if you were planning a series of lessons with the group you are observing or teaching.

Comment
1 This will be a much more useful activity if you have a particular group in mind. It would be useful to select the unit to adapt from the coursebook you use with your TP group.
2 If you do the activity with one or two colleagues (each of you looking at a different book), you can compare the advantages and disadvantages of the coursebooks you evaluate.

Task 2

Aim
To design a task to go with a piece of authentic material that would be suitable for your TP class.

Procedure
1 Find a piece of authentic material that you could use with the class you are teaching on TP.
2 Decide whether you need to shorten the text and/or add a glossary.
3 Consider which language and/or skills aims you could achieve.
4 Design a task for the materials which will fulfil these aims.
5 Show the material and your task to fellow trainees, and invite their comments.
6 Try out the material with your TP group.

Comment
Is the task that you designed authentic as well as the material? You may like to consider the advantages and disadvantages of making the task an authentic one.

Further reading

Cooper, R., Lavery, M. and Rinvolucri, M. 1991 *Video* (OUP)
Cunningsworth, A. 1995 *Choosing your Coursebook* (Heinemann)
Griffee, D. 1992 *Songs in Action* (Prentice Hall International)
Grundy, P. 1993 *Newspapers* (OUP)
Hardisty, D. and Windeatt, S. 1989 *CALL* (OUP)
Hedge, T. 1985 *Using Readers in Language Teaching* (Prentice Hall International)
Stempleski, S. and Tomalin, B. 1990 *Video in Action* (Prentice Hall International)

Chapter 5   Developing skills and strategies

Language learning is not only concerned with acquiring knowledge (about grammar and pronunciation systems, for example) – it is not just something we learn *about*. Rather, it is a *skill*, or a set of skills – something we learn to *do*, like riding a bike. So, students need meaningful, interactive practice in the skills in order to learn to use the language.

Traditionally we speak of four language skills: two 'receptive' skills – listening and reading, and two 'productive' skills – speaking and writing. The receptive skills have a number of things in common and the classroom techniques for reading and listening are often similar. In the same way, there are a number of similarities between lessons that practise the productive skills of speaking and writing.

Within the skill areas there are a number of 'microskills' or strategies which language learners use to communicate with others. Many of these skills are common to all languages – although students may have to be made aware that skills they already use in their first language can be transferred to the language they are learning. Other strategies may have to be introduced: for example, ways of getting the meaning across when you don't know the precise word for something in the foreign language.

Increasingly it is recognized that besides language skills students may also need to have learning skills – they may need to know *how* to learn. 'Learner development' (or 'learner training' as it is sometimes called) is concerned with helping students to become better, more independent learners.

In this chapter we begin by looking at how the various skills are usually integrated in a lesson. Ways of teaching the different skills are then discussed: first the receptive skills of listening and reading; then the productive skills of speaking and writing. Finally, we look at how we can help students develop their learning skills, both inside and outside the classroom.

1   Integrated skills

In real life the language skills of listening, speaking, reading and writing are generally integrated rather than occurring in isolation. When taking part in a conversation, for example, we both listen and speak; when we fill in a form we read and write, and taking notes from a lecture involves listening and writing. Often the use of one skill leads on naturally from another – we often read a novel or see a film and talk about it later to a friend. Or we may take part in a meeting and write a follow-up report.

How can you integrate skills in the lesson?

In lessons, as in real life, skills are often integrated – with one activity leading on to another. For example, a lesson for intermediate level students based around a newspaper article might have the following stages:

speaking → reading → writing

In the speaking stage the teacher introduces the topic (perhaps by showing a picture) and elicits what the students know and/or think about the subject. The students could discuss what they would expect to find in an article on the topic in question. In the reading stage the students read the newspaper article. Tasks could focus on assisting comprehension and perhaps a more detailed study of some of the vocabulary, or on the style of the article. In the writing stage the students could write a letter to the editor in response to the article, or write an article on the same subject from a different perspective, or in a different style.

A lesson for lower level students about finding accommodation could start with the reading of a newspaper advertisement (with a focus on some of the special vocabulary), go on to a roleplay/information gap activity in which the prospective tenant telephones the landlord/lady to ask questions and to make an appointment to see the flat. A listening text of someone being shown round the flat could follow. Finally, the students could write a letter to a friend describing their new flat. Such a lesson would have the following stages:

reading → speaking → listening → writing

Why is it useful to integrate skills?

- An integrated skills lesson allows for the practice of language in a way which is closer to 'the real world' and assists in the development of a full language *user*.
- Integrated lessons where one thing leads on to the other are more satisfying, less bitty, for the learners.
- A lesson which integrates a number of skills has more variety.
- It gives an opportunity for a topic to be fully explored and for vocabulary connected to the topic to be practised and recycled.
- Because one context or one text can be used for another activity the teacher does not have to spend time setting up something new.

For these reasons it is a good idea to choose reading and listening texts that are generative – that can be used for lessons in which a number of skills are integrated.

Can skills practice be integrated with the introduction and practice of language items?

Yes. Skills practice is also often integrated with the introduction, practice and revision of language items – grammar or functional structures, vocabulary or pronunciation. (See Chapter 6: *Presenting and practising language.*)

Planning a skills lesson

Although you may want to practise a number of skills in any one lesson it is important to be clear in your own mind what the overall aims of the lesson are and what the specific aims are for each stage. Your lesson may have the practice of one skill as its main aim, with other skills playing a subsidiary role, or there may be an equal balance of skills. Make sure that you and the students know what the focus is at any one stage in the lesson. This is particularly important if you are sharing a class with other trainees or teachers. (See Chapter 8: *Planning lessons*.)

2   Receptive skills: listening

How can you help students to improve their listening?

- Think about what you say in the classroom. Many things that happen in the classroom involve the student in listening – both to the teacher and to other students. In one lesson a learner may have to listen to and understand greetings, instructions, explanations, opinions, correction and feedback, and so on. The teacher is an invaluable source of listening practice. For that reason you should always think about what you say and how you say it from the students' point of view. (See Chapter 2 Section 4: *Teacher talk and student talk*.)
- Encourage students to talk and *listen* to each other. (See *How can you encourage good group dynamics and interdependence between students?* on p57.)
- Provide texts and activities which will develop listening skills and strategies at the same time as providing input for language acquisition.

How can you choose a suitable listening text?

When selecting a text with the purpose of practising your students' listening skills, ask yourself the following questions:

- What is my *main* aim: do I want to use the text mainly for skills development, or do I want to use the text as a resource for language (ie does it contain language that students can usefully acquire or learn?).
- Will the students find the topic and the text interesting?
- Is the text at the right level – just beyond the present competence of the students, so there is enough new language to make it worthwhile, but not so much that they will find it daunting?
- Will it be useful – something they may have to understand and respond to in 'real life'?
- Is it *generative*? Will it lead on to further skills work – perhaps speaking or writing (ie will it stimulate the wish to communicate)?
- What kind of text – a radio extract, a video, a song, an interview, a real story told by the teacher or one of the students, etc?
- What type of listening do I want them to do: what skills do I want them to practise?
- Am I going to use a recording or use my (or another speaker's) voice?
- How difficult will the text be for the aim I have in mind and what will the difficulties be?
- How much of the text do the students have to understand in order to achieve the aim?
- How much support will I have to provide in order for the aim to be achieved?

If you want the listening to be stimulating and challenging, and your students are of intermediate level and above, you will probably want to choose an authentic or 'semi-authentic' listening text – either found (and maybe adapted) by yourself or from published materials. (See Chapter 4: *Using materials.*) If your students are beginners or at elementary level a 'made-up' text is often more suitable – a wide choice of interesting, authentic-sounding texts are available in published materials and these are often accompanied by useful activities.

A balanced general English course should include a variety of types of listening with accompanying activities: different interaction modes – monologues, dialogues; different contexts and situations – social events, meetings, shops/restaurants/banks, etc; different styles – formal or informal, with friends or strangers; different accents, etc.

What makes a listening text easy or difficult?

Generally, listening texts are easier if:

- they are fairly short;
- they have only one speaker, or two speakers who are easy to tell apart;
- the speaker(s) speak slowly (though naturally), in a standard accent, and use simple grammar and vocabulary;
- the speakers can be heard clearly – there is no distracting background noise;
- the speaker(s) can be seen and are 'live' or on video rather than recorded solely on audio;
- the topic is familiar;
- the structure of the text is simple and straightforward but not too dense – there is repetition, pausing, etc;
- the students are interested and prepared for what they will hear.

How can you help the students to understand a listening text?

Choose a text which will interest the students and formulate aims that are suitable for their level and needs. Examples of specific aims are:

- to develop global listening skills (ie to get a rough idea of what's going on);
- to develop intensive listening skills;
- to set the context for a roleplay;
- to introduce a vocabulary 'set' in a natural context.

If your main purpose is to develop listening skills then the text should be just above the students' present level of competence. If, however, your main purpose is to use the text to focus on a new language item then the rest of the text should contain language the students already know. (See Chapter 6: *Presenting and practising language.*)

Often in a skills lesson it isn't essential that students understand every word of a listening text. In general, if students have an overall idea of the meaning, and understand how the different parts fit together to make one piece of discourse, they can more easily go on to a more detailed understanding. So focus on *general* or *global* understanding before detailed understanding. It is essential to build up knowledge of the text gradually – to start with what the students already know in order to tackle the new, to begin with the easy aspects and go on to the more difficult.

Encourage the students to use what they already know (their knowledge of the world and of English) to help them infer meaning. Before they listen, help them to predict what they are going to hear by activating any knowledge they may have of the topic or situation. Elicit the sort of language they expect to be used. It may be helpful to revise or teach some key items of vocabulary that appear in the listening if they are important to an understanding of the text.

Remind students of the listening strategies they employ in their own language. For example, encourage them to guess how the speakers are feeling by their intonation (do they sound angry or frightened? amused or sad?); to get information about the structure of the text from the intonation (are the speakers asking or answering questions? telling a series of events?); to guess the situation from any background noises; to use any visual clues available; to listen out for familiar words which give a clue to the topic or situation; to guess any unknown words from the context.

Give plenty of support, especially with lower level students or those who are not confident about listening. For example, some teachers like to let students read the tapescript for an authentic text if it is available, usually after they have listened to it or while they are listening to it a second time. Occasionally a weak class or one at the beginning of the course can read a tapescript, or part of it, in advance. They can do activities such as sorting out the jumbled lines in tapescripts, or filling in gaps in tapescripts, to help them prepare for what they are going to hear. You can play recorded texts in small chunks and do prediction work at the end of each chunk. You can ask students when they would like you to stop the tape recorder or let them control it, or you can play the tape as many times as the students would like.

Motivate your students by choosing texts that are interesting and that provide a real incentive for the students to understand and to contribute their own ideas and opinions. You may not want to restrict questions about the text to those that require factual answers; you can explore ways of getting your students to infer meaning or express their own views on the matters under discussion.

Choose tasks for the students to do before and while listening rather than afterwards. In that way you are focusing on understanding rather than just good memory – don't ask your students to remember details that a proficient speaker of the language couldn't! Make it clear what degree of attention is required in order to accomplish a particular listening task. For example, do the students need to listen to all the text in order to get the overall gist (as in a story), or do they need to listen out for and remember key details only (as in an airport announcement)? These are sometimes referred to as *sub-skills*.

At the end of the lesson, get feedback from the students about the text, the tasks, any problems, etc. You may also want to ask how they would like to work on a listening text next time.

What are the main stages in a listening skills lesson?

There is no one way of doing a listening skills lesson – it depends on such factors as the aim, the text type, the level of the students, etc. The following are guidelines on *one way* of conducting a listening skills lesson.

Before listening

1 *Arouse interest and set the scene*

Before a listening activity, encourage the students to think about and discuss what they are going to hear. Or create a 'need to know' by telling them how the listening task fits in with a later activity they are going to do.

Use prompts such as realia, visuals, questions, references to your or the students' experiences, a short discussion task to arouse the students' interest, to activate any knowledge they have about the topic and to help them predict what they are going to hear.

Example

If you are going to hear something about a famous person's life, show a picture and elicit facts the students know or can guess about the person. You write the facts on the board (perhaps under two columns: *Facts we are sure about/Facts we aren't sure about*). After listening you can check which facts were mentioned. A picture – even of an unknown person – can give rise to a lot of speculation.

Don't worry about 'mistakes' during these lead-in activities – the aim here is not to focus on accuracy but rather to create real interest which will motivate the students to listen.

2 *Teach key words/phrases before listening*

It may be helpful to teach a few key words – without which the listening would be very difficult to understand. Even if you do not provide this support it is important that you recognize the troublesome words and have a strategy for dealing with them. (See Chapter 6 Section 2: *Vocabulary* for how you might teach these words or expressions.) It is rarely a good idea to teach in advance more than about five words out of context. Remember: the context can make the task of understanding easier!

Proper names, such as the names of people or places, can really throw low-level students, so it is useful to pick those out, write them on the board, and tell the students how they are pronounced.

First listening

1 *Set a task to help focus on overall understanding*

This can be in the form of two or three questions, or a task.

Example

These pictures tell a story. Listen and put them in the correct order.

Don't make the completion of the task dependent on the students catching every detail. You may want to tell the students that you don't expect them to understand every word.

2 *Give the listening text for the first time (either play the recording or read the text)*

Whether you do read the listening text yourself or play a recording, it is probably better not to pause – this is more realistic and helps the students concentrate on getting the whole picture.

3 *Feedback*

Possibly ask the students to discuss their answers and opinions in pairs or groups before you elicit them. If the listening is recorded you can ask the students whether they would like to hear the whole or part of the text again before they go on to focusing on the text in more detail.

Second listening

1 *Set a task to focus on more detailed understanding*

Whether you are using published materials or devising your own activities, try to vary the tasks. If you ask questions, in addition to those which call for a factual answer, try to introduce some which require the students to infer meaning – particularly at the higher levels.

2 *Give the listening text for the second time*

This time you may want to make the task easier by pausing – especially if the students have to write notes, for example. Monitor and assess how well they are doing the task.

3 *Feedback*

Again, encourage the students to work together before eliciting their responses.

4 *Personal response*

Try to encourage a personal response from your students by asking questions like *What did you think of what the woman did? Would you have done that?* etc. In this way listening work can be naturally integrated with speaking practice.

Finally, if you are going to use the text to lead into language work it might be useful to let the students read the tapescript while they listen to all or part of the text again.

Is listening to a video different from listening to an audio tape?

Although using a video tape is very similar in many ways to using an audio tape, there are differences that you ought to think about when planning a listening skills lesson:

- Video is generally easier to understand because of the visual clues available. In fact sometimes no listening skills are needed to understand the action.
- Video is very useful if more than one person is speaking: in a conversation with overlapping dialogue, unfinished sentences, interjections, etc. Monologues are fine on audio tape but conversations, particularly if they are authentic, are often very difficult to follow – even for proficient speakers of the language.
- Video is more like real life. Unless they are on the telephone or radio, we can usually see the person we are listening to. As a result, watching video is usually more motivating.
- The viewer has to watch the screen to get all the available information. For this reason it is not easy for them to complete 'while-viewing' tasks that require a lot of writing (filling in a chart, etc). In this case it is usually better to let the students view once without writing and then do the task the second time they view.
- Video tapes (especially if they are authentic) tend to be long. You need to be very careful about the length of the video or extract you show and choose aims and activities that are appropriate. Video can be popular with students but you have to ensure that useful learning outcomes result and the students don't just use the opportunity to go to sleep!

Can you use a listening text to introduce or practise language points?

Yes. After helping students get a general understanding of a text you may want to go on to pick out and examine some of the language in the listening: a point of grammar or pronunciation; a functional or vocabulary focus. Using a listening text is a very good way of introducing and practising language in context. (See Chapter 6: *Presenting and practising language*.)

Task 1

Aim

To practise writing questions to go with an authentic listening text.

Procedure

1 Record a text of between one and two minutes. A short item from the radio, for example the news, is ideal.
2 Write questions suitable for students at intermediate level to fit into the following stages, in a lesson whose aim is to develop listening skills:
    1 Set the scene and arouse interest in the topic of ...
      (Write three questions.)
    2 Focus on the overall or general comprehension of the text.
      (Write three 'gist' questions.)
    3 Focus on the understanding of more detailed aspects of the text.
      (Write six questions – two factual, two inference and two opinion.)

Comment

Play your text and show your questions to a colleague for comments. After making any suggested improvements you could try the activity with a group of students.

Task 2

Aim

To consider the staging of a listening lesson.

Procedure

1 The activities, instructions and questions A–P on p93 refer to the authentic listening text at the top of p93. Which order do you think they should come in?
2 Compare your decision with a colleague and discuss the reasons for your recommended order.

Comment

1 To make this activity easier you can photocopy the material and cut it into sections that can be moved around.
2 You may decide that more than one way of ordering the activities can be justified. It might depend on the level of the group of students listening to the text. You may also want to add or omit some instructions or activities.

Listening text

Talking about telepathy ... I've never experienced anything myself but recently, erm, my father went into hospital for an operation. And, er, he was having a knee operation at a particular time a few days ago. And my uncle, apparently, who's his brother, they're not twins but they're brothers, and as they've got older they've got a lot closer; they didn't use to be very close when they were young. And, erm, ... he was telling me the other day that he was at work – he's an electrician – and he was working, and on Monday morning as he was working, he got this strange pain in his le..., in his left leg. He maintains that this is true. And my father at that time was having an operation on his left leg. And the pain got gradually worse as the morning went on so that by lunchtime he had to go home from work and rest his leg. Yeah. And he said – well it turns out that it was at the same time that my dad was having his operation. And he found it very strange and I mean – so did I.

From *Signature Intermediate* by Phillips and Sheerin (Nelson 1991)

A 'Read these statements. Some are true and some are false. Listen to the cassette and decide which are true and which are false.'
Teacher writes the statements on the board or gives them to the students on pieces of paper.
1 *Angela's father and uncle are twins.*
2 *The brothers have a better relationship now than in the past.*
3 *Angela's uncle had an operation on his left leg.*
4 *Angela's uncle had a pain in his left leg.*
5 *Angela and her uncle think something strange happened.*

B 'Listen to this account about telepathy. The story is told by someone called Angela.'

C Teacher writes these questions on the board: *How many people are involved in the story?*
Who had the operation?
Who had a pain in his leg?

D 'Compare your answers in pairs.'

E 'In pairs, correct the statements that are wrong.'

F 'Write the story that Angela told in your own words. You can use the statements (including those you corrected) to remind you of the story. You can do this in pairs.'

G The teacher elicits the groups' opinions.

H The teacher draws a picture of two heads on the board and links them with a line labelled *thoughts*. The teacher writes the word *telepathy* on the board next to the picture of the two linked heads.

I 'Do you think Angela's account is true?'

J The teacher elicits any stories the students may have.

K The students discuss in groups.

L 'Have you or anyone you know ever experienced anything that you cannot explain?'

M The teacher elicits the answers.

N The teacher plays the cassette.

O The teacher elicits the answers.

P The teacher plays the cassette.

3 Receptive skills: reading

How can you help your students improve their reading?

As reading, like listening, is a receptive skill, a lesson based around the comprehension of a reading text is similar in many ways to that designed to practise listening skills. Almost all the questions you have to answer when choosing a listening text also apply when choosing a reading text (see Section 2: *Receptive skills: listening*).

There are some significant differences, though, which in some ways make reading easier and in some ways make it more difficult than listening:

Listening	Reading
A listening text can seem 'unstructured'	A reading text is usually more obviously organized
Unfamiliar regional/national accents can cause problems	For some students the written script is unfamiliar
Meaning is conveyed by the stress on key words and the intonation of the voice	In a reading text the fact that English words are not always spelled like they sound can cause difficulty
If the students can also see the speaker (live or on video), gesture and expression will also aid understanding	
Students have to listen in 'real time' (ie go at the speaker's speed)	Students can take their time, check back on details, puzzle out meaning
Listeners are normally expected to participate (eg reply) immediately	
All students have listening skills in their own language	Not all students may be skilled in reading their own language
One important aspect that is common to listening and reading: Both listeners and readers have to infer meaning, using their knowledge of the world	

What makes a reading text easy or difficult?

Generally, reading texts are easier if:

- they contain 'simple' language – structures and vocabulary familiar to the students;
- they are short;
- they contain short, simple sentences;
- they are clearly organized – eg there is a straightforward storyline or a clearly signposted argument;
- they are factual;
- they are in standard English – with no specialized vocabulary;
- the topic is concrete and familiar;
- there is support in the way of layout, titles, pictures, graphs, etc.

What are the different 'ways' of reading?

We read different texts in different ways, depending on our purpose. For example:

Skimming

When reading a newspaper we often glance over the headlines until we find an article that catches our interest. If we are in a hurry we read through the article quickly – probably not reading every word, maybe reading only the first sentence of each paragraph. When we do this we are *skim* reading for the general sense or the *gist* of the article. We want to know what's in the article but only on a rather superficial level.

Scanning

Next we may want to see what's on television this evening at 8 o'clock. We are unlikely to start reading from the beginning of the list of programmes – starting with what's on at 6 o'clock in the morning! Instead our eyes move quickly over the page until we find 8.00 pm and then we start reading the details of the programmes. In other words, we *scan* the page until we find what we're looking for.

Intensive reading

In the same newspaper we may find something that we want to read in detail. Perhaps the article we *skim* read at first is really interesting and we want to read it again, more slowly, taking in the information and perhaps even making a mental note of some of the details to tell someone about later. Or we may do the crossword – paying close attention to the clues in order to solve the puzzle. In both these instances we are *reading for detail*.

Extensive reading

This is the way we usually read when we are reading for pleasure – perhaps a novel or a biography.

You will probably want to introduce your students to a variety of different reading texts and give them practice in employing the appropriate reading strategies. Sometimes we can use a text to practise more than one type of reading approach; for example, skimming an article then reading all or part of it for detailed information. However, be very careful not to set a task which involves a reading strategy which is inappropriate for the text.

How can you help students to understand a reading text?

As with listening, choose a text and formulate aims that are suitable for the students' level and interests: challenging – but manageable with support. See the list on p94 for factors that make a reading text easier. How much of the text the students need to understand depends on your aim. The most important skill is to be able to identify what the text is about – what is the writer trying to say? When reading for gist or overall understanding it often isn't essential that the students understand every word of a reading text, though there shouldn't be too much which is unfamiliar. If the students can get an overall idea of the meaning they can more easily deduce unknown words and go on to a more detailed understanding. So focus on their *general* or *global* understanding before their grasp of detail.

Encourage the students to use what they already know – their knowledge of the world and of English. Before they tackle the text, help them to predict what they are going to read by activating any knowledge they may have of the topic or text type. Elicit the sort of language they might expect to meet. Start with what the students already know in order to tackle the new; begin with the easy aspects and go on to the more difficult.

Remind the students of the reading skills they employ in their own language. For example, discuss the ways of reading outlined above and encourage them to use strategies appropriate to the text and the purpose of reading. Encourage them to use any visual clues available – layout, pictures, etc.

Help the students understand the structure of the text by focusing, for example, on the key sentences and the way sentences are linked. Encourage the students to deduce the meaning of unknown vocabulary by guessing the meaning of the word from clues in the context; identifying the grammar of the word (is it a verb, noun, etc?); separating the root of the word from any affixes and seeing if it is like a word they already know. Help the students use a dictionary efficiently to find the meaning of unknown words and expressions. (See also Section 6: *Learner development and study skills.*)

Give plenty of support, especially with lower level students or those who are not confident about reading:

- Encourage the students to work together and help one another.
- You may want to ask the students if they need more time to read the text or part of the text again.
- You can let the students work on the text at home before tackling another task in a later lesson.

Motivate your students by choosing texts that are interesting and that provide a real incentive for them to understand and to contribute their own ideas and opinions. You may not want to restrict questions about the text to those that require factual answers, but you can explore ways of getting your students to infer meaning or express their own views on the matters under discussion.

Is it useful for the students to read aloud?

It can be – but it's rather different from the activities listed above as it involves speaking as well as reading. It is quite difficult for the speaker to pay attention to the *meaning* of a text when reading aloud, particularly in public. It is also often not comprehensible to the other students who carry on reading rather than listening to the student reading aloud. So don't ask your students to read aloud in class and then expect them to answer comprehension questions. However, some students like to read aloud on their own, as they listen to a text on cassette. It helps them to associate the spelling of the words and the pronunciation, and improves their fluency. There are a number of simplified readers with accompanying cassettes that can be used in this way.

What are the stages in a reading skills lesson?

There is no one way of doing a reading skills lesson – it depends on such factors as the aim, the text type, the level of the students, etc. The following are guidelines on one type of reading skills lesson, one in which the students are going to read a fairly short text – perhaps a newspaper or magazine article. The ultimate aim is that the students can understand the text well enough to discuss it with a friend – giving their personal reactions to the article.

Notice the many similarities (and the few differences) between these guidelines and those for a listening comprehension.

Before reading

1 *Arouse interest and help prediction*

Encourage the students to think about and discuss what they are going to read. Or create a 'need to know' by telling them how the reading fits in with a later activity they are going to do.

Don't worry about grammar 'mistakes' during these lead-in activities – the aim here is not to focus on grammatical accuracy but rather to interest and motivate the students to read.

Use such prompts as realia, visuals, references to your or the students' experiences, and questions to arouse the students' interest, to activate any knowledge they have about the topic and to help them predict what they are going to read.

Use any clues afforded by the text layout and format. Is it a magazine article, a letter, a theatre programme, etc? Are there any photographs or pictures accompanying the text that can help the students predict what the text is about?

2 *Teach any key words*

Consider whether there are any key words which you want to teach before the students read the text. As in a listening text the context makes the task of understanding individual words and expressions easier. However, unlike a listening text, the students can see the words so it is not as difficult for them to identify proper names or to take the time to puzzle out the meaning of unfamiliar vocabulary.

First reading

1 *Set a task to assist overall understanding*

This can be in the form of two or three gist questions, or a task.

Example
Choose a headline from a choice of three to go with the article.

Don't make the completion of the task dependent on the students reading in too much detail.

Give advice about the type of strategies the students might employ.

Example
Don't try to read everything. Just read the first sentence in each paragraph and try to get a general idea of what it's about so that you can answer the questions on the board/choose an appropriate headline. You have two minutes.

2 *The students read the text*

You may want to give a time limit – this may discourage students from reading for detail when they should be skimming. On the other hand you may want to give them as much time as they feel they need.

3 *Feedback*

Ask the students to discuss their answers and opinions in pairs or groups before you elicit them.

Second reading

1 *Set a task to focus on more detailed understanding*

Whether you are using material from published materials or devising your own activities, try to vary the tasks – including tasks which require the students to 'read between the lines' as well as answer questions which call for factual answers.

2 *The students read the text for the second time*

Again, give them some idea of how long they have to do this and how they should set about the task.

Example

You have three minutes; don't forget to look carefully at the linking words – they'll help you work out the order of events in the story. You can use your dictionaries if you wish.

3 *Feedback*

Again, encourage the students to work together before eliciting their responses.

Follow-up

You will probably want to encourage a personal response to the text from your students.

Example

What did you think of the man's idea? Would you have done that?

In this way reading can be naturally integrated with speaking practice.

It may be appropriate for you to read, or to play a recording of all or part of the text so the students read and listen simultaneously. By doing so the sounds and spelling of the language are linked. If the resources are available students often enjoy doing this as a self-access activity. Or you could use part of the text as a dictation activity, perhaps as a revision activity in a later lesson.

As with a listening text, you may want to go on to use a reading text as a context for the introduction or practice of specific language: a point of grammar or pronunciation, a functional or vocabulary focus. (See Chapter 6: *Presenting and practising language.*)

Task 1

Aim

To design an activity to go with a piece of authentic reading matter that would be suitable for your TP class.

Procedure

1 Find a piece of authentic reading matter that you could use with the class you are teaching on TP: for example, a magazine article, a menu, a holiday brochure.
2 Consider which skills aims you could achieve.
3 Design an activity (or activities) for the reading materials which will fulfil these aims. (Consider which reading strategy or strategies the students should employ to do the activity efficiently.)
4 Show the reading matter and the activity to fellow trainees and invite their constructive criticism.
5 Try out the material with your TP group.

Comment

Is the task that you designed authentic as well as the material? You may like to consider the advantages and disadvantages of making the task an authentic one.

Task 2

Aim

To practise identifying key words in a reading text.

Procedure

1 Find a reading text that you could use with the class you are teaching. Identify those words which are key to the understanding of the text.
2 Decide which, if any, you would need to teach before the students read the text for the first time.
3 Compare your list with a partner. Explain why you chose your words.

Comment

You can go on to discuss *how* you would teach the words as quickly and efficiently as possible.

4 Productive skills: speaking

Every opportunity for speaking in the classroom should be taken. It is by trying to communicate that students realize their need for language and by speaking that they increase their fluency and confidence. At first students may be self-conscious and reluctant to speak in front of a lot of people. However, there are ways (repetition work and pairwork activities) of providing a safer, less public environment in which the students can begin to practise speaking.

What do we mean by speaking skills?

Speaking has many different aspects. It is useful to look at them under these headings:

1 Accuracy

Accuracy involves the correct use of vocabulary, grammar and pronunciation. In *controlled* and *guided* activities the focus is usually on accuracy and the teacher makes it clear from feedback that accuracy is important. Ongoing correction is often appropriate during accuracy activities. In *freer* activities the teacher is hoping for the correct use of language but is also keen to encourage the students' attempts to use the language they have in order to communicate. (See below.)

In feedback the teacher will probably comment on correct use of language but also on how successfully the students communicated. (See also Chapter 6: *Presenting and practising language*.) Even in free activities students can be encouraged to be as accurate as possible so long as their anxiety to 'get it right' doesn't interfere too much with their fluency and ability to communicate. In any particular activity the teacher can make it clear to students in which areas accuracy is expected, and to what extent. (See also Chapter 7 Section 2: *Correction techniques*.)

2 Fluency

Fluency can be thought of as 'the ability to keep going when speaking spontaneously'. When speaking fluently students should be able to get the message across with whatever resources and abilities they've got, regardless of grammatical and other mistakes.

Normally, students should not be corrected during fluency activities. However, in feedback afterwards you can comment favourably on any strategies the students used to increase their fluency. For example:

- the use of natural-sounding 'incomplete' sentences: *When did you go? On Tuesday* (not *I went on Tuesday*);
- the use of common expressions like *I see what you mean, Never mind, What's the matter?*
- the use of 'fillers' and hesitation devices: *Well, Let me think, Let's see;*
- the use of communication strategies, such as asking for clarification: *I don't understand. Do you mean ...?*
- the ability to paraphrase – 'put it another way' or explain/describe what they want to say if they haven't got the right language. This can involve using gesture or even mime;
- the use of useful expressions such as *That reminds me ... /By the way ... /Talking of ...* etc when introducing a topic; *Still ... /Anyway ... /Strange, really ...* etc when finishing with a topic; and *Well, I must go/Nice talking to you,* etc when finishing a conversation.

Some of these aspects are more difficult to focus on than others. Students obviously transfer many of the speaking skills they have in their own language when they are speaking English. However, don't forget that some conventions of conversation are not universal and it can be very useful to focus on particular aspects in class. For example, Japanese people consider it impolite to interrupt – especially someone older or of a higher status. With more advanced students who have to take part in discussions and meetings with native speakers of English, it can be helpful to teach Japanese students how to interrupt in English in a way which is considered acceptable by native speakers.

What types of speaking activities can we use in the classroom?

Interactive activities can be divided for convenience into the following categories:

1 Controlled activities

For example: repetition practice or set sentences prompted by picture or word cues – to improve the accurate use of words, structures and pronunciation, and to foster confidence.

2 Guided activities

For example: model dialogues which the students can change to talk about themselves and to communicate their own needs and ideas; tasks which the students carry out using language (structures and/or vocabulary) which has been taught beforehand.

3 Creative or freer communication

These activities are usually designed to give either creative practice opportunities for predicted language items, or general fluency practice, where the specific language focus is less relevant.

The students are given the opportunity to experiment, to see how far they can communicate in situations where all the choices of language used are made by the people speaking; to practise the fluent use of language they know. In general these activities both increase the students' motivation, since the students talk for themselves, and help bridge the gap between the rather artificial world of the classroom, with its controlled language practice, and the real world outside.

Of course, any situation the teacher sets up in the classroom for such experimentation will, to a certain extent, determine the language used. For any limited communicative situation one can predict some of the language items likely to occur and teachers often plan a freer stage to follow the introduction and more controlled practice of language items. For example, a discussion about favourite television programmes can follow the presentation and practice of vocabulary items such as *comedy, soap opera, documentary*.

The most important point to remember is that the students must have a *reason* for speaking in order for the activity to be truly communicative; there must be a 'gap' between the speakers to be filled – either an opinion gap (*I don't know what you think about this topic*) and/or an information gap (*you have some information I need to know*). The existence and bridging of this 'gap' must be carefully planned for a successful speaking lesson. (See below.)

Inevitably lots of mistakes are made. They can be seen as part and parcel of learning to communicate. Although it is not usual to stop students in order to correct them in a free communication activity, it is important to note mistakes that you may want to discuss with students later.

How can you encourage students to speak?

1 Encourage student interaction

Many of the points answering the question *How can you encourage good group dynamics and interdependence between students?* (see p57) involve increasing the amount students speak in class. You should aim to create a comfortable atmosphere where students are not afraid to speak and enjoy communicating with you and their fellow students.

2 Give plenty of controlled and guided practice

Generally, the lower the level of the students the more controlled and guided practice, compared with freer practice, you will do. However, even quite advanced students often welcome the chance to get their tongues round new vocabulary and grammar structures, expressions and model sentences before using them 'for real'.

3 Make speaking activities communicative

The aim of communication activities is to encourage purposeful and meaningful interaction between students. Communicative tasks are designed so that students have a reason or a purpose for speaking: they are bridging an information or opinion gap; they are asking for or giving real information or finding out about the opinions of their fellow students. Not only are these activities motivating in the classroom, but they offer a challenge which mirrors real-life interaction.

Even quite controlled activities can be made communicative if the students are talking about *real* events and opinions.

Example
When students are practising talking about likes and dislikes they can choose from the list of vocabulary (going to the theatre, playing football, etc) – things they *really* like doing rather than mechanically repeating *I like playing football* when they don't!

In freer activities students have to listen and respond in real time without knowing what is about to come next and successful communication is of greater priority than complete grammatical accuracy.

4 Plan speaking activities carefully

Speaking activities need to be very carefully structured at first, especially at lower levels, so that the students have few demands on them. It is often difficult for students to come up with ideas at the same time as having to cope with the language. They need something to speak about, such as a picture; or a purpose – like performing a roleplay from the context of a reading text. As they become used to doing controlled and guided activities students become more sure of themselves and more adventurous so that freer activities can be attempted.

Freer activities, however, still need careful planning if they are not to fall flat. Carefully set up tasks (roleplay, picture description, debate, problem-solving, ranking tasks, etc) provide the reason, purpose and guidelines within which students can speak more freely. Examples of these activities are given below.

Guidelines for a free/creative speaking activity

Before the lesson

- Decide on your aims: what you want to do and why.
- Try to predict what the students will bring to the activity and any problems they might have. Will they have something to speak about? Are they capable of doing the activity successfully? Do they have the necessary language? Will the students find the activity interesting, useful, fun?
- Work out how long the activity will take and tailor it to the time available.
- Prepare the materials.
- Work out your instructions.

During the activity

- Arouse the students' interest through visuals, a short lead-in talk, a newspaper headline, etc. Try to relate the topic to the students' own interests and experience.
- You may want to remind students of any structures or vocabulary that might be useful – perhaps leaving them on the board for reference.
- Set up the activity so that the students know the aims of the activity and what they are to do. This means giving clear instructions and checking that they have been understood.
- Make sure the students have enough time to prepare, perhaps in pairs or groups, before asking them to tackle the main activity. Don't be tempted to cut down on the time needed for this. Don't forget that the students are probably getting useful speaking practice at this stage too.
- Make the activity even more 'process' rather than 'product'-based by encouraging rehearsal if appropriate, particularly with roleplays.
- Monitor the activity: don't interrupt except to provide help and encouragement if necessary; try to keep a low profile. Watch the pace – don't let the activity drag on and remember to leave time for feedback.
- Evaluate the activity and the students' performance in order to provide feedback later but don't jump in with instant corrections.

After the activity

Provide feedback:

- Indicate how each person communicated, comment on how fluent each was, how well they argued as a group, and so on.
- Sometimes you might record the activity on audio or video cassette and play it back for discussion. Focus on possible improvements rather than mistakes – in fact if it is taped, sometimes they can be asked to do a rough version first, then discuss improvements, then re-record.
- Note down glaring and recurrent errors in grammar, pronunciation, use of vocabulary. Individual mistakes might be discussed (in private) with the students concerned and you might recommend suitable remedial work to do at home. Mistakes which are common to the class can be mentioned and then practised another day when you have had a chance to prepare a suitable remedial lesson. (For more ideas on how to provide feedback, see Chapter 7: *Giving feedback to students*.)

Examples of guided and free speaking activities

For convenience these activities have been grouped under five headings: *interaction or information gap activities; roleplays; simulations; discussions; games*, although there is obviously an overlap of features and techniques between the categories.

Interaction or information gap activities

These are carried out in pairs or groups and usually depend on one or more students either having incomplete information or no information at all, and the other(s) having the information needed to complete the task. The aim is for the 'haves' to communicate their information to the 'have nots' or the 'have nots' to extract it.

Examples

1 *Giving directions*

Aim: to give freer practice using the language of directions (for example, *Go straight on, Turn left ..., It's on the right*, etc).

Procedure: The students do the activity in pairs. Both students have a map of the same town. On Student A's map some of the places are not marked. Student A asks Student B for directions to these places, Student B gives the directions and Student A marks them on his or her map.

If Student A has places included on his or her map that are not on that of Student B the roles can be reversed – with Student A giving directions to Student B.

2 *Making an appointment*

Aim: to provide an opportunity for the students to use the language of *suggestion, excuse, acceptance* and *confirmation* as used in making an appointment.
Procedure:

STUDENT A

You are a teacher and you want to meet the father/mother of one of your students. You must make an appointment with them. Here is your diary for next week. Do not show it to your partner.

	Morning	Afternoon	Evening
Monday	teaching class 3		opera
Tuesday		teaching class 2	
Wednesday		teaching class 3	dinner with headteacher
Thursday	teaching class 2		
Friday	teachers' meeting	teaching class 3	going away for the weekend

---

STUDENT B

You are the mother/father of a student. You want to talk to the teacher. You must make an appointment with him/her. Here is your diary for next week. Do not show it to your partner.

	Morning	Afternoon	Evening
Monday		driving lesson	
Tuesday	dentist		dinner with friends
Wednesday	interview for new job		
Thursday			theatre 'Macbeth'
Friday			

As the two students take the part of the parent and the teacher this activity could be viewed as a roleplay (see p105).

Roleplays

A roleplay is when students take the part of a particular person: a customer, a manager, a shop assistant, for example. As this person they take part in a situation, acting out a conversation. It is unscripted, although general ideas about what they are going to say might be prepared beforehand. These might well come out of a text or a previous context. Roleplay can be used to:

- remind the students of situations they might be in;
- give the students an opportunity to try out language recently introduced or revised and practised in a more controlled way;
- give the students the opportunity to improve their fluency, through a wide range of language, in a variety of situations and with different speakers;
- help you plan which areas to work on through the diagnosis of the strengths and weaknesses of the students' English.

Example 1

Simple roleplays where students are put in situations they may be faced with when they stay in an English-speaking country (for example, buying things from a shop, asking for directions, etc) are very useful, particularly at lower levels. In such roleplays there is no need for detailed character definition. The activity works best if there is no fixed conclusion to be reached, or if there is something awkward or unexpected in the exchange.

Step 1: Prepare the following cards:

STUDENT A	STUDENT B
AT THE STATION	AT THE STATION
You want to get to London by 3 o'clock.	You are a ticket clerk.
It is now 12.15.	To get to London, passengers must change at Cambridge.
You are hungry and would like to have lunch, either at the station or on the train.	There is at train at 12.30 which arrives at 2.30 and one at 1.15 which arrives at 3.15.
Ask the ticket clerk about the trains to London.	Passengers can buy sandwiches and drinks on the train.

Step 2: Establish the context of a railway station, perhaps using a picture or by talking about the students' experiences.

Step 3: Divide the class into pairs. Each pair consists of Student A and Student B.

Step 4: Student A and Student B read their cards silently and digest the information written down without giving anything away to the other.

Step 5: Check that the students (particularly the weaker ones) understand what they have to do, and answer any individual queries.

Step 6: Get the students to act it out in pairs. Monitor unobtrusively.

Step 7: Possibly get one or two pairs to act it out in front of the others.

Step 8: Provide general feedback.

Before the pairs of A and B students get together you can add an additional step. Divide the students into pairs of two As and two Bs and ask them to discuss their role cards together and practise some of the things they might say.

Example 2

More complex roleplays are usually more suitable for higher levels. For example, the students might play the various characters at a trial, or at a business meeting. In these cases, much of the work on the context needs to be done in greater depth – perhaps even over a series of lessons, particularly if the whole class is to be involved in an extended discussion. The students may need to prepare certain aspects of their role beforehand, perhaps for homework.

For this type of roleplay the students need to have clearly in their minds as much knowledge as possible about:

- the full context. This should include the characters – maybe their age, appearance, mood, any mannerisms, etc;
- the reason for the interaction. This will often have some conflict built into it somewhere so that the students have to 'negotiate' in English.

Step 1: Prepare the following cards:

CUE CARD

Situation: Immigration desk. Two characters: an immigration official and a Peruvian doctor trying to enter the country.

Props: a date stamp, a desk, a passport

Problem: The doctor's passport is out of date and his/her money has been stolen on the plane. He/she has to persuade the official to let him/her in.

CHARACTER A

You are an immigration official. You are working overtime because one of your colleagues is sick. You are tired and you want to get home. You like everything to be simple and straightforward. You are irritated by the doctor and his/her problem.

CHARACTER B

You are a Peruvian doctor. You have come to Britain to attend your son's graduation at university. You have had a long journey. You are fed up and cold. Your passport is a week out of date and you have had your money stolen on the plane. You want to see a police officer.

Step 2: To warm them up to the topic discuss with students the problems any of them might have had going through immigration.

Step 3: Check they understand one or two words like *out of date* and *fed up*, if you think they don't know them and they are crucial to the roleplay.

Step 4: Give out a copy of the cue card to each student. Get them to read the cards silently and check that they understand what is written on them by asking one or two comprehension questions.

Step 5: Allocate roles – half the students are A, and half B – and give out the character cards. Check that individual students have understood who they are without giving the whole game away to the other students.

Step 6: Put pairs or groups of As and Bs together and ask them to discuss what sorts of things they are going to say.

Step 7: Put the students into pairs – one A and one B in each pair – and give out the props, or objects to represent the props.

Step 8: Get them to rehearse the situation in pairs.

Step 9: Ask one or two pairs to go through the roleplay again in front of the class.

Step 10: Discuss with the whole class how it might continue and what other characters might be needed (eg a police officer, the son).

Step 11: Build up a picture of the characters with the whole class, perhaps writing notes on the board.

Step 12: Assign roles to as many students as possible.

Step 13: Continue the roleplay in front of the class.

Step 14: Discuss the roleplay and provide feedback, making special note of the fluency strategies used by the students. (See also Chapter 7: *Giving feedback to students.*)

Simulations

A simulation is slightly different from a roleplay in that the students are not playing roles but being themselves. They are confronted by a task to do or a problem to be solved and they must do what they would do in the circumstances. Some simulations are quite complex, with new information being fed in as the activity proceeds. There are a number of commercially available simulations – especially in the form of computer software. Simulations, however, can be quite simple. Generally the more realistic they are, the more likely the students will be to participate.

Example
This task could be given to intermediate-level students, in groups:

The bar/restaurant in your school or college is losing money and will have to close soon if changes are not made. In your group make some suggestions of what could be done to keep the restaurant/bar open.

If possible, the students should refer to the bar/restaurant in their school or college. If it doesn't have one you will have to feed in some information: what it sells, prices, opening hours, staffing, etc.

Discussions

Most fully-fledged discussions (as opposed to small ones that arise naturally in response to something immediate like the day's news) take a lot of preparation if the teacher is not going to dominate. However, discussions with a class can be successful if you can ensure that:

- the students are interested in the subject and have ideas of their own about it;
- the activity has sufficient motivating factors in its structure to create the need to speak;

- the students have the language to discuss what they are supposed to discuss – this may include particular structures and vocabulary;
- the students have been prepared for the discussion and have been given time to organize their thoughts. Some of the preparation can be done in an earlier lesson and the students given time to prepare at home, or it may be part of a previous stage of the lesson. For example, often discussions arise from reading or listening texts (see also Section 1: *Integrated skills*);
- the activity is managed so that the discussion is not dominated by one or two students.

If you don't think about these factors you will end up doing all the talking!

How can you stimulate discussion?

These are a few examples of ways of structuring discussion. Many more ideas are included in books referred to at the end of the chapter.

Modifying statements
The students are given a list of, say, ten controversial statements around the topic of 'parents' (if that is a relevant theme): for example, *Parents should teach boys to cook and girls to mend the car.* Groups are then asked to modify the statements so that all the members of the group agree with them. If there is time, groups can then compare their statements with other groups.

Sequencing statements
The students are given a list of, say, ten non-controversial statements: for example, *It's important to put children to bed early if they have school the next day.* They are then asked, in groups, to sequence them (1–10) in order of priority for the successful bringing-up of children.

Defending statements
Different controversial statements are written on pieces of paper and then put into a box: for example, *Children should be encouraged to leave home at sixteen.* The students are told to pick out a statement and then spend a few minutes preparing arguments to defend it. One of the students can be made chairperson. All the students then have to present their arguments in turn, answer questions and defend themselves from attack. This usually leads to a lively discussion. You may want to end the activity with a vote to decide on the most convincing defence. It is sometimes a good idea, if there's time, to give the students a chance to say what they *really* think about the statement they had to defend.

Problem-solving
Students can be presented with a puzzle or problem and given a set time to discuss possible answers to or explanations of the puzzle.

Example
Last Monday Katy left for college at 8.30 as usual. She went out of the front door, closing it behind her. A few seconds later she rang the door bell. When her father opened the door Katy said 'Thank you' and then turned to go to college.
(The explanation is given on p124.)

Either the teacher can present the problem, or the problem and solution can be given to one of the students, who can answer questions (*yes* or *no*) from other students in the group. A number of such problems are to be found in *Challenge to Think* by Frank, Rinvolucri and Berer (OUP 1982).

Moral issues

The students are given details of a problematic situation and are asked to discuss the situation and make a decision. Such decisions as 'Whose fault was the accident?' 'Who should get the job?' 'What is the appropriate punishment?' 'Which charity gets the money?' can be discussed.

Example

(from *Non-Stop Discussion Workbook* by Rooks, Newbury House 1981)

You have four remaining spots in your first year medical school class. You must choose four from eight highly-qualified applicants.
(Details of the applicants are given.)

Describing and comparing

These activities work particularly well in a multinational class. Ask each student to prepare some information on something which varies from country to country.

Example

The students tell about the ages at which people in their country can drink alcohol, marry, vote, drive a car, ride a motorbike, join the army, leave home, get a credit card, smoke, be sent to jail, etc. In groups the students compare the information about their countries and come to a group decision about which set of rules they think the most sensible – or they can decide on their own.

How can you organize discussion in large classes?

Groupwork

Rather than try to include the whole class in a discussion, it is often better to divide the class into groups so that a number of parallel discussions can take place. In this way more students get a chance to speak, although it is more difficult for the teacher to monitor. At the end of the discussion phase there can be a period when the whole class comes together to compare conclusions. Each group can choose a reporter to take notes and report back on the discussion that took place in his or her group. The groups can also report back using an OHT or a poster to show the others.

Taking turns

In a smaller class the teacher can introduce a rule whereby no one who has already spoken can speak again until all the members of the group have had a turn to speak. This is rather an artificial constraint but it ensures that the discussion is not taken over by one or two students right from the start.

The pyramid technique

Another way to structure a discussion in a large group is via the 'pyramid' or 'snowballing' technique. For example, each student might list the five most important qualities a good parent must have (patience, a sense of humour, etc). The students then form pairs and agree on the list of five things. Then pairs form groups of four and have to agree on their five things – and so on until there are few enough groups for a list to be elicited from each group and put on the board, or the whole class is discussing the topic together. The pattern is shown in the diagram at the top of p110.

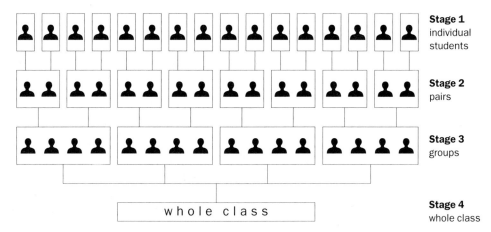

Stage 1 individual students

Stage 2 pairs

Stage 3 groups

Stage 4 whole class

Games

Many conventional games can be adapted to foreign language teaching. As with any communication activity the areas of language produced may be predictable, and therefore useful as a guided activity, or less predictable and suitable for a freer stage.

Games are particularly useful with younger learners but are generally popular with students of all ages, especially if they appreciate how they can help them improve their English. (See also Section 6: *Learner development and study skills*.)

In multinational classes some games can be a problem if some students know the game and others have never heard of it. The latter are at a disadvantage at first. Try to make sure that if you have people from different parts of the world the game does not depend on too much general knowledge. Frequently their general knowledge does not overlap!

Examples

Type 1: Predictable language

Twenty Questions

For low-level classes, to give freer practice of inverted form (for example, *Is she alive?*) and short-form answers (for example, *No, she isn't*).

Instructions: A student chooses a place, a famous person or an object and the rest of the class has to guess what or who it is by asking a maximum of twenty questions that demand the answer *Yes* or *No*.

- Make the game competitive. In most classes competition increases motivation and interest considerably. Divide the class into teams and have a scoring system to record the wins and losses of each group. The group with the most points wins.
- Have a quick run-through with you choosing a person or an object first and with you answering the students' questions. This will provide the students with a model for the activity. Then pass the game over to the students as far as possible. You can also get the students to do the scoring.
- Make sure you have checked all your instructions sufficiently.
- Make sure you have allowed the right amount of time for the game. It is very difficult to have to follow on from one that has petered out. Equally, it is very frustrating for the students to have to finish before the game has come to an end.

- Get all the students involved.
- Make the game fun!

Type 2: Less predictable language

The Objects Game
For intermediate and advanced students.

Instructions: Each student in the group is given, or chooses, a profession: one might be a doctor, another an architect. Each group has a pack of cards – each card depicting an object, eg a bucket, a dictionary, an umbrella, a portable telephone. The cards are turned over one by one. The students in turn have to convince the others of why they might need that object. The person who puts his or her case most convincingly wins the card. The student with the most cards at the end is the winner.

- Make sure that each student has time to argue his or her case.
- Give credit for creative expression and skills of persuasion.
- The students might need time to prepare for the game by practising some expressions: for example, *I'd use it to ...*, *It would be really useful for -ing ...*, and the language of one or two 'turn-taking' expressions (for example, *Listen, sorry I don't agree ...*).

Task 1

Aim
To evaluate speaking activities in a coursebook.

Procedure
1 Choose a unit in a coursebook – perhaps the one you are using with your TP class.
2 Look at each speaking activity and categorize it as 'controlled', 'guided' or 'freer/creative'.
3 Compare your ideas with a colleague.
4 Decide how each activity should be monitored and how and when you would correct/give feedback.

Comment
You may decide that the balance of activities could be improved to suit your class: ie you may need to add an extra controlled practice activity or extend the practice with a more creative exercise. If so, try to find/create such an activity.

Task 2

Aim
To give some idea of the kind of language necessary to carry out an activity.

Procedure
1 Select an interaction activity suitable for pairwork – one with an information gap.
2 Each member of the group then privately writes down the language items that they think will be used to complete the activity.
3 The activity is then given to two members of another group to carry out and the language they use is recorded on paper or on tape.
4 The predictions and the actual language used are then compared.
5 You may then want to give the same activity to your TP students to see what language items they use to complete it.

Comment

1 Don't be too discouraged if you find a huge difference between what is expected and what actually occurs.
2 Noting the language down on paper as the activity is carried out is less time-consuming than going over tapes; on the other hand, taping can rule out fruitless arguments.

Task 3

Aim

To experience and evaluate the 'pyramid' discussion technique.

Procedure

1 Write down six controversial statements about EFL teaching (for example, *Vocabulary teaching is more important than the teaching of grammar. It's better for students to be fluent than accurate. Pronunciation teaching is a waste of time*).
2 Give the list to your group and ask them individually to modify the statements so they can agree with them.
3 Modify them for yourself.
4 In pairs, compare the modified statements and modify them again so that you can both agree with them.
5 Repeat the procedure in groups of four.
6 Double up the groups until the discussion involves the whole group.

Comment

1 Did discussion take place, involving all members of the group?
2 Were you happy to discuss the sentences so many times – and if not, at which point did it get boring?

Task 4

Aim

To give some idea of the length of time a roleplay will take.

Procedure

1 Select two roleplay activities, one at intermediate or advanced level and one at a more elementary level.
2 Work in groups of three, with two carrying out the roleplays and the third timing them.
3 Repeat the roleplays more than once.
4 Discuss the time each took and estimate how long it might take with learners of the appropriate level.
5 Discuss the preparation needed to set it up and the length of time it would take with a group of students.
6 Discuss whether it was useful to do the roleplay more than once.

Comment

This activity might be more useful if done in a foreign language which would mean grouping yourselves according to languages you speak.

General comment

Communication activities are by their nature something involving thought on the part of the people involved. They can all, therefore, usefully be tried out in pairs or groups of teachers before being given to students.

5   Productive skills: writing

Writing is often not as important to many students as speaking and it tends to get rather neglected in many classes, unless the students are working for a written examination. In TP there is often not enough time to complete a long written task as the process may need to extend over several lessons. However, there are many ways in which the importance of writing can be impressed upon students and a number of activities to help them improve their written skills.

It is useful to consider what types of writing your students may want or need to do – in other words, the reasons they may have for writing: for example, letters to request information or to complain, forms and questionnaires, lecture notes, exam essays, reports, etc.

As with speaking, activities to improve writing skills can range from very controlled to free or creative.

What do we mean by writing skills?

Writing involves many different aspects. It is useful to look at them under these headings:

1 Handwriting

This may be a problem for students who are not familiar with Roman script: Far Eastern and Arabic-speaking students, for example.

2 Spelling

Again, usually more of a problem for speakers of non-European languages. However, speakers of languages where the spelling and pronunciation are consistent, for example Spanish, also need help with spelling.

3 Punctuation

The conventions of English capital letters and punctuation are not universal and might have to be taught.

4 Sentence construction

The construction of sentences that are grammatically correct, using the correct word order.

5 Organizing a text and paragraphing

Dividing the information into paragraphs. Knowing when to start a new paragraph. Ordering the paragraphs to present a logical argument, tell a story, etc.

6 Text cohesion

The appropriate use of linking words and phrases so that the organization of the text is clear to the reader.

7 Register/style

Using language (structures and vocabulary) appropriate to the formality and style of the text.

You will notice that with many of the skills the emphasis is on *accuracy* – controlled and guided practice activities can help improve accuracy. However, it is also important to see writing, like speaking, as a means of communication – a way of getting ideas across – and to encourage *fluency* and communicative impact. In order for the writing to be truly communicative, wherever possible students should write for a purpose, with a reader in mind. Freer and more creative activities can help students write more fluently.

How can you encourage students to write?

1 Have a positive and co-operative attitude towards writing

- Encourage real writing tasks in the classroom. For example, for the birthday of a member of the class write greetings cards.
- Plan sufficient time for writing activities and give them due importance in the programme of work.
- Encourage the students to show each other their writing and to ask each other for advice.
- Try letting the students write in pairs or groups sometimes.
- Give encouraging feedback. (See Chapter 7: *Giving feedback to students,* especially p169.)
- Be selective about the kind of mistakes you are going to mark so that you don't have to mark every mistake made.
- Display finished tasks on the wall or in a class book.

2 Prepare students for writing

Help the students gather ideas from reading, listening and talking to one another. Point out those aspects of written texts that can be used as models for their own writing: the layout of letters, for example. The analysis of a text in a reading skills lesson can lead on to students writing a text along the same lines, and often students' writing can arise naturally as a response to a listening or reading text. (See Section 1: *Integrated skills.*)

3 Structure writing activities

Plan writing activities carefully so that tasks progress from the more controlled, through guided to freer, particularly with students who lack confidence in their writing.

One way in which students get controlled practice, particularly at lower levels is by copying from the board. So make sure you:

- provide a clear model;
- make it clear when you want students to copy from the board;
- give them time;
- monitor carefully, especially with low-level students, as mistakes often occur at this stage;
- show that you think neat, accurate writing is important.

Practice activities can be very controlled but still be challenging. Ordering jumbled sentences and writing them out in the correct order can give useful copying practice, for example.

4 Plan guided and freer practice activities carefully

As with speaking activities you can decide whether to focus mainly on accuracy or fluency. You may want to structure writing activities carefully at first, especially at lower levels, so that the students have few demands on them. However, activities that involve creative writing can be used with quite low-level classes: for example, *Write me a letter telling me about someone in your family.* The feedback for this activity would be concerned with the communicative content of the letter rather than with grammatical accuracy. (See Chapter 7: *Giving feedback to students.*)

As students get used to doing controlled and guided activities and become more confident, freer activities can be attempted. Even freer writing activities, however, need careful planning if the students are to be motivated to produce work which is of worth and which will serve to improve their writing skills. In order to provide this structure you need to focus on the *process* of writing – the steps necessary for successful, communicative writing – rather than on the finished *product*. Students are encouraged to make rough drafts which they improve on before they write out their finished 'product'. Of course the final product is important, but the students learn by being led through the necessary steps rather than by being given a title for a piece of writing and left to get on with it!

Guidelines for a process writing activity

1 Introduction

Stimulate interest: through a listening or reading text, a speaking activity such as a roleplay, visuals, etc. Create a situation where a piece of writing is required. Discuss the text type – is it a letter, a poster, a story, etc? Think about the reader(s). Who are they? What will interest them? What do they need to know?

2 Working with ideas

- Get ideas from the students – through brainstorming, using word pools, mind maps, etc.
- Note down ideas.
- Develop the ideas.
- Choose those ideas to keep and those to be rejected.
- Order the ideas.

This can be done as a class on the board or OHP, in pairs or individually.

3 Planning

Remind students of the typical features and structure of the text type they are writing; a model is very useful here.

Examples

Letter of complaint
– layout of the letter
– introducing the subject and giving any background
– making the complaint
– stating what you want done

Argument essay
– introduction to the topic
– arguments for
– arguments against
– writer's conclusion

Help the students to use this knowledge to make a plan, dividing their ideas into paragraphs.

4 Drafting

The students write a first draft, perhaps in pairs, from their notes/plan. They may need to refer to dictionaries, grammar reference books and model texts for some conventions: for example, the salutations and standard phrases used in formal letters.

5 Reviewing/editing

The students correct and improve their first draft – looking at content, language accuracy, organization, style, etc. At this stage you can take the work in and make comments.

6 Re-writing

The students write out the final version and then, if possible, give it to the intended reader(s). The intended reader may be the teacher (especially if it is a practice examination). You then have to decide what form feedback is going to take and to what extent and how you are going to correct the text. You may want to respond in writing – by writing a letter in reply to a letter, for example. (See Chapter 7 Section 1: *Giving positive feedback*, especially p164.)

Word-processing

Using a computer for writing is becoming more and more usual and some students may be proficient at word-processing. There are many writing tasks that lend themselves to word-processing – for example, amending texts, moving text around, summarizing, expanding – and many students are more motivated to write if they can do it on a computer.

Task 1

Aim
To consider the types of authentic writing tasks your students may need to do and to plan a process writing lesson.

Procedure
1 In pairs make a list of the type of writing tasks the students in your TP class may have to do in English. (The need may be immediate or in the future.)
2 Choose one type of writing from the list. Discuss the problems your students might encounter when attempting such a piece of writing. How could you prepare the students for the writing and what activities would you ask them to do?

Comment
You could develop your ideas into a lesson which you could try out with the class.

Task 2

Aim
To design an activity using word-processing in order to provide practice for an aspect of writing.

Procedure
1 Choose a text which your TP class has read recently. It could be from their coursebook or it could be an authentic text.
2 Put the text, or part of it, onto the computer.
3 Modify the text in some way. For example, one of the following changes could be made:
  – To focus on correct punctuation: take out the punctuation and capital letters.
  – To focus on words used to link sentences and clauses: take out the linking words such as *so, then, however, also.*
  – To focus on how paragraphs are ordered to form a coherent piece of writing: jumble the paragraphs.
  – To focus on the effect that adjectives can have in a piece of descriptive writing: take out the adjectives.
  – To focus on the tense form (for example, the past simple and past continuous in a narrative): put all the verbs in the infinitive form.
4 Ask some of your fellow trainees to restore the text to its original form.
5 Get feedback from them and then, if possible, try out the activity with your TP class.

Comment
Clearly this activity can only be done if you and the TP class have access to a number of computers (one between two or three students) and the students have been introduced to word-processing techniques.

6 Learner development and study skills

Ideally one of your tasks as a language teacher is to encourage your students to take responsibility for their own learning both inside and outside the classroom. The aim of many of the techniques (pairwork and groupwork , self- and peer-correction, etc) described in other chapters is to foster independence from the teacher.

In order to be more independent and efficient learners the students need to be aware of how languages are learned and what their own preferred learning style is – how they learn best. They also need to be aware of certain study skills and strategies for learning so they can choose which work best for them and use them to continue learning outside the classroom and after their course.

To a large extent you are limited in the amount of influence you have over the development of these learning skills in TP. You may not see the students from the beginning of their course, they may come to you with a wide range of attitudes towards learning and a variety of language-learning skills and techniques already in place, and your time with them is limited. However, many of the activities you can do to promote more efficient learning can be integrated within lessons whose main aim is concerned with learning particular language items or practising particular skills. Promoting learner development is often achieved by making your attitude to learning clear to the students and by incorporating the introduction of strategies and techniques into your everyday teaching.

Awareness and responsibility

How can you encourage the students to be more aware of how they learn a language?

- Make the aims and objectives of your lessons clear to the students so they know *what* you and they are doing, and *why*. Ask them what they think they learned in a lesson, and from time to time get feedback on activities, materials and your own teaching techniques. (See also Chapter 7 Section 3: *Evaluation and testing.*)
- Help the students to explore their own attitude to learning: ask them to think about *why* they want to learn English, for what purposes they want the language – for their job or studies, for interest, or for some other reason; whether any particular aspects are more important than others – ég do they need to be able to write the language or is it sufficient to be a fluent speaker?
- Encourage them to think about *how* they like to learn; which activities interest them and help them make progress.
- Help them to assess their strengths and weaknesses.
- Help them to set realistic and achievable goals.
- Encourage them to monitor and review their learning through: self-assessment and correction, self-testing to check learning, and reviewing and revising language learned.

How can you help raise the students' awareness?

Awareness-raising can be done in many ways:

Examples

1 Through questionnaires with such questions as:

How often do you:

- listen to English on the radio?
- read an English magazine?
- listen to a song in English?
- watch a film in English?

2 Through 'credo sheets' – lists of statements which the students discuss and agree or disagree with. For example:

- If I learn all the grammar rules of English, I will be able to speak the language well.
- When you're reading a book in English, it's a good idea to look up every word you don't know in a dictionary.
- It doesn't matter if you make mistakes – it's more important to be fluent.

3 Through ordering activities. For example:

Put these ways of storing new words in order: Most useful for me → Least useful for me:

- Writing them down in alphabetical order in a vocabulary notebook.
- Recording them on tape.
- Putting the words in groups according to topic – one page per topic.
- Putting the new words in sentences.
- Writing a dictionary definition next to the new word.
- Writing the new word on one side of a piece of card and the translation on the other.

4 Through discussing and writing 'advice for language learners' or when deciding on 'class rules'. For example:

- Always speak English in class.
- Ask a friend to check your homework before giving it to the teacher.
- Look through work you did in class every evening.
- Try to learn ten new words a day.

For more ideas, see also those suggested in the study skills section below.

These activities have the advantage of providing authentic topics for discussion and useful skills practice at the same time as raising students' awareness. Some are particularly useful at the beginning of a course when you and the students are getting to know each other, and others can be used later as a means of helping the students think about their learning both in and outside the class, and their progress. With very low-level students in a monolingual group these activities can be conducted in the first language.

How can you help students to be more independent, and responsible for what goes on in the classroom?

- Teach them the language they need to understand instructions in English right from the start. For example:
  Turn to page 45.
  Get into pairs.
- Teach them useful expressions they can use in class:
  to get attention – *Excuse me*
  to ask for repetition – *Sorry?*
  for clarification – *I don't understand; What does .... mean? How do you pronounce this word? How do you spell .... ?*
  for particular words in English – *What's that in English?*
  to check – *Can you say '....' in English?*
  These expressions can be written on card and put up on the wall of the classroom for constant reference.
- Encourage them to use resources other than the teacher: for example, dictionaries, reference materials, other students. (See also the section on study skills below.)
- Ask them to bring in their own materials for use in class: for example, interesting magazines they have found in English which could be used for a reading task; photographs of their friends and family for use in a speaking lesson focusing on description; a song in English for a listening lesson. By contributing something to the classroom 'product' and taking some responsibility for the success of the lesson they are investing more of themselves.
- You may also want students to take responsibility roles in the classroom: for example, one student looks after the register; one is responsible for collecting homework; one is responsible for filling in a record of work.
- Give the students responsibility for part of the lessons: co-ordinating groupwork; chairing a group discussion; reporting back on work done as a group. You can also delegate part of the teacher's job. This may be at the level of operating OHPs or tape recorders.
  At advanced levels, you might ask students to prepare lessons which will teach the others something specific (like a grammar point some of them are shaky on).

At intermediate levels, you might ask students to prepare short talks on some aspect of their country and customs, or where all the students are of the same nationality their job or their special interest – for example, photography.

- Give the students more responsibility for the timetable. You may get them to help you prepare their timetable for the coming series of lessons. Such discussion encourages them to be much more involved in their learning and helps you to realize what they think they need.

It is important to note that students of a certain age or from certain educational backgrounds may be more resistant to the notion of learner responsibility than others. In this case discussion and the gradual introduction of change is needed.

Learning strategies

Students need to be made aware of learning strategies they might find effective. You can point out techniques and strategies which other language learners have found successful. Many of the following strategies are detailed in the sections above (Sections 2–5).

You can encourage students to use a number of strategies when practising *language skills* – strategies which they can employ when they are using the language independently of the classroom and the teacher. Some examples of these techniques or strategies are:

Listening

- making an effort to predict what they are going to hear;
- choosing the appropriate 'way' of listening depending on the purpose, eg for overall understanding, or specific details. This choice can be encouraged by the teacher in class;
- using techniques of facilitating listening when taking part in a conversation (eg asking for repetition, clarification).

Reading

- choosing appropriate 'ways' of reading depending on the text and the purpose for reading (eg skimming, scanning). When giving an authentic text to read the teacher can ask the students how they would read a similar text in their own language;
- using strategies for deducing the meaning of unknown words in a reading text;
- using dictionaries efficiently (see also p122).

Speaking

- using strategies for facilitating speaking such as paraphrasing, appropriate 'fillers', etc.

Writing

- making notes and organizing them before doing a piece of 'free' writing;
- making a rough draft first and going back and trying to improve it;
- identifying their own mistakes in their written work after their teacher has indicated mistakes by symbols such as the ones at the top of p121.

v	verb form, tense
ww	wrong word
wo	word order
prep	preposition
sp	spelling
agr	agreement of verb and subject
~~	unclear, I don't understand

The following are some strategies you can encourage students to use when learning, practising and revising language (see also Chapter 6: *Presenting and practising language*):

Vocabulary

- deciding which words or expressions they want to learn/remember: choosing vocabulary that they think will come in useful and not worrying too much about the rest!
- using a method of recording vocabulary which suits them (for ideas, see p151);
- developing methods for memorizing vocabulary – for example, using visual imagery. An English-speaking person could remember the German word for *town hall*, which is *Rathaus*, by visualizing a Lord Mayor in full regalia standing on the steps of a building from which hundreds of rats are running.

Grammar

- looking for patterns and generalizations in language;
- noting when structures are the same (as is the case with conditional sentences in a number of European languages) and when they are different (for example, the use of the present rather than a future after *when* in the sentence *I'll tell him when he comes*);
- compiling 'personalized' grammar notebooks to note down particular grammar points, perhaps with explanations in the student's own words and their own example sentences;
- using dictionaries for grammatical information (see also below).

Pronunciation

- being aware of their own individual/nationality problems in relation to English pronunciation;
- recognizing phonemic symbols so that information in dictionaries about the pronunciation of words can be accessed.

Study skills

As well as strategies peculiar to language learning there are also a number of more general study skills that you can encourage learners to use. Many of these are reference skills which they can use when studying other subjects.

Examples
1 You can suggest and discuss ways in which learners can organize their files and notebooks, record new grammar and vocabulary, keep a record of the work they have completed, and organize their revision.

2 You can encourage them to make full use of a coursebook by helping them use such features as the contents page, tapescripts, grammar reference section, student workbooks and student cassettes.

3 You can teach them how to use grammar and other reference books. Familiarize them with grammatical terminology – the parts of speech, the names of the tenses, etc so they can use reference books independently; practise using the contents and index pages, and cross-references to find entries and exercises.

4 You can teach them to use dictionaries. When using monolingual dictionaries practice looking up entries to find:

- headwords and sub-entries including idioms and multi-word verbs;
- meaning – definitions, examples;
- information about pronunciation (the phonemic and stress symbols);
- spelling – including information about irregular plurals, double letters, etc;
- grammar – eg whether verbs are regular or irregular, whether nouns are countable or uncountable, etc.

Many of these study skills can be naturally integrated into language and skills work: for example, you can use grammar reference books when doing grammar practice, or dictionary work when tackling reading or writing tasks. Or the skills can be focused on separately for part of a lesson. To what extent you need to concentrate on these study skills will obviously depend on the age, circumstances and educational background of your students.

7 Students working outside the classroom

As part of TP you may be responsible for setting or suggesting work that students can do outside of lesson time. For some students, especially those who can only spend a few hours a week having lessons, the work they do outside the classroom forms an important part of their learning programme, and many students expect to be set 'homework'.

What type of work can students do outside the classroom?

1 Practice activities from coursebooks or workbooks

It is often a more efficient use of time, after introducing a new language item, to ask the students to do some controlled practice activities at home. This gives them time to review the language and do the exercises at their own pace. During the next lesson their answers can be compared in pairs before, perhaps, going on to do some freer practice.

2 Writing

In a process writing activity, after the interest of the students has been raised and they have had a chance to exchange ideas and note down their thoughts, they can be asked to organize their notes and write a first draft at home. Then, after this draft has been shown to and discussed with the teacher and/or other students the final piece of work can be written up outside class time.

3 Preparation

Students can often be asked to do some preparation work at home. For example, if the class is reading an extended text such as a novel together it saves a lot of time if the students can read a section before the class so that time in class can be spent on exchanging ideas about the text. Sometimes it is useful to give an activity to guide the students in their reading.

You can set different preparation activities for different students. For example, if you have a student who is very weak and lacking in confidence you can ask him or her to read the tapescript of a listening text you plan to do the next lesson. Students can prepare for an oral presentation they give in class, perhaps on a topic of their choosing. They can spend time out of class planning what they are going to say and perhaps finding pictures to illustrate their talk.

However, unless you can be sure of your students, it is not a good idea to plan a lesson which totally depends on all the students having done the preparation work.

4 Research

Students can be asked to research a grammar point or some vocabulary items out of class in order to report their findings in class. This is particularly useful if they have access to a library or self-access centre. This activity encourages them to be more independent in their learning. (See also Section 6: *Learner development and study skills*.)

5 Making use of the outside world

Students can be encouraged to explore other ways of accessing the language. Even in non-English-speaking countries students may be able to use videos, satellite television, radio, English-language newspapers, magazines and pop songs in English.

6 Project work

Once project work has been set up in class the students can be asked to complete certain tasks out of class time and show or report their findings in a later lesson. For example, they might design a questionnaire in class and conduct a survey among their friends and family, other students in the school or college or even, if they are studying in an English-speaking country, with members of the public.

7 Revision

You can encourage the students to go over at home what they have done with you in class by:

- asking them to look at any notes they made in their vocabulary or grammar notebooks;
- advising them to look back over any activities in the coursebook covered that day;
- suggesting that they re-read any texts dealt with in class;
- setting them some vocabulary to learn and perhaps testing them the next lesson;
- asking them to study the grammar section, if such a section is included in their coursebooks;
- suggesting that they keep a learner diary. You can offer to look at the students' diaries or they may wish to keep them private;
- setting regular progress tests based on work they have done with you in class. (See also Chapter 7 Section 3: *Evaluation and testing*.)

Task 👤

Aim

To raise your awareness of your learning style and the learning strategies you employ.

Procedure

Answer these questions about the course you are doing and/or your own TP. Do the task individually and then if possible compare your responses with your fellow trainees.

	True or false?	**T**	**F**
1	I prefer to know in advance what the sessions on the course are about so that I can prepare for them.		
2	I like to be asked my opinion about sessions on the course or on methods of TP feedback.		
3	I prefer to take an active part in sessions and in TP feedback.		
4	I like it when the trainer gives us detailed written notes.		
5	I like problem-solving and brainstorming activities.		
6	I prefer to work on my own rather than in pairs or groups.		
7	I think I know my strengths and weaknesses as a teacher.		
8	I always review the day's work and make notes about things I need to remember.		
9	I expect too much of myself.		
10	I value feedback from colleagues about my work and my lessons.		
11	My notes and folders of work are well organized.		
12	I tend to leave homework assignments to the last minute.		
13	It is sometimes relaxing to be able to sit back and listen to the trainer.		
14	I set myself realistic goals and usually achieve them.		
15	I like to research teaching techniques thoroughly before putting them into practice.		

Comment

1 You may want to modify the statements in order to make them clearly true or false for you.
2 You may find that your idea of yourself does not accord with that of your colleagues.
3 Do you think you are a 'good student'?
4 What could you do to make yourself a better student teacher?

Answer to the puzzle on p108

Katy had got her scarf trapped in the door as she closed it behind her. (Thanks to Jill Cosh who told me about this incident which happened to her daughter.)

Further reading

Listening

Underwood, M. 1989 *Teaching Listening* (Longman)
Ur, P. 1984 *Teaching Listening Comprehension* (CUP)

Reading

Greenwood J. 1988 *Class Readers* (OUP)
Grellet, F. 1981 *Developing Reading Skills* (CUP)
Holme, R. 1991 *Talking Texts* (Longman)
Nuttall, C. 1996 *Teaching Reading Skills in a Foreign Language*, new edition
    (Heinemann)
Wallace, C. 1992 *Reading* (OUP)

Speaking

Bygate, M. 1987 *Speaking* (OUP)
Byrne, D. 1986 *Teaching Oral English* (Longman)
Byrne, D. 1987 *Techniques for Classroom Interaction* (Longman)
Dougill, J. 1987 *Drama Activities for Language Learning* (Prentice Hall/Macmillan)
Klippel, F. 1984 *Keep Talking* (CUP)
Maley, A. and Duff, A. 1980 *Drama Techniques in Language Learning* (CUP)
Maley, A., Duff, A. and Grellet, F. 1980 *The Mind's Eye* (CUP)
Morgan, J. and Rinvolucri, M. 1983 *Once Upon a Time* (CUP)
Nolasco, R. and Arthur, A. 1987 *Conversation* (OUP)
Porter Ladousse, G. 1987 *Role Play* (OUP)
Rixon, S. 1981 *How to Use Games in Language Teaching* (Prentice Hall/Macmillan)
Ur, P. 1981 *Discussions that Work* (CUP)
Wessels, C. 1987 *Drama* (OUP)
Wright, A., Betteridge, D. and Buckby, M. 1979 *Games for Language Learning*
    (CUP)

Writing

Byrne, D. 1988 *Teaching Writing Skills* (Longman)
Davis, P. and Rinvolucri, M. 1988 *Dictation* (CUP)
Hadfield, C. and Hadfield, J. 1990 *Writing Games* (Nelson)
Hedge, T. 1990 *Writing* (OUP)
White, R. and Arndt, V. 1991 *Process Writing* (Longman)

Learner development and study skills

Ellis, G. and Sinclair, B. 1989 *Learning to Learn English* (CUP)

Chapter 6　Presenting and practising language

One of the teacher's main roles is to introduce, or 'present', and practise new language and to revise language that the students have met before. Presentation and practice techniques are particularly useful at lower levels where much of the language that students come across is new. Of course some of this new language will be acquired naturally through exposure to native speaker discourse, but learners also need and want important areas of language to be highlighted by the teacher: to be explored or illustrated in terms of meaning and form (including spelling and pronunciation), and then practised. The relative amount and the type of presentation and practice depends on a number of factors which are explored in the rest of this chapter under the following headings: *1 Structures: grammar and functions*, *2 Vocabulary*, and *3 Pronunciation*.

It is convenient to categorize language under these three headings, but it must be noted that the *principles* behind the presentation of language items (as opposed to the development of skills as discussed in Chapter 5) apply – whether we are dealing with structures, vocabulary or pronunciation. So there are many areas of commonality and overlap in the approaches and techniques described in these three sections.

1　Structures: grammar and functions

Although it is recognized that people learn languages in different ways, it seems that many people can learn a language more easily if they can perceive regularities or patterns. Many of the patterns that students learn are particular grammatical items: verb forms such as the past simple, modal verbs such as *will* or *could*, particular combinations such as the first conditional (for example: *If she gets the job she'll move to London*). A list of grammatical items which are regularly focused on in language classes can be found in the contents list of any good learner's grammar book such as *An A-Z of English Grammar and Usage* by Leech (Nelson), *Practical English Usage* by Swan (OUP) or *The Heinemann English Grammar* by Beaumont and Granger (Heinemann).

Language can not only be seen in terms of grammatical form; it can also be seen in terms of 'what it does' or its 'function' in communication. Often, one language item can be used to perform more than one function in communication: for example, *Can* for both requesting – *Can you pass the salt?* – and expressing ability – *Can you swim?* And one function can often be performed by using more than one grammatical structure: for example, *Let's ... What about ... ? How about ...?* all perform the function of suggesting. (There is no definitive list of functions as there is for grammatical structures.)

Many coursebooks aim to have an *integrated* syllabus – one which combines certain grammatical structures with the functions thought most useful for students at a particular level. So at beginner level the present simple is introduced with the function of describing 'facts': *My name's Marta. I'm 18 and I live in Mexico City. I have three brothers.* At intermediate level the same verb form can be introduced with a different use – timetabled events in the future: *The plane leaves at 10.00 am. We arrive at Orly Airport at noon. From there we go straight to the hotel.* Then at advanced level we may want to introduce the use of the present simple to tell stories and anecdotes about past events: *So there I am, in the café, when up comes Jeff. He picks up my drink and he pours it all over my head.*

Some books may be designed with particular groups of people in mind, and introduce structures with functions thought most useful for the students' special needs and situation. For example, books targeted at business people usually focus on the language needed for making introductions, for arranging meetings, for negotiating, and other business-oriented functions.

What aspects of a structure should you consider?

When focusing on a structure, either for the first time or for revision, the following can be considered:

1 The form

- the parts of speech. For example, is it made up of a verb plus a preposition (*to put off*)?
- whether it is regular or irregular. For example, a regular simple past ends in *-ed* (*listened*), irregular verbs have different forms (*heard, spoke, read, wrote*);
- the spelling;
- the pronunciation. For example, does the structure contain contractions (*I'm, haven't, should've*)?
- the word order and whether the item follows or is followed by any particular words or structures. For example, does the verb usually have to be followed by a noun (*I bought the car*)?

You need also to decide how many aspects of the form you want to focus on at any one time: for example, when presenting a new verb form, you probably wouldn't want to introduce the affirmative, the question forms, the negative, short answers and question tags all in the same lesson!

2 The meaning

The exact meaning(s) you are concentrating on. This is particularly important to consider if a structure can be used to perform more than one function. For example, the past simple tense can be used to talk about the past (*Last year I was in China*), to ask a question politely (*What was it you wanted?*), to report what someone has said (*Mary said it was her birthday tomorrow*).

3 The use

How and when the language item is appropriately used; in what contexts, by which people, on which occasions? Is the structure widely used in a range of contexts and situations or does it have a more restricted use? For example, compare *Would you like to come to the cinema on Saturday?* (an invitation) and *Would you come with me?* (an instruction).

4 Potential problems

- Are there any special difficulties related to the structure's form or meaning? An example of a difficult *form* is *should not have had*, as in *I shouldn't have had that third piece of cake* – with its number of 'parts' and the double *have*. There may be difficulties of pronunciation, depending on the first language of your students. Structures which contain problematic sounds such as /ə/ or /θ/ will need special attention. An example of a difficulty of *meaning* is *needn't have +* past participle, especially when confused with *didn't need to;* or *I used to do ...* and *I was used to doing ...*
- Can the language structure be confused with any other item in English, or with an item in the students' mother tongue?

How do you decide what approach to take?

Once you have decided what structure to teach, the way you aid the students' understanding and practise the language can depend on a number of factors:

- whether the structure is completely new, is familiar to at least some of the students but has not been focused on before, or has been presented before and is now being revised. Generally, the less familiar the language item the more controlled practice you need;
- whether one or more structures are being presented and whether or not they are being compared;
- the nature of the language: for example, whether it is the meaning and use or the form which is complex. The *use* of the present perfect is difficult to grasp for many students (*I've been here since 3 o'clock* – where in many languages it would be *I am here since 3 o'clock*). On the other hand, it is the complexity of the *form* rather than the meaning of the third conditional, with its many 'parts', which generally causes difficulty (*If my alarm clock hadn't been broken I wouldn't have been late for the lecture*);
- whether the structure is more likely to be written or spoken. Some structures are mainly found in the written form and do not lend themselves to spoken practice activities – for example, this sentence from a formal letter: *I enclose (the invoice/brochure/estimate)*. On the other hand, the students need practice in *saying* such utterances as *It's a great (party/day/show), isn't it?*
- the students:
  - their level;
  - their age;
  - whether you can or want to use their mother tongue for explanation;
  - the attitude of the group – how confident the students are, whether they feel they already 'know' the language item, etc;
  - their language-learning background and expectations of how language is presented – whether, for example, they expect a 'traditional' teacher-centred approach;
  - their preferred language-learning style – for example, some students like to study grammar in an overt way while others (particularly children) are not interested in talking about the language and using such labels as *gerund* or *demonstrative adjective*.

What approaches can be used to present or revise language structures?

There are a number of different approaches. The factors mentioned in the previous section will help you decide what kind of approach to take – different ways may be suitable, depending on the students and the language being dealt with. One of the ways in which the approaches differ is in the amount and type of practice activities used: for certain language items and with certain students much more controlled practice is required, whereas on other occasions the practice can be freer. It's also important to remember that a variety of approach is interesting and motivating for students – so it's a good idea to try to vary the ways you present and practise language.

Visual/oral contexts

Pictures, mime and realia can be used to illustrate the meaning and to establish a context in which the target structure is set. Often the context is built up orally by the teacher with the help of visual aids and elicitation from the students.

Example

To present:
Structure: past simple – some irregular verbs: *went, had, fell, broke, took, was/were*
Function/use: telling a story/anecdote (about a skiing accident)
Visual aids: a postcard of a ski resort and a series of hand-drawn pictures showing 'me', the teacher (*I went skiing/I fell/I broke my leg/They took me to hospital/I was in hospital for Christmas*) and the scar on the teacher's leg!

The teacher can introduce the topic by showing the postcard and asking if any of the students know the resort, etc, and by establishing that this happened in the past – *last year, just before Christmas.*

By showing the pictures and by mime the teacher elicits any words the students know, tells the story and introduces the target language (ie the past simple of irregular verbs). After the context has been established the verbs are highlighted and practised. (For a further example of this type of lesson, see *What are the possible stages in a lesson using the inductive approach?* on p136.)

When is it useful to present language through a visual/oral context?

The introduction of structures in this way is often used:

- if the students are at a low level and the teacher wants to keep extraneous language to a minimum;
- if the students are young and would not be so interested in an overt focus on the grammar rules of the language item;
- if the meaning and use of the language is complex and so a clear, simple, but generative context is needed: you can create a context which provides a number of examples of the target language, which allows students to have plenty of controlled practice;
- if a single language item is being introduced;
- if you want to create a context that the students can relate to: if the situation is personalized in some way it will be more interesting and memorable to the students;
- if you want the situation to be unambiguous (unless there is a good reason to be ambiguous).

What are the disadvantages of this approach?

- The language can be contrived and artificial.
- It can be time-consuming to set up a new context for *each* new language item (although often 'mini-contexts' can be set up to illustrate the meaning of two or three words – see Section 2: *Vocabulary*).
- It is quite teacher-centred, as the teacher is 'up-front' at the beginning of the lesson.
- It demands a lot from the teacher by way of a 'performance'.
- Higher level and/or older students may feel this approach is 'less serious' than one which explains the 'rule' at the start, as described below.

Texts

As was pointed out in Chapter 5, as well as providing a means of practising listening and reading skills, texts can provide a natural context for language exploration and a pool from which particular language items and structures can be drawn, analysed and practised. The texts can be very varied: reading texts such as newspaper and magazine articles, stories, biographies, information leaflets and booklets, letters, reports, notices, etc; listening texts such as conversations, interviews, short talks, radio or television programmes, songs, etc. Texts which are intrinsically interesting and which give the students something to communicate about are especially useful as a vehicle for introducing and practising language.

Clearly, written texts provide a more suitable context for language which is mostly found in the written form: for example, *I look forward to … (your reply/our meeting/receiving your estimate)* – as in a formal letter. And listening texts are more useful for introducing language which is generally spoken, for example: *See you …(later, soon, tomorrow, next week, etc)*.

When is it useful to present language through texts?

The presentation of language in this way is often used:

- when students are of intermediate level and above. Because the texts from which the language is taken are often authentic or adapted from authentic material, this way·is especially suitable for students who already have some language. Authentic texts give exposure to language as a whole and not just grammatical structures in isolation, providing opportunities for natural acquisition of less familiar language as well as learning/studying of the focus language area;
- if the meaning and use of the structure is complex and the meaning of the new item is clearly illustrated by the context present in the text;
- if the new structure is being introduced in contrast with language which is already familiar and which is also present in the text;
- if a number of items are being introduced – perhaps several exponents of a function (for example, several ways of giving advice in a conversation between friends);
- if the structure has been encountered before. A way of revising language is to take it from a new and interesting context. Texts can always contain new vocabulary, even if the structures have been met before. This helps get over the 'not the past simple again!' problem – ie when students need revision of areas that they have practised before and feel they are not making progress;

- if you want the presentation and practice of a particular structure to be integrated naturally into skills work. The language item can be drawn from a reading or listening text, isolated and focused upon, and then practised naturally in, for example, a speaking or writing activity. In other words, you can use the same text very often as a basis for speaking or writing tasks where the structure can get used more freely;
- when you use the students' coursebook. Many modern coursebooks contain texts chosen (or adapted) from authentic material to illustrate particular structures which fit into the structural syllabus of the course.

Are there any problems in using texts for presenting language?

If they are not available in the coursebook it isn't always easy to find authentic texts or to create texts which contain natural examples of the structure you want to introduce, particularly if the surrounding language is to be of the 'right' level, ie 'comprehensible'. For this reason it's not so easy to introduce language through texts to lower level students. Texts which are specially written to illustrate the target language and which are simple enough for the students to cope with are often very contrived and unnatural.

However, this approach should not be ruled out. If they are well chosen, there is no reason why short authentic, or at least 'semi-authentic' or simplified texts, should not be used with low-level students. You may have to adapt a reading text, or construct a semi-authentic listening text by getting someone (perhaps another trainee or a teacher) to record a monologue using the structures you want to illustrate. If you give the person some notes to work with but let him or her speak spontaneously, you can get a more authentic-sounding listening text.

It does take a relatively long time to use this kind of material. The overall meaning of the text must be within the grasp of the students before individual language items are picked out; the text may contain language which has to be dealt with *before* you can concentrate on the target language. This is only all right if the lesson is seen as consisting of skills work leading on to a focus on particular language items, and time is allowed for these stages.

If you choose a text for skills work the structures it illustrates well may not be the ones that fit into the structural syllabus of the course the students are following. Bear in mind that particular text-types lend themselves to the presentation of particular structures: for example, simple stories contain the simple past, and a text of someone talking about his or her personal experiences will usually contain natural instances of the present perfect.

Another disadvantage with authentic texts is that they often don't give you enough examples of the target structure.

Short dialogues

Dialogues are a type of text – a spoken text which we listen to, although for teaching and learning purposes we also look at them in their written or transcribed form. Although they are a type of text, it is worth considering them separately from reading and other listening texts as they are often used as a model for speaking practice of structures.

Dialogues are often used as an alternative, or in addition, to introducing language through visual means, especially with lower level students.

Example

This dialogue could be used with low-level students to introduce the question form and the short answer of the verb *to be* in the present simple. It also revises *Sorry?* as a way of asking for repetition.

At the airport Customs

Customs officer:	Is this your bag?
Woman traveller:	Sorry?
Customs officer:	Is this your bag?
Woman traveller:	Yes it is.

Usually the teacher introduces the characters and the situation through pictures/board drawings and elicitation – *Who's this? Where are they?* etc. The understanding of the new language is checked (see p138). The students repeat the lines of the dialogue after the teacher and then take turns to play the roles, perhaps in open pairs first, then in closed pairs. It is a generative situation in that new vocabulary items can then be introduced (in this dialogue, for example, *suitcase, camera, handbag,* etc) and more sentences containing the same structures can be elicited and practised: *Is this your suitcase?* etc.

When are dialogues useful?

Dialogues are useful from time to time, particularly at elementary level, mainly for the following reasons:

- You can write the dialogue so that it focuses on the language you want to introduce and doesn't include distractions such as unknown vocabulary.
- You can make the language vivid and memorable, with a clear situation and location, and sharply distinguished characters, often aided by pictures and props.
- Dialogues provide a controlled setting for language items and conversational features.
- They are very useful for introducing language functions, for example, asking the way, at lower levels.
- Dialogues can be used to generate a number of practice sentences. For example, with the dialogue above, the teacher, by using picture prompts, can elicit these questions from students: *Is this your suitcase? Is this your camera?* and get the same replies from 'the woman'.
- It is easy to introduce pairwork practice, as the dialogues naturally have two parts. Pairwork practice often begins with repetition/imitation of the 'model' dialogue, but often this controlled practice can be followed by freer, more 'meaningful' communication. Dialogues lend themselves to information gap activities in which each student in the pair has access to different information which he or she can feed into the dialogue.
- They can be a springboard for more improvised language practice. If the practice tasks can be made more creative and open-ended the students have some degree of choice over what they say. For example, the last sentence of a dialogue can be left open.

Example

This dialogue practises language for making suggestions:

It's Rosie's birthday next week. What shall we get her?/What about ... (the students choose). *That's a good idea because ...* or *No, because ...*

A dialogue can often lead into a cued roleplay, such as the one in Task 3 on p43. See also *Setting up activities* on p44. Dialogues can also be used to illustrate the different social identity and the relationship between the speakers, and the kind of language they would use. For example, the way you ask a close friend to lend you enough money to buy a cup of coffee would be different from the way you ask a bank manager for a large loan.

What are the disadvantages of using dialogues?

- If dialogues are uncommunicative, predictable and not mixed in with other approaches to presentation they can be boring.
- They are rarely useful for students above elementary level, who benefit from seeing language within a wider context, not in isolated chunks.
- Because they are idealized, they don't prepare students for the unexpected – in real life people don't always play their part as set down in the dialogue practised in class! For example, the Customs Officer in the dialogue on p132 is just as likely to say *Your bag, is it?* as he is to say *Is this your bag?*
- It is not always easy to find or create a dialogue which is naturally generative, and in order to make them generative the dialogues can often be rather artificial and repetitive.

Giving or working out the 'rule'

In this way of presenting a structure, the teacher explains the rules or patterns of form and use and maybe, in a monolingual group, translates the structure into the students' mother tongue. You can start the lesson by telling them explicitly what language you are going to deal with: for example, *Today we are going to look at how we use the third conditional: for example – If you'd woken me on time I wouldn't have been late.* Then you can go on to give the rules of grammar and use then set up some practice.

Alternatively, you can give some example sentences containing the structure and encourage the students to work out or suggest the rules for themselves. For example, a number of paired sentences can be given and the students encouraged to say when *for* and when *since* is used with the present perfect:

a *I've been here for six hours.* **b** *I've been here since 3 o'clock.*

a *They've lived in this country for ten months.* **b** *They've lived in this country since October.*

The 'rule' can be elicited and then practice can be given. This approach is sometimes referred to as *guided discovery* and is particularly useful if you think the students have some familiarity with the target structure or if you want to revise the structure.

When is it useful to give or to elicit the 'rule'?

Giving or eliciting the 'rule' is useful:

- if the meaning of the item is easy to understand (perhaps it is very similar to the students' first language) but the structure is complex from a 'form' point of view: for example, the comparative and superlative forms of adjectives: *difficult, more difficult, the most difficult* compared with *easy, easier, the easiest*;

- if a different aspect of, say, a verb form is being presented after a stage in which the tense has already been introduced, perhaps via a text or a visual/oral context. For example, if you have introduced the affirmative and question forms of the regular past simple it is quicker, and often more efficient, simply to elicit or give the rules for the formation and use of the negative before going on to practise using it;
- if the students come from a very traditional educational background and expect a grammar/translation approach;
- if the students are at a higher level and can more easily cope with a discussion about language.

Are there any problems with this approach?

- It can seem dry and uninteresting, especially to younger learners.
- It is not so suitable for low-level multilingual groups where the students may not have enough language to understand the explanation, or the language to express it themselves.
- It isn't so suitable for language which is complex in meaning and use: it may be that there is no clear 'rule' to discover! For example, it is difficult to explain why such nouns as *fruit, money, information* and *news* are uncountable in English but countable in many other languages.

Test–teach–test

In this approach the teacher sets a communicative activity for the students which is designed to find out how well they can understand and use a particular area of language; it can be a creative activity such as taking part in a roleplay or writing a story. The teacher monitors and evaluates the activity in order to assess whether the language structure he or she wants to focus on is being used correctly and appropriately or not. It is also important to note if the students seem to be avoiding the structure. If the students have no problem with the structure the teacher can then go on to something else. If they are having problems or avoiding it altogether then the teacher can revise the target language. Practice activities which consolidate the students' ability to use the language can follow until the teacher is happy with the students' performance.

The first phase is the 'test' where the teacher finds out what the students can and cannot already do; 'teach' is the second phase when the language is revised, and the second 'test' is when practice activities are done to see if the students can use the language better than in the first phase.

What are the advantages of this approach?

This approach is particularly useful:

- at higher levels where very few, if any, language structures are new to the students;
- with confident (over-confident?) students who claim to 'know' the target language;
- with classes when you are not sure what the students have done previously and what they already know;
- when you want to focus on more than one structure – perhaps a number of exponents of a function, or the different forms of a tense;
- if you want to compare and contrast structures.

What are the disadvantages?

This type of approach, if it is done in one lesson, requires a considerable degree of flexibility on the part of the teacher. He or she has to respond instantly and appropriately to the first stage – giving feedback and picking out aspects of language to revise and consolidate. However, it may be possible to do the first phase on one day and the revision and practice activities, if it is thought necessary, on another day. In this way the teacher has time to evaluate what the students need and can plan accordingly.

If, during the first phase, the students show that they can use the target language competently, then the teacher has to have alternative activities and materials planned to replace the revision and consolidation phase.

Student-based research

Here the students are encouraged to do their own research into language areas using grammar reference books; they then report back to the class. The research can be done in or out of class time, individually or in groups. The report can take a number of forms: an oral presentation, a written report, a poster, etc. The students may also teach the structure to their fellow students and/or provide practice activities; in other words, the students 'present' the language. This approach puts much more of the responsibility for their own learning on the shoulders of the students.

When is student-based research useful?

This approach is particularly useful:

- if the students are at a high level where few, if any, structures are new;
- if they have been encouraged to be independent learners – capable of using reference books for their own research (see Chapter 5 Section 6: *Learner development and study skills*);
- if individual students have difficulty with particular structures. In this way the teacher need not focus in class on language most of the students in the class have no trouble with.

What are the disadvantages?

- This approach depends on having students of a high enough level, with good reference skills and a strong motivation and interest.
- The students have to have access to reference materials.
- You also need to have the class over a period of time.

For these reasons this approach is not always practicable in the TP situation.

'Inductive' and 'deductive' approaches

Two of the basic approaches to the presentation of language items are sometimes referred to as *inductive* and *deductive*.

When an *inductive* approach is used, a context is established first from which the target structure is drawn. So, the approaches described under *Visual/oral contexts* (p129), *Texts* (p130) and *Short dialogues* (p131) could be called inductive. When a *deductive* approach is used an example of a structure and the grammatical rule is given first and then the language is practised, as described under *Giving or working out the 'rule'* on p133.

What are the possible stages in a lesson using the inductive approach?

As noted above there are a number of variations on a theme, but this is an example of one way to proceed:

1 Create the context – with a text which has already been used for skills practice, with a dialogue, or with a short visual/oral context.

Example

This is an extract from a lesson introducing comparative adjectives via a visual context (pictures or drawings) to a class of low-level students:

The teacher shows a picture of a tall, thin man labelled *Sam*, and indicates by hand gesture that Sam is tall and elicits *Sam's tall*. The teacher shows a second picture of an even taller, even thinner man labelled *Tom* and elicits *Tom's tall*. The teacher then puts the two pictures side by side and says *Sam's tall and Tom's tall, but Tom's taller than Sam*. The teacher can do the same for *thin* and introduce more pictures and adjectives – *fat, short*, etc.

If you set up the context through a picture or short dialogue, rather than using a text, you may want to ask some simple questions to make sure that the students have a general understanding of the context. In the example dialogue given on p132, for example, the teacher would need to check that the students understand that the people are at an airport, that one is the Customs Officer and the other is a traveller.

2 The situation should lead naturally to a sentence using the language to be taught – the *model* or *target* sentence.

Example

In the lesson presenting comparative adjectives above, the target sentence is *Tom's taller than Sam* and other sentences can be generated using the pattern *X's ... er than Y*. You can then say the target language and/or write it on the board.

3 Check that the students have grasped the meaning of the structure. (See *How can you check students have understood what is being presented?* on p138.)

4 Practise saying the target language. Concentrate on the pronunciation. (See Section 3: *Pronunciation.*) Let the students repeat after you or from a model provided on cassette. They can do this together and then individually. (If the structure is one that is usually written but not spoken, this stage can be omitted.)

5 Give further practice. This is usually less controlled than the repetition practice and can involve pairwork or groupwork.

6 Then write up⋆ the language structure. At this stage a clear record of what has gone on before is given. Try to make the record the students copy from the board as memorable and integrated as possible (not just a list of unrelated sentences). Whenever possible elicit from the students the language you write on the board. This serves as a further check that they understand and remember what you have presented. Name the structure/function using clear headings, and give information about the form and/or use where appropriate.

⋆ *When* you write the language up on the board depends to some extent on the students – some feel more secure if they can see the target language written up as soon as it is focused on. You can put the target or model sentence on the board (in Step 2 above) and then add to it after oral practice (in Step 6). Or you can write up the sentence but rub it off before oral practice. In this way the students are listening to, rather than reading, the sentence and their own pronunciation is likely to be better as a result.

For example:

- note whether the words in the structure are nouns, adjectives, pronouns, etc;
- mark the sentence stress and intonation and note any contractions (see Section 3: *Pronunciation*);
- give the grammar rule (in this lesson: *to make comparative adjectives of words of one syllable, add -er);*
- note any special features of the spelling (if the word ends in a single consonant letter, double it: for example, *fat → fatter, thin → thinner*).

If you are using translation with a monolingual group you can also write up the translation, if appropriate. Give examples of the language item in sentences, perhaps in the form of a *substitution table*. If possible, try to make the examples personal and memorable for the students.

Example

I am (I'm)		Sonja.
You are (You're)		Tomas.
Rick is (He's)	taller than	his brother.
We are (We're)		our parents.
On average Americans are (They're)		Mexicans.

Other means of helping to understand and remember the meaning can be added – by using 'time-lines', for example (see p138). Give the students time to copy the information in their note books or to make a note of where the information is recorded in their coursebook.

Whether you want to do more than this depends on the language item and the class. Further practice may be needed in the form of guided and/or freer practice, integrated into skills work – as part of the same lesson or on another day. You may also want to set some homework to practise the new language. In the lessons that follow you can try to build in activities that will re-activate the language item. Often students need a little time for the new item to 'sink in' – they may recognize it, but often delay putting it into active use.

What are the possible stages in a lesson using the deductive approach?

Again, there is no one way of presenting a structure using a deductive approach. However, one possible way of staging such a lesson is as follows:

1 Present the structure and explain the 'rule' in a way that involves the students.

Examples
In order to compare ways of talking about the future you could put two sentences on the board: *I'm seeing her tomorrow* and *OK, I'll see her tomorrow* and ask the students to discuss the difference in the situation and the meaning.

With a function you could give the students a number of exponents and ask them to group them – perhaps according to degree of formality – and then discuss when and with which people you would use such expressions. For example, with requests – *Open the window. Can you open the window? Open the window, would you? Do you think you could open the window? Would you like to open the window? I don't suppose you could open the window for me, could you?* etc.

2 Write up the language structure(s). (See Stage 6 in the inductive lesson above.)

3 Set up some activities so that the students can practise using the language in a meaningful context – perhaps in a roleplay, a discussion or in a piece of writing. The practice can often be integrated into skills work.

How can you check students have understood what is being presented?

There are a number of ways you can check that the students have understood the meaning of a language item and the way it is used. It makes sense to check their understanding *before* any controlled practice – otherwise they may just be repeating parrot-fashion!

Visuals

In addition to *illustrating* meaning, visuals can be used to *check* understanding.

Examples
Students can be asked to choose the picture that best illustrates the meaning of a particular word or sentence; to put pictures in order to show a sequence of events; or to match pictures and sentences, as in this example which compares the past simple and the past perfect.

Which sentence goes with which picture?
They started the meeting when she arrived.
They'd started the meeting when she arrived.

Time-lines

Time-lines are graphic ways of illustrating the use of tenses. For example:

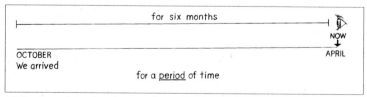

We've been here for six months.

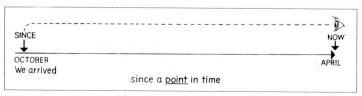

We've been here since October.

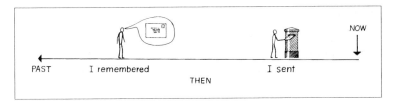

I remembered to send him a birthday card.

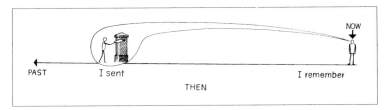

I remember sending him a birthday card.

You can check students' understanding by asking them to select the correct time-line, to label or even draw time-lines.

Concept questions

Concept questions are questions you ask students to check whether they understand the meaning of a language item. If you consider the concept questions when thinking about the language you're going to teach this should help you get the meaning clear in your own mind. Until you have had considerable experience you will need to write the questions in your lesson plan and have them to hand at the appropriate stage of the lesson.

They should be:

- simple and short. The language level should be below that of the students and certainly simpler than the language item you are focusing on. Try to design questions which only require a *yes/no* or a one-word answer from the students. One-word questions, for example – *Past?* and gestures such as a thumb over the shoulder to indicate the past together with a questioning expression are not only acceptable, they are preferable;
- in language that does not include the language being checked in either the question or in the answer. If students don't understand what you are checking, then your question will be meaningless and will not guide the students towards understanding;
- varied and numerous. Often more than one question is needed for each aspect so that more than one student can be asked without the others picking up the 'right' answer from the first student. However, concept checking must be done efficiently – you've got to find a balance between asking too many questions and asking enough to satisfy yourself that the meaning has been grasped;
- asked often and spread around the class. It is not usually possible to ask all the students in the class, but if you make sure you ask at least one of the slower students, their answers should give you a good indication of how well you have managed to get the meaning across.

Examples

1 Past perfect to indicate an action that took place *before* another action in the past:

They had started the meeting when she arrived.

Was she there at the beginning of the meeting? (No)
Did they start the meeting before or after she arrived? (Before)
Did she miss the start of the meeting? (Yes)
Did she miss the meeting? (No, not all of it, just the beginning)
Was she late for the meeting? (Yes)

2 A polite request – a young man to a woman who is sitting near him in a restaurant:

Would you mind if I smoked?

Does the man want a cigarette? (Yes)
Does the man know the woman very well? (No)
Why does he ask her? (He is polite. He doesn't want to upset her)
Does everyone like smoking? (No)
Is he asking before or after he has the cigarette? (Before)
How would you ask a friend the same question? (Is it OK if I smoke? etc)

(See also Section 2: *Vocabulary* for examples of 'concept' questions used to check the understanding of vocabulary items.)

Translation

This is only possible with monolingual groups but it can cut down on lengthy, laborious explanations – particularly at lower levels. You can check the students' understanding by asking them to translate words or sentences. However, it is dangerous for students to assume that a word-for-word translation is always available. Often the connotation of a word which is looked up in a dictionary is not fully appreciated and consequently the word is used inappropriately. Also, you may not want students to get into the habit of translating every language item they meet.

Task 1

Aim
To give practice in drawing 'time-lines' to illustrate the meaning of structures.

Procedure
1 Draw time-lines to illustrate the meaning of the following structures:

   a I've been here since four o'clock.
   b He was going round the corner when he lost control of the car.
   c This time next week we'll be lying on the beach in Florida.
   d I'm using this office while mine is being decorated.

2 If possible, show your time-lines to a colleague, a high-level student, your supervisor, someone not in EFL for their comments.

Comment
Of the people who were shown your time-lines, who understood them easily, who had the most difficulty? Why do you think this was?

Task 2

Aim

To give practice in writing questions to check that students understand new language.

Procedure A

1 Write concept questions to check the understanding of particular language items. For example:

  a I wish they'd come.
  b He used to go fishing every week.
  c She must have gone out.

2 Swap questions around and get each set modified or developed by others in your group.

3 Discuss.

Procedure B

1 Write concept questions for a particular structure.
2 Ask colleagues to try to guess what is being checked.

Procedure C

1 Get each person in your group to prepare concept questions for different items.
2 Shuffle the items and questions.
3 Get the whole group to match them.

Task 3

Aim

To consider the most suitable approach to use when presenting and practising a structure.

Procedure

1 Think about a class you are familiar with – perhaps your TP group or a class you are observing.

2 Which approach would you use – inductive or deductive – to present or revise the following structures? How would you illustrate and check the students' understanding of the meaning of the structures?

  a The present perfect to talk about experience of events before 'now': for example, *I've seen 'Cats' six times.*

  b Ways of expressing likes and dislikes: for example, *I really like ..., I hate ..., I absolutely adore ..., I can't stand ...,* etc.

  c A comparison of the uses of *so* and *such*: for example, *He's such a good dancer. He's so good. We had such good weather. The weather was so good. That's such good news.*

3 Compare your ideas with a colleague.

Comment

1 You may, of course, consider that these structures are not suitable for your class, or that you would choose different examples to illustrate the language.

2 You may be able to try out your ideas in a lesson with the class.

2 Vocabulary

The importance of vocabulary

Vocabulary is important to students – it is more important than grammar for communication purposes, particularly in the early stages when students are motivated to learn the basic words they need to get by in the language. Also, as the lexical system is 'open', there's always something new to learn when students have 'done' the grammar. So more advanced students are motivated to add to their vocabulary stock, to understand nuances of meaning, to become more proficient in their own choice of words and expressions.

A learner's receptive vocabulary is generally much larger than his or her productive vocabulary: language learners can usually understand many more words than they actively use. And students are idiosyncratic in the way they remember vocabulary – no two students are exactly the same. In particular, as students become more advanced, their individual interests and needs will help determine what kinds of words they will want to understand, remember and use.

Acquisition vs. learning of vocabulary

Vocabulary can be 'acquired' (or 'picked up') by students who listen to and read authentic language. If a text is at such a level as to be generally comprehensible the students can often grasp the meaning of new words from the context. The more often a vocabulary item is encountered, the more likely it is that the full meaning will be understood and remembered.

It is also clear that there are certain ways in which students can consciously 'learn' as opposed to 'acquire' vocabulary. Words are generally easier to remember if the meaning is well understood; so a clear presentation by the teacher can be helpful. Also memory is aided if the learner can be encouraged to make as many cues or 'memory triggers' as possible when committing the vocabulary item to memory. These cues can take the form of:

- a visual reminder such as a picture or diagram (the use of colour can be very effective);
- the sound and rhythm of the word (this is why repetition practice is helpful);
- the inclusion of the item in a sentence which is bizarre and/or personal;
- a translation of the item in the student's first language.

Most importantly, the association of one item with other items aids memory.

Examples
1 Words which are associated with the same topic such as clothes or food at lower levels and ecology or the law at higher levels (these are known as *word fields* or *word sets*).
2 Words which have the same prefix or suffix – for example, *unhappy, unlucky, unfriendly.*
3 Synonyms or near-synonyms with illustrations of the differences in use – for example, *unhappy, sad, miserable, wretched*, etc; antonyms – *tall/short, fair/dark.*

So it helps if words that have associated features are presented together. And it is helpful to point out to students study/review techniques that make use of word association – like ordering their personal vocabulary books according to topic.

What makes a vocabulary item easy or difficult?

How 'easy' or 'difficult' a vocabulary item is can depend on a number of factors:

Similarity to L1

The difficulty of a vocabulary item often depends on how similar the item is in form and meaning to the students' first language. Obviously speakers of Latin and Germanic languages have a huge advantage over other students where learning English is concerned. And a long, uncommon word such as *augmentation* may be much easier for, say, a French speaker than a short word like *mud*.

However, words which are similar in the first language and English may be misleading rather than helpful. There are many examples of these 'false friends' in European languages; someone described as sensible in English will be understood to be sensitive by many Europeans and if you say you're embarrassed to a Spanish speaker, they may well think you're expecting a baby! At first it's not easy to know which words students will find difficult and which they will find easy, especially if you are not familiar with their first language.

Similarity to English words already known

Once students have some English then a word which is related to an English word they are already familiar with is easier than one which is not. For example, if students have already met the word *friendly* they should be able to guess the meaning of *unfriendly*.

Connotation

Another difficult aspect that learners have to get to grips with is the connotation of the word. For example, does the word have a positive or negative connotation to a native speaker? Either *skinny* and *slim* could be used to describe someone who is thin – but these words are very different in their connotation and by choosing one rather than the other the speaker conveys a particular attitude. Sometimes, however, native speakers do not even agree about the exact nuance of a word. For example, to be *a patriot* may be considered good by some and bad by others, depending on their political viewpoint.

Spelling and pronunciation

The spelling of many English words can cause problems for students who speak languages with very regular spelling systems (Spanish, for example). Particular spelling patterns can also cause confusion where the pronunciation is concerned. For example, it is easy to understand why many students confuse the meaning, spelling and pronunciation of these words: *through, though, thought, tough, thorough*.

Multi-word items

A lexical item may consist of more than one word, as in a compound noun such as *tennis shoes* or *sports car*, or a phrasal verb such as *to put someone up*. Phrasal verbs are notoriously difficult for learners of English because they are made up of simple words (often prepositions or adverbs) which are easily confused. There is a world of difference between *putting someone up* and *putting someone down*. Phrasal verbs also cause grammatical problems: eg *look up the chimney* vs. *look chimney up* (in the dictionary).

Collocation

How a lexical item *collocates* (or 'goes with' other items) can also cause difficulty. For example, people are *injured* or *wounded* but things are *damaged*, and we can say a *strong wind* and *strong coffee* – but it's a *light* wind not a *weak* wind and *weak* coffee not *light* coffee. The way some grammatical structures are formed depends on knowing which words go with others and which do not; for example, a learner may know the expression *to be interested* but say *I'm interested of that* rather than *I'm interested in that*.

Appropriate use

When to use vocabulary appropriately is also problematical. Some words and expressions are restricted to use in particular contexts (for example, we can use *pushing* to mean *almost* in *He's pushing fifty*. But *pushing* is only used in this way with older people – we do not say *He's pushing three!*). Also it is important that students know whether the word or phrase has a marked *style* – informal or formal. Students have to take care with the use of colloquial and slang expressions, for example. Some language is so restricted we talk about it belonging to a particular *register*: for example, English for commerce (eg *bill of lading, free on board*); medical English (eg *abdomen* instead of *stomach, fracture* instead of *break*), and legal English (eg *easement, in fee simple*).

What aspects of a vocabulary item should the teacher consider?

As with a structure it is useful to think about the *form*, the *meaning* and the *use* of any new vocabulary item that you introduce to students:

The form

- What part of speech is the word – noun, verb, preposition, etc?
- How is it spelled – is it regular or irregular?
- Does it belong to a 'family' of words, for example *electricity, electrical, electrician*?
- How is the word, or combination of words, pronounced and, in words of more than one syllable, where is the stress? (See Section 3: *Pronunciation*.)
- How does the word collocate with surrounding words? Is it part of a set expression?

The meaning

- Many words have more than one meaning. What exact meaning(s) in which context do you want to focus on?
- What is the connotation of the item?
- Could the vocabulary item have different meanings for different people?

The use

- How is the vocabulary item used?
- Does it have a restricted use? Does it belong to a particular style or register?

Increasingly compilers of dictionaries are using computer concordance programmes based on written and spoken corpora to discover how language is used by native speakers in real life.

How do you decide what vocabulary to teach?

If vocabulary (or lexis) can be defined as 'all the words in a language', how do you decide what to teach?

Type of lesson

Firstly, it is worth distinguishing between the 'teaching' of vocabulary that you, the teacher, bring into the class and the development of strategies for helping students to understand and remember vocabulary (use of dictionaries, helping students deduce words in context, etc).

There is a difference between a 'vocabulary lesson' (where, for example, the main objective is for the students to learn and use a number of vocabulary items) and a lesson in which vocabulary comes up as part of another activity (where, for example, the teacher helps the students deal with vocabulary they may meet in an authentic listening or reading text). You will make different decisions about what vocabulary to present, depending on the type of lesson.

For receptive or productive use?

Secondly, you should think about whether the vocabulary items you have chosen to present are for *receptive* or *productive* use. Is it enough for the students to be able to recognize the vocabulary when they meet it in context, or do you want them to be able to use it? If you want the students to be able to use the vocabulary, what practice activities are you going to set up?

Lexical syllabus

Thirdly, you may have to consider the order in which vocabulary items are introduced, particularly at low levels. If you are using a coursebook, the lexical syllabus – the vocabulary items and the order in which words and expressions are introduced – will have been considered by the authors. However, you may want to add or omit items depending on the teaching context and the needs of your students.

With a General English class it is usual to introduce:

- the 'easy' words before the 'difficult' (see above);
- the concrete before the abstract;
- the most frequent before the uncommon;
- the most generative, or 'all-purpose', before those that have a more restricted use (for example, it would probably be a good idea to introduce *chair* before *armchair* or *highchair*).

You have to think about this process of grading language when you are choosing vocabulary items to teach to the class and when you are considering how to deal with the vocabulary in any authentic materials you include in your lessons.

Presenting, practising and revising vocabulary

As with structures (see Section 1: *Structures: grammar and functions*), there are a variety of ways of introducing, practising and revising vocabulary.

Presenting a vocabulary set via a visual/oral context

As with the presentation of structures, introducing vocabulary through a visual/oral context is very effective, especially with lower level students and with children. It is particularly useful when the teacher wants to present a set of 'concrete', demonstrable words and expressions on a particular topic. You can proceed in a way which is very similar to that outlined in the inductive approach to presenting a structure (see p129), with a few notable changes:

Example
The teacher wants to elicit the words for food and drink that the students already know and then introduce some new items of vocabulary before going on to practise ordering food in a restaurant.

1 Illustrate the meaning using visual aids (pictures and drawings or, if possible, real food and drink).
2 Say the words. Don't forget to include any grammar words that make up the lexical item: for example, the preposition *of* as in *a bottle of mineral water*. At this point you can write the words on the board, or you can leave this step until later.
3 Check the students' understanding of the meaning of the items. (For ideas on how to do this, see below.) In steps 2 and 3 involve the students as much as possible: elicit what they already know and encourage them to help one another.
4 The students practise saying the words. Concentrate on the pronunciation – the sounds, the word stress and, in items of more than one word, the way the words link together (see Section 3: Pronunciation). Let the students repeat after you or from a model provided on cassette, together and/or individually.
5 If you haven't already done so, write the words on the board. Mark the word stress, note what parts of speech the items belong to, any spelling points worthy of note, contractions, punctuation and capital letters where appropriate. Write down examples of the language item in sentences – try to make the sentences personal and memorable to the students.
6 Give the students time to make a note of where the information is recorded in their coursebook or to copy the information in vocabulary notebooks under the topic heading of *Food and Drink*. You can encourage the students to include any 'memory triggers' – a picture or diagram, a translation, information about how the word is pronounced, the use of different colours for different parts of speech, etc.
7 Any further practice activities you organize will depend on the vocabulary items and whether you expect the vocabulary to be for receptive use only (ie students can understand the word or expression if they see it written or hear it spoken) or for productive use (ie they should be able to use the item correctly and appropriately). For the former it may be enough to give some controlled or guided practice activities: filling gaps in a text with words from a given list or matching words and definitions, for example.

If you want to provide freer productive practice you may plan to integrate work on vocabulary with some productive skills work. For example, after you have revised and introduced some food and drink vocabulary the students can take part in a roleplay set in a restaurant where they read a menu and choose and order food.

In addition, you may often want to set vocabulary-learning homework. You can decide on the words and expressions to learn and give a short test during the next lesson. Alternatively, you can ask the students to choose, say, ten words or expressions from the day's lesson to learn. The next lesson you can then put them in pairs and ask them to test each other. In this way they learn their own list and get further practice in the words their partner has chosen to learn.

Vocabulary in texts

One very effective way of introducing new vocabulary is through listening or reading texts, as it is from specific contexts that words and expressions derive their particular meaning. Often in integrated skills lessons one of the teacher's aims is to introduce and practise a number of lexical items on a particular topic or theme.

Example
A lesson suitable for intermediate students on the theme of holiday resorts. After introducing a number of words and expressions on the topic through a short text from a holiday brochure, the teacher can then ask the students either to plan and deliver a talk about a resort in their own country and/or to write an entry on their own town for a holiday brochure or travel guide. The procedure for such a lesson could be as follows:

1 Introduce the topic by showing the students a real holiday brochure, elicit the words *holiday brochure* and ask students what kind of information a holiday brochure contains.
2 Give each student a copy of a short passage which describes a particular holiday resort. Ask a few general questions to check that the students have an overall understanding of the text (for example, *Is it a good place for a holiday? Is it a place for people interested in culture or just relaxation? Would you like to go there?* etc).
3 You can then pick out vocabulary from the text and introduce some related vocabulary (for example, the text might mention *beautiful coastal scenery* and you could introduce *mountain scenery, desert scenery*, etc).
4 The rest of the lesson could follow on from Step 2 in the sample lesson outlined on p146 in *Presenting a vocabulary set via a visual/oral context*.

Test–teach–test

It is sometimes useful to adopt a 'test–teach–test' approach to vocabulary, especially with more advanced students. This approach is very useful when you want to revise vocabulary items or to remind students of words they may have already met before you go on to do some skills work.

1 Set a production activity for the students which is designed to find out how well they can understand and use vocabulary which is suitable for the task. It can be a creative activity – perhaps taking part in a discussion on a controversial topic such as *Banning smoking in public places*, or writing a letter to a friend describing a new job.
2 Monitor and evaluate the activity in order to assess whether the students are

using the vocabulary accurately and appropriately. It is also important to note if the students seem to be avoiding any vocabulary that would be appropriate to fulfil the task.

3 If the students have no problem with the language you can then go on to something else. If they are having problems or avoiding it altogether then you can revise the vocabulary by focusing on the form, meaning and use.

4 Practice activities which consolidate the students' ability to use the language can follow. As when this approach is used to revise structures, the activities need not all take place on the same day.

Recycling vocabulary

Often students need a little time for the new item to 'sink in'– they may recognize it but often delay putting it into active use. For this reason it is useful to plan activities that recycle and reactivate the new vocabulary in subsequent lessons. You, or your fellow trainees, can introduce texts that contain some of the new language and organize speaking and writing tasks that require the students to use it. It is often appropriate to start off the lesson by doing a short activity which revises a lexical set presented the day before. Quick vocabulary revision games are a good way to warm up students at the beginning of a lesson.

Examples
Some ideas for five- or ten-minute activities include:

1 Put the students into groups of four or five. Ask them to recall as many words and expressions as they can from the last lesson on the topic of ..... The group which can remember the most words is the winner.

2 Remind the students of the topic and ask them all to stand up, in a circle if possible. Clap out a beat and say *One, two, three*, followed by a word on the topic. After the next three beats the next student in the circle gives a word related to the topic, and so it continues. Anyone who can't think of a word or repeats a word already given has to sit down and it's the turn of the next person. The winner is the last to remain standing.

3 To revise occupations write the words *doctor, hairdresser, truck driver*, etc on cards and get the students to mime the job. The person who guesses correctly does the next mime. This can be done in front of the whole class or in smaller groups.

4 This revises occupations with higher level students. Attach a label, with an occupation written on it, to the back of each student: *lawyer, politician, engineer*, etc. Ask them to mingle and ask each other questions until they guess the word on their back: for example, *Do I work with people? Do I wear a uniform? Is it a well-paid job? Would you like to do this job?* etc. (It also, of course, revises the present simple.)

5 This game to revise the vocabulary of appearance and/or clothing is fun (but can be a bit wild!). Seat the students in circle. Start by saying *All those (wearing jeans/with fair hair/who wear glasses, etc) change places*. After a few goes, give a command and then take one of the chairs away, leaving a student standing in the middle of the circle. This student must then give the next command and find a seat when the others change places. The student who cannot find a seat gives the next command.

Conveying meaning and checking understanding

As with the presentation of a structure, there are a number of ways of conveying the meaning of vocabulary and checking the students' understanding. Asking *Do you understand?* is not always helpful even if they say *Yes* because students may think they understand when they don't! Or they may be trying to please the teacher, or prevent the teacher from doing more work. So it is important to check the understanding of vocabulary which you think may be new to the students.

Realia and visuals

For concrete items it is usually much quicker to show the item than explain the meaning. Especially at low levels a quick board drawing is an efficient way of getting the meaning across. When you plan to introduce a vocabulary set take time to prepare some visuals rather than relying on wordy explanation and discussion. Visuals in themselves make the lesson more interesting and lively and can be put on the wall, with labels, as a constant reminder of the vocabulary. In addition to illustrating meaning, visuals can be used to check understanding: for example, students can be asked to match the picture to the word or phrase.

Mime and gesture

Mime is particularly useful to illustrate actions such as brushing teeth, riding a bike, painting a wall, etc. Some teachers seem to be particularly gifted in this area but practice makes perfect. Mime may seem frivolous at times but it is efficient and memorable.

Action by the students can tell you whether they understand. You can ask them to point (to one of the pictures on the board), to touch or hold up something, to make a face or gesture (to indicate *yes* or *no*, perhaps). This approach is particularly successful to check the understanding of actions and of concrete objects, with children and lower level students.

Give examples

Often the meaning of more abstract or 'umbrella' terms can be conveyed by giving examples of their attributes or of what they do and do not 'contain': for example, to illustrate the word *clothing* you can list *shirt, jeans, jacket,* etc and you can ask questions to check that the students have understood the meaning (see also 'Concept' questions on p150): *Is a skirt a piece of clothing? (Yes.) And a bag? (No.)* etc.

Explanation or definition

Giving an explanation, definition or paraphrase is often the least successful way of conveying the meaning of a vocabulary item, especially at low levels where the words you need to explain or define may also be unknown. Also students may know the meaning of a word but be unable to explain it. So it can be very frustrating for them if you try to check their understanding by asking them to explain vocabulary.

If you know there are words you are going to explain, try to make sure you give the 'whole picture': when the word(s) can be used appropriately, in which contexts, how they collocate, etc. Giving partial information can be misleading rather than helpful. For example, if you tell students that, in Britain, *white* means *with milk* without telling them that it is only used to describe coffee, they may think you can also say *white tea*.

It is often better to get students to use a good learners' dictionary in order to find a definition of an unknown word, rather than always giving a definition yourself. Training in using such dictionaries will help the students find out about vocabulary independently of the teacher. (See below and also Chapter 5 Section 6: *Learner development and study skills*.)

Translation

It is much easier to use translation in a monolingual group, but even in multilingual groups it is worth spending some time helping students to make the most of their translation dictionaries.

Concept questions

Concept questions are particularly useful to check the understanding of vocabulary items. (See also the use of concept questions with structures on pp139-40.) If your aim is to check understanding of a vocabulary item such as the noun *building*, the questions would have to determine what the word doesn't signify as much as what it does signify. In other words, you are checking and clarifying the limits of the meaning of the item. For example, here are some questions you could ask, though you probably won't want to ask all of them:

What are buildings used for? (Homes, hospitals ...)
Is a school a building? (Yes, usually)
A tent? (No)
Are they usually there for a long or short time? (Long)
Do birds make buildings? (No)
What are buildings made of? (Stone, brick, wood ...)
Can you give me some more examples of buildings?

You eliminate those things that could be confused with a building and leave the students with a clear impression of what a building actually is – something permanent made of bricks, concrete, wood, etc with walls, in which people live or work.

Developing students' skills and strategies

It is important that students should be encouraged to take responsibility for their own acquisition and learning of vocabulary and it is usually easier for them to be independent in their learning of vocabulary than in their learning of grammar or pronunciation.

Ways the teacher can foster this independence both in and out of the classroom include:

1 Encouraging strategies for dealing with unfamiliar vocabulary in texts

An important aspect of the skills of listening and reading is to be able to deal with unfamiliar vocabulary. This becomes increasingly important as students become more proficient in the language and 'acquire' a lot of new vocabulary from authentic texts.

There are a number of ways in which teachers can help students to develop the necessary strategies. Students need practice in deciding which words are crucial to the overall understanding of the text and which they can ignore. For example, you can provide a reading text which contains a number of words which will almost certainly be unknown to most of the students and ask them to choose three or four words which they most want to know the meaning of. They can do this individually and then compare their lists in pairs or groups. The process of selection and deciding on a priority will force the students to examine which words they need to understand. You can then illustrate the meaning and check the students' understanding using one or more of the ways discussed above in *Conveying meaning and checking understanding.*

Students also need help and practice in deducing the meaning of words: by comparing words with those in their own language; by looking at the parts of the unknown word and comparing it with English words which contain the same root or affix (for example, guessing the word *unelectable* from their knowledge of the root *elect*, the prefix *un-* and the suffix *-able*); by guessing the word from the context provided by the sentence and/or the whole passage. These strategies can be discussed and a number of vocabulary items picked out of the text which lend themselves to these processes of deduction.

2 Developing reference skills

If they meet words or expressions which they cannot deduce from the word itself or from the context (if they are 'unguessable'), or if they want to check that their guesses were correct, students need to be able to use dictionaries quickly and effectively. Activities which improve the students' reference skills can be very helpful in improving their ability to deal with new vocabulary. There are a number of workbooks designed to be used with learners' dictionaries which contain such activities.

3 Encouraging the use of vocabulary records

You can demonstrate and discuss ways in which students can keep their own vocabulary records. For example:

- putting the words in groups according to topic – one page per topic;
- putting the new words in sentences;
- writing a dictionary definition or a translation next to the new word;
- using colour, symbols and pictures to distinguish categories of words;
- putting the words and expressions on one topic in a 'spidergram' to which new words can be added:

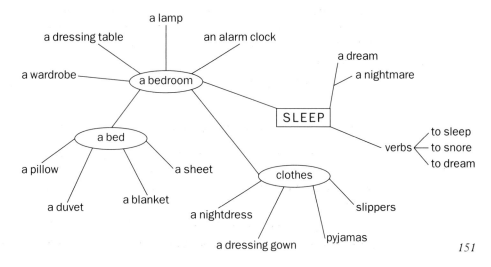

4 Demonstrating and discussing ways of memorizing vocabulary

You can teach the students mnemonics such as the rhyme to help spelling – 'i before e except after c'. You can explain the system of visually linking the word to be learned to a bizarre and memorable image – for example, an English speaker might remember the Spanish word *col*, meaning *cabbage*, by visualizing a huge cabbage, with a rucksack on its back, going over the col of a mountain.

You can encourage the students to find ways of 'learning' vocabulary. For example:

- recording words and expressions on tape and listening to them on a personal stereo or in the car;
- keeping a small box containing cards with the English word on one side of a piece of card and the translation on the other (the learner can test him- or herself and when the word is memorized the card is taken out of the box);
- sticking up words around a mirror or on the wall above the desk in the student's own room.

5 Giving choice

Different students often choose to note and remember different vocabulary items, depending on their interests and needs, and when you revise vocabulary you will probably find quite a variation in what individual students have remembered. You can foster student independence and responsibility, even at low levels, by sometimes giving students a choice as to how many or which items they note down and learn. They are much more likely to be motivated to remember words which they have selected and which they are interested in.

6 Helping learners devise their own revision plan for reviewing and learning vocabulary

This is particularly useful if they are using a coursebook which contains lists of words to learn. You can help the students by notifying them in advance of any tests you plan to give.

Task

Aim
To devise a vocabulary revision game.

Procedure
1 Think of a topic that the class you are teaching during TP is familiar with.
2 Write down about ten words or expressions that they have met which are related to that topic.
3 Devise a game or short activity that will revise that vocabulary.
4 Play the game with the class.

Comment
You may like to do this activity with a colleague and try it out with fellow trainees before doing it with the students.

3 Pronunciation

Work on pronunciation is important for two main reasons: to help the students understand the spoken English they hear, and to help them make their own speech more comprehensible and meaningful to others.

What elements go to make up pronunciation?

The various elements that go to make up pronunciation can be looked at under the following headings, although it is not necessary to teach the elements in this order.

Individual sounds

Each language has its own set of sounds or phonemes. There are 44 English phonemes. Sounds differ depending on how they are formed in the mouth, throat and nose and whether they are 'voiced' (when the vocal chords are used – as when you hum) or 'voiceless' (when the vocal chords are not used – as when you whisper). All vowels are voiced but some consonants are voiced and some are voiceless. The most common sound in English is /ə/ – the 'schwa' or 'weak' sound. A table or list of phonetic symbols and the sounds they represent can be found in most learner dictionaries. Phonetic conventions vary slightly; the most commonly used system is the International Phonetic Alphabet (IPA).

Word stress

In words of two or more syllables, one syllable is normally stressed more than the other(s). This is the primary stress. For example, in the word *pronunciation* the stress is on the *a*, the fourth syllable. Often, sounds that are not stressed are pronounced with the /ə/ sound: the first *o* and the *io* in *pronunciation* /prənʌnsıeıʃən/, for example.

Sounds in connected speech

In spoken sentences or utterances certain changes take place to some of the sounds as words are said at normal speed and linked together to make connected speech:

- The 'weak' forms of words are used: *was* becomes /wəz/ not /wɑz/; *of* becomes /əv/ not /ɑv/.
- Some sounds are often not pronounced, for example the *or* in *comfortable,* the *d* in *handkerchief,* the *t* at the end of *first* in *first thing*, etc. This is known as *elision.* When the missing letters are replaced by apostrophes they are known as *contractions*: for example, *I am* becomes *I'm, could have* becomes *could've*, etc.
- In order to make linking of words easier we sometimes insert a sound that is not present in the spelling. For example, *a banana* /r/ *and two* /w/ *apples and three* /j/ *oranges*. These are called *intrusive* sounds: /r/, /w/, /j/.
- Sometimes when words are linked one sound is changed into another sound. For example, *good morning* becomes *gubmorning*, and *Great Britain* sounds like *Grapebritain*! This process is known as *assimilation*.

Rhythm and stress in utterances

English is generally considered to be a *stress-timed* language: some words – usually the 'content' words or those that carry information (for example, nouns and main verbs) – are stressed and others are not. For example: *Throw the ball to Ben.* However, sometimes the speaker can choose to stress 'non-content' words as in this utterance: *Throw it to him, not at him.*

It is often said that in English we try to keep a fairly steady rhythm – spending about the same time to get from one stressed syllable to the next each time. To do this the unstressed syllables are 'squashed up' through devices such as contractions and weak sounds (see *Sounds in connected speech* on p153).

Intonation

Intonation is a pattern of rise and fall in the level (the pitch) of the voice, which often adds meaning to what is being said: for example, when we want to show interest or surprise in something, the pitch of our voice often rises.

Change of pitch takes place in the most strongly stressed word – on the 'tonic' syllable. The word containing the tonic syllable is often at the end of an utterance, but the speaker can shift the stress to affect the meaning of the utterance. (See the examples in *Indicating intonation: By making marks on the board* on p160.)

Together with change of pitch, the quality or tone of voice we use when we speak conveys meaning. Even if we don't understand the words of a language, we can usually tell if someone is speaking angrily, tenderly, sadly, etc.

How do you know what aspects of pronunciation to focus on?

There are some aspects of pronunciation which need to be focused on with all groups: for example, stress in new words; contractions and weak forms; the intonation used for a particular function (a request for a stranger to pass the salt will have a different intonation pattern from a request for the children to stop arguing).

One advantage of a monolingual group is that it is easy to pick out the English sounds which are difficult for all the students in the class. A focus on sounds is more problematical in a multilingual class as students with different mother tongues have different problems. However, there are certain English sounds which many students from a number of different language backgrounds have difficulty with: /θ, ð, ɪ, əʊ, ə/.

If certain sounds are only a problem for some of your students you shouldn't spend long focusing on them with the whole class. Try to pick up any problems and give quick individual correction and practice where necessary, within the lesson, without spending too long on any one student. At times it may be possible to set individual tasks based on specific problems with sounds. Nearly all students will benefit from work done on stress and intonation.

When should you focus on pronunciation?

Wherever possible pronunciation work should be integrated into lessons in which the main focus is the presentation or practice of a grammar point, a function or a set of vocabulary items. Lessons practising the skills of listening and speaking are also excellent vehicles for pronunciation work. Authentic listening texts provide opportunities to acquire pronunciation patterns naturally; you can also use them to point out the techniques that native speakers use to be effective communicators: use of stress, linking and intonation in particular. These techniques can then be practised and evaluated during speaking activities. Also, it is sometimes useful to devote a slot or even a whole lesson to pronunciation work.

Opportunities should be seized for individual correction of pronunciation whenever it is possible to do this without seriously holding up the progress of the lesson. Don't forget, also, to give feedback on the *good* pronunciation of your students. (See Chapter 7: *Giving feedback to students.*)

Raising awareness

The first step is to help the students recognize the importance of pronunciation. It may be useful to do some awareness-raising activities with a group in which, depending on their level and degree of self-awareness, some of the following can be discussed:

How good do you think your pronunciation needs to be – like a native speaker, good enough to be understood by others, etc?
What are the different aspects that affect your pronunciation of English?
Do you know which aspects of your pronunciation you need to work on?
Which English sounds do people who speak your first language usually have problems with?
Are there any aspects of stress and intonation which you find difficult? etc.

Focusing on how things are said

When the focus is on pronunciation it is usual to give the students the opportunity of hearing the language pronounced correctly, perhaps to have certain aspects of the pronunciation pointed out to them, and then have a chance to practise the word or utterance themselves.

Often, especially if the classes are taking place in a non-English-speaking country, an important model for pronunciation is the teacher. Obviously, clear modelling is important and is especially important in any lesson in which new language is introduced. (See Section 1: *Structures: grammar and functions* and Section 2: *Vocabulary.*) This is usually done directly by the teacher or with the aid of a recording, although sometimes the model can be provided by one of the students.

It is important to try to use natural speech in the classroom: you can grade your language so that you use simpler language at lower levels and you can speak a little more slowly, but you should avoid giving an unnaturally slow and deliberate pronunciation model. This is easier said than done, but gets easier with practice. So use contractions and weak forms except when analysing the language (see below) and even then make sure the students hear and practise the correct pronunciation immediately afterwards.

When providing a model, it is sometimes useful to *contrast* certain features of sounds, stress and intonation. A pair of words which differ by only one sound is known as a *minimal pair*: for example, *pin* and *bin* or *hat* and *heart*. A student can more readily perceive that a sound is voiced (the /b/ in *bin*) by placing it alongside a sound that is voiceless (the /p/ in *pin*). Attention can be drawn to stress on a particular syllable by saying it correctly and then repeating the word with the stress on a different syllable. A rising question tag becomes easier to recognize when it is heard immediately before or after a falling one. So, *You haven't seen the film yet, have you?* (with falling intonation because the speaker is expecting confirmation of the statement, not asking a question) can be compared to *You haven't seen my glasses, have you?* – with rising intonation because it is a genuine question. This can be taken a step further and students can be asked to identify which of a pair of words has a particular sound in it, which utterance has the rising intonation, which question starts with a stressed word, and so on.

How can you indicate individual sounds?

Mouthing the word

This involves exaggerated movements of the lips, teeth and tongue so that the students can see clearly what is happening. It can only really be applied to the consonants produced at the front of the mouth, /p, b, f, v, w, m, θ/, but it is very useful to show vowels – where the shape of the lips is important. Silently mouthing before saying a vowel sound focuses attention on how it is formed.

Using gesture

If you ask students to say some sounds with their hands on their throats or over their ears they will notice the difference between those that are voiced and those that are voiceless. For example, you can contrast /sssszzzzzssss/ as a continuous sound, switching the voicing on and off. Once students have learned about voicing then you can indicate that feature of the sound by making a gesture to remind them of it: for example, you might place your hand on your throat to indicate that the sound is voiced.

Emphasizing the syllable containing the sound

This has the advantage of bringing it clearly to the students' attention but the disadvantage of possibly distorting the stress pattern of the word, as well as possibly changing the production of the sound as it would occur in connected speech. This is a particular disadvantage in the case of sounds in unstressed syllables (the schwa /ə/ is often heard as the weak form of another sound).

It is best, then, to follow the simple rule that if you stress sound unnaturally for any reason, it should immediately be repeated normally. In this way the final thing which stays in the students' mind is the sound produced as it would be in the context from which it has been taken.

Finger indication

A word can be broken down into sounds and each segment associated with one of your fingers. You can then point to the appropriate finger and say the sound:

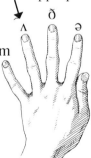

The sound can be isolated by going through the word slowly, finger by finger, then going back to the finger representing the important sound and getting the students to pronounce it in isolation. At the end you should always put the sound back in its context in the word by either giving a sweeping gesture across all the fingers or closing the fingers and giving a clear, normal model.

Visuals

A diagram of the mouth can be put on the board or displayed on the wall and used whenever a problem occurs with a particular sound.

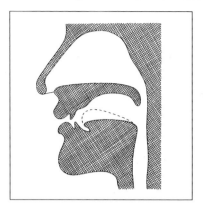

Pictures representing problem sounds: for example, a picture of a man called Jim to represent /ɪ/ can be put next to one of a woman called Jean /iː/, and the students asked *Is that a Jim sound or a Jean sound?* Pictures representing other words containing that sound can be added below when they occur: for example, *fish, lips, swim* under Jim and *meat, knee, ski* under Jean. This is obviously more useful in classes where pronunciation problems are common to the group. This activity is also useful in pointing out the fact that the same sound can be spelled in different ways.

A chart can act as a useful reminder of sounds and their spellings. As new words are presented to the class students can suggest which column they should be added to and write them in:

feet /iː/				
ee	ea	ie	ey	e
bee	*meat*	*thief*	*key*	*she*

Hands

For consonant sounds such as /ð/ one hand can represent the top teeth and the other hand the tip of the tongue to show the light contact the tongue has with the teeth.

Phonetic or phonemic symbols

Students and teachers alike are often put off by the apparent difficulty of a phonetic, or more correctly, a phonemic transcription. It is worth remembering that the symbols were developed as a kind of short cut, a way of representing sounds without having to give an explanation each time. They are also in common use in dictionaries and in coursebooks. Even if you don't feel you have time in TP to teach all the symbols to a class of students who don't already know them, it is useful to have a chart on the wall for reference and to be able to introduce and refer to the symbols for common or difficult sounds: for example, /θ, ð, əʊ, ɪ, ə/.

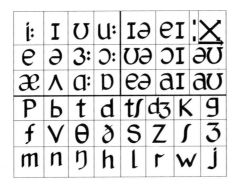

From *Sound Foundations*
by Adrian Underhill (Heinemann 1994)

Indicating stress in a word

You can indicate word stress to students in a number of ways:

1 'Where's the stress?'

It is important that students realize that words consist of one or more syllables before you work on word stress in the classroom. You can demonstrate the number of syllables by clapping out the word – students generally get the idea very quickly. You can then say, for example: *In 'hotel', where's the stress – first or second syllable?* You can also point out where parts of words are not pronounced: for example, the word *vegetable* has three, not four, syllables as the second *e* is not pronounced.

2 By overstressing

This technique makes stress in words more easily perceived and experience suggests that there is little danger of them repeating the exaggeration outside the classroom. There is also little danger of distortion, unlike when a particular sound is stressed.

3 By gesture

This is done by any of the following ways:

- moving the hand, like a conductor, on the stressed syllable;
- clapping the word – with a louder clap on the stressed syllable;
- clicking the fingers on the stressed syllable;
- tapping the desk.

4 By using Cuisenaire rods

Each syllable in the word can be represented by a rod. A taller one is used for the stressed syllable.

5 By making marks on the board

There are a number of possible ways. For example, take the word *hotel*, where the stress is on the second syllable:

a Capitalization: hoTEL
This could be confusing for students having difficulty with the Roman script.

b Underlining: ho<u>tel</u>
This is simple. However, you may want to save underlining for showing stress within a sentence or utterance.

c Stress marks: ho'tel
These are used by most dictionaries for word stress, with marks at the top indicating primary stress and those at the bottom indicating secondary stress. However, these can easily be confused with apostrophes and speech marks in sentences.

d Boxes: hotel
This is useful because the pattern can be shown without the word, like this:

Be careful to place the box above the vowel in the syllable, as this is where the stress takes place.

Whichever you choose, your system should be clear and immediately understandable to students. It is advisable to keep it consistent within any one teaching institution to reduce the possibility of confusion.

Indicating rhythm and stress in sentences/utterances

Some of the same techniques for indicating stress in words can be used to indicate rhythm and stress in utterances: overstressing, gesture (this is particularly useful to indicate the rhythm), Cuisenaire rods (a rod for each word) and marking on the board.

When marking on the board it might be useful to indicate stress in the utterance differently from stress in the word – although the two overlap. For example:

<u>How</u> about <u>going</u> to the <u>cinema</u> this <u>evening</u>?

Indicating intonation

1 By exaggeration

When you exaggerate the main features (for example, a falling tone in some *wh-* questions) the pattern is more easily recognized and more memorable for students. It also encourages them to widen their own range. When they try to imitate it, however, it is important that they don't make it too silly or they won't think of transferring it to their normal speech behaviour.

In long utterances it is useful to use a technique called *backchaining* to maintain the intonation pattern and at the same time practise a long sentence in manageable chunks. For example, in the utterance *If I'd <u>caught</u> the <u>bus</u> I wouldn't have been so <u>late</u>* – you can say the whole sentence then get the students to repeat after you in sections, beginning at the end of the sentence: *so late* (students repeat), *I wouldn't've been so late* (students repeat), *caught the bus I wouldn't've been so late* (students repeat), *If I'd caught the bus I wouldn't've been so late* (students repeat).

2 By gesture

It is possible to 'draw' an approximation of the whole intonation pattern in the air with your hand, but this is usually unnecessarily complicated. It is far easier, and perhaps more useful, to give a clear sweep of the hand either up or down in order to indicate the general direction the voice should take on a particular syllable. Hands can also be used to show whether the voice starts on a high or low pitch.

3 By making marks on the board

Again, there are a number of possible ways. For example, take the sentence *It's a lovely day, isn't it?* with a fall on each part.

Curved writing

It's a lovely day isn't it?

This is difficult to do neatly, but what it means is clear. However, it can interfere with students' writing development.

Arrows

It's a lovely day, isn't it?

This is clear and simple and can be used by students. If it is tied in with sentence stress it emphasizes the fact that pitch change takes place on the tonic (or most stressed) syllable:

It's a lovely day, isn't it?

This is particularly useful when you want to indicate that sentences have different meanings, depending on where the tonic syllable is. For example:

1 Is that your little girl?

2 Is that your little girl? (not your big girl?)

3 Is that your little girl? (not someone else's girl?)

4 Is that your little girl? (not this girl)

5 Is that your little girl? (are you sure?)

Again, select one system according to the sophistication, the level and the needs of your students, and stick to it.

Task 1 👥

Aim
To think of some minimal pair words which can be used to contrast two sounds.

Procedure
1 Write down three minimal pairs for each the following:

/ p / / b /
/ v / / w /
/ l / / r /
/ ɪ / / iː /
/ ɑ / / ɔː /

For example: /b/ /v/ *boat/vote*; *beer/veer*; *bet/vet*; *lubber/lover*; *hobble/hovel*.

2 Compare your minimal pairs with those of another trainee.

Comment
Could your minimal pairs be used with students at a low level? Would they know the words? Is it useful to use words which the students don't understand?

Task 2 👤

Aim
To practise marking the stress on words on the board.

Procedure
1 Choose one of the methods for marking word stress described on p159.
2 Write these words on the board and mark the stress:
photograph, photographer, photographic
music, musician, musical
politics, politician, political

Comment
1 What do you notice about the position of the stress in these words which have the same root?
2 How many 'weak' sounds are there in each of the words?

Task 3 👥

Aim
To practise indicating stress and intonation.

Procedure
1 Decide how you might say these utterances (it's possible to say them in more than one way):
What's the time?
They're always late.
Is Alice coming?
2 Mark the stressed syllables.
3 In each utterance, decide which syllable is the tonic (most stressed) syllable and mark whether your voice goes up or down on this syllable.
4 Practise saying the utterance and getting your colleagues to repeat it after you.

Comment
Did you manage to be consistent in the way you said the utterances each time?

Further reading

Ur, P. and Wright, A. 1992 *Five-Minute Activities* (CUP)

Grammar

Aitken, R. 1992 *Teaching Tenses* (Nelson)
Frank, C. and Rinvolucri, M. 1991 *Grammar in Action Again* (Prentice Hall International)
Harmer, J. 1987 *Teaching and Learning Grammar* (Longman)
Morgan, J. and Rinvolucri, M. 1988 *The Q Book* (Longman)
Rinvolucri, M. 1984 *Grammar Games* (CUP)

Vocabulary

Gairns, R. and Redman, S. 1986 *Working with Words* (CUP)
Howard-Williams, D. and Herd, C. 1986 *Word Games with English* (Heinemann)
Morgan, J. and Rinvolucri, M. 1988 *Vocabulary and Language Teaching* (Longman)
Taylor, L. 1990 *Teaching and Learning Vocabulary* (Prentice Hall International)

Pronunciation

Bowen, T. and Marks, J. 1992 *The Pronunciation Book* (Longman)
Kenworthy, J. 1987 *Teaching English Pronunciation* (Longman)
Tench, P. 1991 *Pronunciation Skills* (Prentice Hall/Macmillan)
Underhill, A. 1994 *Sound Foundations* (Heinemann)
Underhill, A. 1994 *Sound Foundations Chart and Guide* (Heinemann)

Chapter 7 Giving feedback to students

Giving feedback is one of the most important responsibilities of a teacher. By providing ongoing feedback you can help your students evaluate their success and progress. Feedback can take a number of forms: giving praise and encouragement; correcting; setting regular tests; having discussions about how the group as a whole is doing; giving individual tutorials; etc. Some of these types of feedback are easier to incorporate into the TP situation than others.

The type and extent of feedback and its timing depends on a variety of factors:

- individual students. Different students respond to different types of feedback. Unconfident students may need more coaxing and encouragement, whereas students who are more self-confident and perhaps have an external exam to pass usually appreciate more direct correction from the teacher – advanced students usually feel they don't get enough correction;
- the culture you are teaching in and the expected roles of the teacher;
- the stage of the lesson and the type of activity. For example, structured or controlled activities require a different type of feedback from guided or freer activities. Written activities require a different type of feedback from oral activities;
- the stage in the course.

In this chapter we look at the role of feedback (including correction) in TP, and practical correction techniques are described. We also examine ways of evaluating and testing student performance and progress.

1 Giving positive feedback

The aim of feedback is to bring about self-awareness and improvement. Everyone thrives on genuine praise and encouragement. When giving feedback on oral or written work, always be on the lookout for positive points to comment upon. For example:

- successful communication – where students have expressed themselves clearly (and been understood by others);
- accurate use of grammar points recently learned;
- use of new vocabulary, appropriate expressions;
- good pronunciation – expressive intonation;
- language in the appropriate style – good use of colloquial expressions in conversation;
- good use of fluency strategies in conversation;
- handwriting, spelling and punctuation in written work.

Try to find areas of improvement in individual students' work and also comment on progress made by the class as a whole – work successfully completed and achievements made.

The ways you give positive feedback can include the informal *Well done*; praising individual achievement privately or in front of the class; 'publishing' good work by displaying it, including it in a class magazine or using it as a model; operating a more formal grading system as part of a system of keeping track of student progress. You may even consider giving merit marks or small rewards or prizes for good work – though this is more appropriate with a group of children.

2   Correction techniques

How do you decide whether the student has made an error or made a mistake?

In teaching EFL it is common practice to distinguish between mistakes and errors. A mistake can be thought of as a slip of the tongue or the pen. The student is able to correct it himself or herself, either completely unprompted or with the guidance of the teacher or other students. Native speakers make mistakes all the time, even though the correct form is usually known.

An error is much more deeply ingrained. The student might:

- believe what he or she is saying or writing is correct;
- not know what the correct form should be;
- know what the correct form should be, but not be able to get it right.

Errors are usually produced regularly and systematically, so be on the lookout for frequent errors. Asking the student to try again is often the best way of helping you decide whether the incorrect form is an error or a mistake.

Error correction is usually thought of as relating to the form of the language but obviously students can say something incorrectly if they choose an *inappropriate* thing to say on a particular occasion, or because they have misunderstood the meaning of something when they listen to or read a text. Generally, you should consider an error that shows the student doesn't understand the *meaning* of the language as more serious than one where the student is not able to produce the correct *form*.

Are errors always bad?

Obviously both you and the students would rather they didn't commit errors. However, there are positive aspects to be considered:

- At least the students are trying – this is preferable to being so unsure of themselves that they don't want to take part at all.
- By making errors learners are testing out their ideas about the language – they are experimenting. Making errors is part of the learning process: by receiving appropriate feedback students gradually get to know the difference between correct and incorrect language.
- By noting the errors that the students make you can see what needs focusing on in future lessons. Errors that reveal misapprehensions about meaning can help you assess the students' understanding. The extent to which students make errors in 'freer' practice activities can tell us how much new language has been absorbed and how much more practice is needed.

How can you anticipate and avoid errors?

Obviously students are less likely to make errors of meaning if the language has been presented well – with adequate highlighting, clarifying and checking of understanding. And they are less likely to make mistakes with the form if they have been given sufficient controlled practice in saying and writing the language.

One way of helping yourself cope with errors that occur in the classroom is to try to anticipate any that might come up. If you know what *might* come up you are likely to be more alert to the errors that *do* come up.

Familiarize yourself with all aspects of an item of language you are focusing on. For example, likely pronunciation problems can often be worked out by writing out the item in phonemic script in your lesson plan beforehand: so *should have* when spoken might be transcribed /ʃʊdəv/, revealing a contraction, a weak vowel for *have* and an absent /h/! The more you know about the language you are teaching the less likely you are to mislead students and cause 'teacher-induced' errors.

Familiarize yourself, too, with the typical grammatical, lexical and pronunciation problems associated with the nationality of the students in your group. This is obviously easier in monolingual classes than multilingual classes. If you have a chance to observe the group you teach, spend time noting the errors made by the different students. See *Learner English*, Swan and Smith (eds.) (CUP 1987).

How do you correct?

The ability to correct – sensitively, efficiently and effectively – is a skill that takes time to perfect. You should aim to maintain a co-operative working atmosphere. Don't let students think they are being picked on – correction can seem threatening if done badly. Try not to 'echo' the errors, even in a mocking, astonished way. Some teachers find this an easy way of indicating an error, but although the humour can be beneficial it tends to reinforce the teacher's superior relationship and inhibit the students' ability to work things out for themselves. The basic principle is that students learn more effectively if they are guided in such a way that they eventually correct themselves rather than if they are given the correct version of something straight away. The struggle to get it right also helps them understand *why* they were wrong.

The main stages in the process are as follows:

1 The student must know something is not accurate

But first let him or her finish the utterance. Students find it disconcerting to be interrupted mid-stream. Make a gesture, like a wave of the finger, or give some not-too-discouraging word like *nearly*. Black looks or shouts of *No!* will only serve to reduce the students' desire to try out the language. (See Chapter 2 Section 1: *Use of eye contact, gesture and the voice*.)

2 The student must know where the error is

So you need to isolate for the student the part of the utterance that is wrong. If the student says *My wife come yesterday* but meant *My wife came yesterday,* then telling him to try again might be of no use. He has put the word *yesterday* in to indicate past time so he may think he has made a correct utterance. What he needs to know is that the word *come* is incorrect. There are a number of things you can say: *the second word; not 'come' but ....?* You can use your fingers, Cuisenaire rods (see p70), or even a row of students to represent each word. When you get to the word that is wrong, indicate that that is where the problem is and see if he or she can get it right.

3 The student must know what kind of error it is

The student will need to know whether the problem is (as above) grammatical, syntactical (for example, a missing word), or phonological (for example, a wrongly stressed word).

You can say, for example, *Verb? Tense? Word stress? Wrong word.* You can also use appropriate gestures. Common gestures used to indicate the type of error can be found on p12 and p156. Finger correction is particularly useful and can be used to indicate **a** an unnecessary word, **b** a missing word, or **c** contraction (see diagrams **a**, **b**, **c** below).

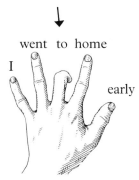

a unnecessary word

b missing word

c contraction

You can no doubt think of other useful gestures. However, it is important that the students understand them and that you use the same gestures each time to represent the same thing. If you share a group of students you may want to get together with the other trainees and agree on a repertoire of gestures to use.

You can also use the board. So if a student says *She buy some apples*, you can write the word *buy* on the board, cross it out and/or write up the word *past* and elicit the correct form.

Who corrects?

Self-correction

Always give the students the chance to correct themselves. If they are going to become more accurate they must learn to monitor themselves. They may have just made a slip and will welcome the opportunity to put it right. Sometimes they need some assistance from you in knowing where the mistake is and what kind of mistake it is, before they can self-correct. (See above.)

Student–student correction

If the student still can't get it right, it's probably because she doesn't know how to. So with a gesture, hold her attention and get another student to help out. This has the advantage of:

- involving all the students in the correction process;
- making the learning more co-operative generally;
- reducing student dependence on the teacher;
- increasing the amount the students listen to each other;
- giving the better students something to do.

Student–student correction must be done carefully. Not *Oh, no! Wrong again, Juan. Go on Sami, tell him.* but *Not quite, Juan. Do you know, Sami?* Even better, do the whole thing by gesture. Indicate *not quite* with your face or hands and gesture to another student to help. Try to choose a student who looks eager to help and don't always resort to the class know-all! Always return to the first student and let him or her say the correct version.

Teacher correction

If neither self-correction nor student–student correction is effective you must assume that either the student hasn't understood what you're getting at or doesn't know what the correct version should be. If it's an important point and the others don't know it either, you may have to stop and teach it to the whole class. If not, and the meaning of the item is clear, your simply saying it and getting the students to say it should be enough.

No matter how you have done the correction, get the student who made the error to say the correct version, if possible in its original context. This is a vital part of any correction process. You can do this by gesture or saying something like *OK, again. The whole thing.*

How much do you correct?

Errors are usually made only by individual students, so correction often has to be on an individual basis too. Even more problematically, in multilingual classes, the types of error can vary according to the students' different mother tongues. The problem for you is how to spend enough time on any one error with any one student without slowing down the pace of the lesson and boring the other students.

To reduce that likelihood, involve the whole class as much as possible in the correction process (see *Student–student correction* on p167); also spend less time correcting what is only a problem for one student and more time on problems common to the whole group.

There is such a thing as over-correction. That is, the more you try to correct something, the worse the student gets. So often it's worth spending a short time correcting some items only and not trying to get everything perfect in one go, and coming back to others on another day. Correction of major errors is perhaps best considered as something that should be done as quickly as possible, but it is likely to be a long-term process over a series of lessons.

When do you correct?

In general it depends on the aim of the activity. If the focus is on accuracy, the teacher's control and the correction will be tight; if the focus is more on fluency, the teacher's direct control and the correction will be less. It is a good idea to think about how much correction you want to do and what form it will take and include a note in your lesson plan. In addition, you can tell students the purpose of the activity: whether the emphasis is on accuracy or fluency, to what extent you are going to correct them, how you are going to provide feedback, whether you are going to give marks or grades for written work, etc.

So, looking at different types of activities, the following guidelines are suggested:

Presentation of new language and controlled practice

For example, repetition practice (drilling). Insist on accurate production from your students. You must judge what you consider to be an acceptable standard of pronunciation. Aim for a high standard at this stage as the standard will inevitably drop during less controlled and freer production.

Structured speaking practice in pairs or groups

Monitor by moving round the class and listening to the students. Either correct errors as you hear them, remembering to include the other students in the group, or make a note of errors, then give feedback on the errors with the class after the activity.

Guided or freer speaking activities

For example, a roleplay or an exchange of personal views on a topic. Don't interrupt the activity and don't expect complete accuracy. Monitor and give feedback after the activity. During feedback do not comment only on grammatical accuracy; discuss whether the students managed to achieve their communicative aim. Did they express what they wanted to say and did they understand each other? (See the monitor sheet in Task 3 on p172.)

Feedback given after an activity can be done in a number of ways:

- Make a note of errors and focus on common ones, or ones of general interest, after the activity. You don't need to say which student made which error.
- Record the activity (either on audio or video cassette) and
  a go through the cassette with the group (though this can be very time-consuming and boring if done too meticulously and too often);
  b select parts of the cassette to examine (in this way common errors can be dealt with or particularly good instances of language use highlighted);
  c transcribe all or part of a cassette and indicate the errors made. The students – usually in groups – play the cassette and, referring to the transcript, discuss the errors. This is very time-consuming for you, but it is usually appreciated by the students. If you choose to focus on particular errors – tense or word stress, for example – you can focus the students' attention and cut down on your workload.
- Give individual students notes of errors they have made with instructions on how to correct them.
- Provide the class with remedial sessions based on errors common to the majority. Make it clear that the lesson was planned as a direct result of the activity done earlier. This is particularly useful for monolingual groups.

Correcting written work

Controlled written exercises

For example, copying, dictations, or exercises where there is only one right answer. The correct answers must be given and the students made aware of any errors they have made. Whenever possible, ask the students to compare their answers before you elicit the answers; you can ask them to write their answers on the board or on an OHT to be checked by the class.

Guided and freer writing

To some extent the way you approach giving feedback on written work depends on the purpose of the writing. For example, if the students are preparing for a written exam they will probably appreciate detailed correction. However, as correcting every error in a piece of 'free' writing can be very time-consuming for the teacher and discouraging for the students, you may want to focus the feedback you give. In general, aim to encourage improvement rather than dwell on mistakes by awarding marks out of ten, etc.

- You should try to react to the writing as communication as an interested reader: for example, *This was very interesting. I didn't know you'd worked in Africa.*
- You will probably want to comment on how well the writing communicates, how well the meaning has been got across: *This was clearly expressed and well-argued.*
- You can focus on particular aspects such as spelling, punctuation, use of tenses, use of linkers, etc. Self- or peer-correction is often appropriate here. (See p170.)
- You can comment separately on different things within the same piece of written work. For example, for a formal letter you could make the following remarks: *Layout – excellent, no mistakes; Style – good, but don't forget that contractions are not used in a formal letter; Grammar – good, just a couple of tense problems; Use of vocabulary – very good, only one collocation mistake.*

As giving feedback on freer written work is part of 'process writing', see also Chapter 5 Section 5: *Productive skills: writing.*

As with correction of oral work, it is worth thinking about *who* corrects:

Self-correction

You can aid self-correction by underlining errors and putting symbols in the appropriate place in the margin and/or giving appropriate page references in grammar books. For an example of a marking scheme, see p121.

The students correct as many errors as they can and submit the work for re-marking. Before submitting the work they can show it to another student for comments. (See below.)

Student–student correction

You can give the students the opportunity to read and comment on each other's work either before you see it or after you have indicated the errors.

Teacher correction

You must judge when students can't correct their work by themselves and give them the correct version – with an explanation if necessary. You can also note errors that are common to the group and prepare a remedial lesson for them.

When is correction not appropriate?

Although students usually like being corrected, there are times when it can be impractical or inappropriate to correct. This is especially true of spoken language:

- when you are trying to build a student's confidence and encouragement is more productive than correction;
- when you are communicating with a student as a friend rather than as teacher to student – when chatting before or after the class, for example. It is better to respond to *I went in Wembley last night to see Italy play England* with *Oh, was it a good match?* rather than *Not in Wembley ...* ;
- when you are eliciting from the students – perhaps to establish the context before introducing a new language structure or to set the scene and arouse interest before reading or listening to a text. Getting too bogged down in correction at this stage is time-consuming and detracts from the main aims of the lesson. It is better to respond positively to suggestions as communication, and ignore mistakes of form. Alternatively, this is an occasion when 'echoing' – but with the *correct* form can be useful. For example, if the teacher is eliciting experiences of unusual holidays from students before reading an article:

  Student: I have been to Iceland last year.
  Teacher: You went to Iceland last year? That's unusual. Did you like it?

- when your main aim is to focus on the comprehension of a text. If students show that they understand but at the same time make, say, grammar mistakes, you may not want to interrupt the flow of the lesson to stop and correct individuals.

Try to remember that students are trying to focus on many things at once; so, when a student is struggling with the form and meaning of a particular structure but makes a vocabulary or pronunciation error:

  Student: So can I say *If I had known about the test, I would have made my homework?*
  Teacher: Yes – except we say *I would have done my homework.*

3 Evaluation and testing

If you give ongoing feedback, and especially if you make the feedback procedure overt, you are going a long way in providing the students with the information they need to evaluate their own level and progress.

Sometimes, however, it is useful to arrange for more formal means of feedback to take place, and it may be compulsory in the institution you are working in.

Tests

It is often appropriate to give tests at different stages in a course: in TP your students may be given a *placement test* to assist the formation of groups of students at the same level, or a *diagnostic test* which is designed to tell you and the students what they do and don't know at the beginning of a course. Teachers often give a weekly *progress test* on the work covered. This can be in the form of a formal written test or a more informal group activity, even a game – as long as it gives information to both you and the students as to how they are doing. You, perhaps with other trainees, can devise a progress test based on the work done over a series of lessons. If the students are following a course leading to an external examination they are usually eager to do *practice tests* to get some idea of how close they are to the required standard.

Tutorials

These can take place with the whole group or with individual students. It is unlikely that you will have time to conduct individual tutorials with students on TP but it might be useful to spend some time, perhaps the last ten minutes at the end of the week, reviewing the work done, discussing the aims of the lessons, how well the students performed the tasks, whether there are any problems, etc.

Evaluation by the students

It can be very useful to ask the students to evaluate the lessons (not the personalities of the teachers) by means of a questionnaire or guided discussion. For example, they can be asked whether they feel that they are getting enough grammar, if the balance of skills work is right, if they think the work is too easy, too difficult or just right. The results of the survey can then be discussed and future lessons considered in the light of students' comments. This process promotes genuine interaction, develops a much greater awareness among students of what is happening in the classroom and helps you understand better how they react to what you do. If the students' English is too poor for this kind of discussion, in monolingual classes it is worth having it in the students' mother tongue.

(See also Chapter 5 Section 6: *Learner development and study skills.*)

Task 1

Aim
To establish the difference between mistakes and errors.

Procedure
1 Ask a couple of students to record three or four minutes of them talking to each other or to write a short composition. (Give them a topic.)

2 Note down which inaccuracies of form you think are slips and which are errors.

3 Go back to the students and see which inaccuracies they can correct for themselves.

4 Compare what they can and can't do with your original list and discuss some of the individual language problems with the students.

Task 2

Aim
To practise breaking up an utterance so as to aid correction.

Procedure A
1 Give the following utterances to a partner:

I see him yesterday.
He likes tennis table.
She's gone to the work.
I must see dentist.
I see you tomorrow.

Your partner is the student who makes these mistakes.

2 Correct them by slowing your partner down when he or she says each utterance, showing that each finger on your hand represents a word. By gesture alone, indicate what the correct form should be in the problem area.

Procedure B
1 Distribute the above utterances to the whole group.

2 Try to correct each one by making a row of 'students' represent the utterances (for example: S1 = *I*, S2 = *see*, S3 = *him*, S4 = *yesterday*), making the appropriate gestures and moving the students.

Comment
Both exercises are great fun and although the above errors are structural, a similar exercise can be devised for pronunciation problems.

Task 3

Aim
To develop awareness of your students' errors.

Procedure
1 Record your students during a speaking activity on audio or video cassette.

2 Play the tape, pausing when necessary, and try to make a list of their errors under such headings as the following:

FORM				MEANING
Grammar	Word choice	Word order	Pronunciation	
I must to go	*I went on a journey to London (trip)*	*I speak well English*	*/liːv/ for live*	*He's a very sensible child - he cries easily.*

Comment

Try this activity again but in 'real time' when you are observing another teacher or trainee teaching the group.

Task 4

Aim

To practise using a marking scheme to help students correct their own written work.

Procedure

1 Collect a piece of written work from a student and make a copy of it.
2 Each partner marks the student's work using the codes on p121.
3 Compare corrected versions and discuss any problems.

Comment

1 You may find there are some aspects of the piece of writing which can't be marked using the symbols. What would you do about them?
2 See also Chapter 5 Section 5: *Productive skills: writing.*

Task 5

Aim

To help with the anticipation of error when teaching new structures.

Procedure

1 As a group, draw up a list of three structural areas (for example: regular past tense, comparative adjectives, *used to + -ing*, etc).
2 In pairs, list as many potential problems as you can in the following grid:

Potential errors of:			
1 Form	**2** Meaning	**3** Pronunciation	Reasons?

3 Compare your list with another pair.
4 Think of other structures where similar problems might occur.

Comment

You will have to consider the first language of the students in your class – what one student may find difficult another, with a different L1, may not. If possible, do this activity with a particular group of students in mind – your TP group perhaps.

Task 6

Aim

To show how common errors can be used as the basis for future work with a class.

Procedure

1 Ask a class of students to do a piece of written work, remembering to give them suitable guidance.

2 Collect it in and divide the work among your colleagues.

3 Each member of the group should make a list of what they consider the most serious errors in their piece of written work.

4 The lists should then be compared and the common errors listed.

5 Prepare a remedial lesson on one or more of the areas of error.

Comment

This exercise can also be done using a piece of recorded oral work, but it takes longer to do.

Further reading

Bartram, M. and Walton, R. 1991 *Correction* (LTP)

Heaton, J. 1988 *Writing English Language Tests* (Longman)

Madsen, H. 1993 *Techniques in Testing* (OUP)

Swan, M. and Smith, B. (eds.) 1987 *Learner English* (CUP)

Underhill, N. 1987 *Testing Spoken Language* (CUP)

Chapter 8 Planning lessons

Although this chapter comes towards the end of the book, it is a good idea to refer to it throughout TP. Many earlier chapters, particularly Chapter 5: *Developing skills and strategies*, and Chapter 6: *Presenting and practising language*, give examples of how to plan and stage specific types of lessons: the presentation and practice of a language item; conducting a listening lesson; organizing a discussion, etc.

Right from the start it is important that you think about and plan each of your lessons. In the early stages of TP you will probably get a lot of help and guidance from your supervisor; but as you progress and become more independent you will have to make more decisions about what and how you teach. You also need to learn how to design a scheme of work for a particular group of students, in which a series of lessons are linked to form a complete programme. In this chapter we look at writing lesson plans, how you can get ready for lessons and steps you can take after the lesson to help you to improve future lessons. We also look at how to analyse students' needs and plan a scheme of work.

1 Lesson plans

The writing of lesson plans has a number of important functions:

1 An aid to planning

Writing down what you expect the students to be able to do by the end of the lesson, and what you intend to do to make that possible, helps you to think logically through the stages in relation to the time you have available.

2 A working document

Having something to refer to in the lesson helps keep you on target, although it should never prevent you from responding to the needs of the moment, if necessary.

3 A record

Suitably amended after the lesson, a lesson plan acts as a record of what the class has done and might form the basis for a future lesson plan with a similar class.

In addition, in the TP situation the lesson plan can form the basis of discussion of the lesson with your supervisor. He or she may wish to look at the plan during the planning stage and/or before the lesson and will usually refer to it during feedback on the lesson.

What should be included in a lesson plan?

Information to be included in a lesson plan can be considered under the following headings: Aims; Procedure; Approach(es) and activities; Materials, aids and equipment; Information about the students; Anticipated problems.

1 Aims

Questions you need to ask (and answer) are not only *What do I, the teacher, aim to do?* but also *What do I expect the students to do and/or to have achieved by the end of the lesson? What specific language will they understand and use?* or *What specific skills will they have developed?*

Example
To present and practise *Why don't you ...?* for giving advice.
The students will understand that *Why don't you* + infinitive can be used to give advice to a friend. They will be able to use the structure with: *go (home), take (an aspirin),* etc. They will be able to give appropriate responses: *OK, I will.*

Often in a lesson you will have a main aim and perhaps a number of subsidiary aims. This is particularly true, for example, in a lesson in which skills are integrated (see *Planning a skills lesson* on p87) or when a listening or reading text is used to introduce a language item. It is important that you (and the students) recognize the main aim of the lesson and of each stage.

2 Procedure

This is the part of the lesson plan which lays out the steps – the stages – in the lesson to ensure that the aim(s) is achieved.

You should indicate on your plan what will be done at each stage and why (the stage aim), the approximate time, the materials you will use, and perhaps details of any complex instructions you are going to give or questions you plan to ask.

In order to do this you have to consider how you will order the stages and the approach(es), activities, and materials you will use at each stage. You will have to answer these questions:
How much time do I have?
Approximately how will I divide up the lesson into stages?
How much time will each stage take?

You also need to ask yourself:
What will be the aim of each stage?
How will the stages be linked?

Example
For the presentation and practice of *Why don't you ...?* a lesson of 35 minutes might be made up of the following stages:

Stage 1 (5 mins)
Introduce the structures. Context: giving advice to someone who has a headache, and the replies to the advice.

Stage 2 (5 mins)
Check students' understanding and practise saying the model sentences.

Stage 3 (10 mins)
Guided practice, using cue cards – in open then closed pairs.

Stage 4 (10 mins)
Freer practice using a new context: giving advice about preparing for a test.

Stage 5 (5 mins)
Students make a record of the form and uses of the structure in their notebooks.

3 Approach(es) and activities

For each stage you will have to think what approach you are going to use and what activities the students will do to achieve your aims.

Questions to ask yourself may include:

If my aim is to present or revise a language item am I going to do it through a text, a visual or oral context (perhaps a dialogue or pictures) or through a problem-solving activity, etc?
For skills development what do my students need before they can listen, read, write or speak? How will I follow up the skills work?
How will I check that the students understand?
What type of practice activities shall I set up: speaking, pairwork, writing?
Have I planned for a balance and a variety of activities and materials – recognizing that different activities make different demands on the students and arranging it so an easy activity is followed by a more difficult one, a very active one with a quieter one, etc?
Are the activities ordered logically – from more controlled to freer?
For each stage what sort of feedback is appropriate?

The approaches and activities you decide upon should be indicated in the Procedure part of your lesson plan. Sometimes it is worth making a note of your intended seating arrangements as well. Throughout the plan, perhaps in the margin, you can include a note of the groupings and the interaction at each stage: teacher/students, student/student, mingle, etc.

4 Materials, aids and equipment

The question you need to ask is:
At each stage which materials, aids and equipment do I need to achieve my aims?
You should make a note on your lesson plan of when you will use these materials and aids and also include a plan of your blackboard or whiteboard at each stage of the lesson. (See Chapter 3 Section 1: *The board.*)

5 Information about the students and the classroom circumstances

It is worth noting at the top of every plan the level of the class, the coursebook they are using, the size of the class and its composition, especially if it is multinational. You may be required to give more detailed student profiles. You should also note how this lesson fits into the students' course programme (the timetable fit) and what knowledge you assume the students will bring to the lesson.

6 Anticipated problems

Although you need to learn to be flexible in class, to be able to think on your feet and adapt your lesson plan according to circumstances, you are less likely to be thrown if you give some thought to some of the things that can go wrong. It is a good idea to make a note on your plan of any anticipated problems – in terms of language or classroom management – that could occur during any of the activities and any strategies you have considered for dealing with these problems. It is particularly useful to include this on the plan you give to your supervisor. In this way you will be given credit for anticipating difficulties, whereas if you mention such problems after the lesson it sounds as if you are making excuses!

You can anticipate what students will find difficult in a particular language item by thoroughly researching the language you are planning to teach. (See *Researching the language* on p182.) Investigate, if possible, the ways in which their language is different from English. For example, will your students have difficulty with the sound /ə/ because it doesn't exist in their language? This is obviously easier to do with a monolingual group. You can also anticipate difficulties by finding out as much as you can about what the students have done in previous classes – their individual strengths and weaknesses in skills work, for example.

There are a number of ways in which the timing and organization of your lesson can be affected. For example, it is a good idea to think about what you would do if:

- the students take a longer or shorter time to do the activities than you had planned;
- they find an activity easier or more difficult than you thought they would;
- some students finish before the others;
- there are some students who need extra support;
- there are uneven numbers for a pairwork activity;
- some or all of the students have already met the material you have based your lesson round: for example, they have already seen the video you were going to show.

Achieving a balance

It is important to be critical of your lesson plans – especially in checking your aims against your planned procedures. You should constantly ask yourself *What is my aim, and will doing this in this way achieve my aim?*

However, as in all things, you need to strike a realistic balance in the amount of preparation you do. If you overprepare this usually means getting stuck in your plan and not responding flexibly to the class; getting obsessed by your 'performance' – by your own ideas and techniques; or not being sensitive to the students, what they are doing and not doing. If you underprepare, this usually results in long silences while you decide what to do next (demoralizing for you and the students!), unclear aims and underexploited activities.

Also, remember that although you influence what happens in the class it is often more a case of 'managing learning' than teaching; it is the pace the *students* work at that needs to be measured, not the pace *you* work at. You can exhaust yourself with a dazzling array of new ideas you are determined to try out and then realize the students are doing hardly anything. In fact, with some well planned and well set-up activities you might need to do very little in the classroom.

Personal aims

For any particular lesson, in addition to the learning aims for your students, you may also wish to set yourself a 'personal aim', perhaps in consultation with your supervisor. This 'personal aim' focuses on an aspect of your teaching which you want to pay particular attention to in this lesson. For example: *To talk less myself and involve the students more,* or *To make my instructions clearer,* etc. If you are being observed by other trainees you could ask them to give you feedback on how well you achieved your aim.

How should a lesson plan be written down/laid out?

You may have to use a set or prescribed lesson plan form for assessment purposes. However, the way you put your lesson plan down on paper for use in the class is up to you, since you are the one who is going to interpret it both during the lesson and later on when you refer back. The format you choose will also depend on the type of lesson you are giving.

Try to keep lesson plans simple. Cut out prose descriptions, number sections clearly and underline or use coloured or highlighter pens to draw attention to important elements. There is no need to script the lesson – that can't be done and shouldn't be attempted. However, there may be times when you want to write down precisely what you are going to say: a model sentence, or a set of complicated instructions, or some questions to check that the students have understood a language point, for example.

Obviously a lesson plan should be legible and there are two kinds of legibility required. The first is for just before the lesson begins, when you'll probably want quickly to run over the aims and the stages of the lesson again. Normal-size writing is appropriate for this. However, there will be other things that you will need to check 'in the heat of the lesson' to remind you of the stages of the lesson. If you don't want to appear to be reading from a script you will probably want to just glance down at your lesson plan on the desk. This means that you'll need to be able to read these items from about a metre or more away. They need to be bigger, possibly with sections written with different coloured felt-tipped pens or marked with highlighter pens.

Instead of using a sheet of paper as your working document you may prefer to set out the main points of the lesson on cards which can be held in the hand – each card being put to the back of the 'pack' as the stage is completed.

You may want to write out a lesson in more detail if you want to keep it for use again. This can be done after feedback when you can incorporate any suggested changes. (See Section 4: *Follow-up* on p183.)

Your TP supervisor will probably tell you how he or she wants you to write your lesson plans. If you are basing your lesson on a coursebook, the lesson plans/notes in the Teacher's Book will be invaluable: make good use of them while writing your plan.

On pp180–1 is one way you might set out a plan for a lesson in which a visual/oral context is used to present and practise a language structure.

Sample lesson plan

The class

Students: 15 (8F 7M)
Level: lower intermediate

Teaching aids

Photographs and pictures

Aims

To guide the students to an understanding of *used to* /juːstə/ + infinitive for habits or states in the past which are no longer true or have changed.

To provide practice so the students can use the structure to talk about themselves.

Model sentences: I used to have long hair (but now I have short hair).
                     I didn't use to wear glasses.

Context

A comparison of the teacher (me) as a student – appearance, habits, likes and dislikes – and me today.

Personal aim

To improve my board work.

Anticipated problems

The students may be confused with *to be used to -ing*.

Procedure   Teacher/students

1. Show a photo of me as a student. Say *Guess who this is?*
   When was this?

2. Give the model, pointing to the photo: *I used to have long hair.*
   Illustrate/check meaning. Ask: *Is this a photo of me now or in the past? Is my hair long or short now?*

5" 3. Give the model again. Students repeat.

4. Write on board: *When I was a student   Now*
   Put picture prompts under the headings to elicit these sentences:
   (see board plan)

I used to drink beer.	I drink wine.
I used to ride a motorbike.	I drive a car.
I used to live in a flat.	I live in a house.
I used to like heavy metal.	I like classical music.
I used to wear leather jeans.	I wear trousers.
I didn't use to wear glasses.	I wear glasses.
I didn't use to have a beard.	I have a beard.

15"

5. Check understanding of the meaning:
   T: Do I live in a flat now?   Ss: No.
   T: Did I live in a flat?   Ss: Yes.
   T: When?   Ss: When you were a student.
   T: Yes, for three years. I used to live in a flat.
   T: Did I ride a motorbike once?   Ss: No, many times.
   T: Did I wear glasses when I was
      a student?   Ss: No.

20" T: No, I didn't use to wear glasses.

6. Use pictures to prompt repetition practice – choral and individual.

7. Write up the sentences in the first column, next to the pictures (see board plan.)

    25″

    Students copy into notebooks.

8. Pairs practice: Students use *used to/didn't use to* to tell each other about themselves when they were at high school. They can use the pictures on the board as prompts.   student/student

    35″

9. If time, students can tell the class about their partner: *He/she used to ...*

    45″

Board plan: Step 4   *photo of me as a student*

When I was a student   *Now*

☐ *pic of drinking beer*   ☐ *pic of drinking wine*

☐ *pic of riding motorbike*   ☐ *pic of driving car*

☐ *(etc)*   ☐ *(etc)*

☐   ☐

☐   ☐

☐   ☐

☐   ☐

Board plan: Step 7

When I was a student

☐ I		drink	beer.
☐ You		ride	a motorbike.
☐ He/she	used to /juːstə/	live	in a flat.
☐ We		like	heavy metal.
☐ They		wear	jeans.
☐ I	didn't use to /juːstə/	wear	glasses.
☐ He		like	classical music.

How can lesson plans be stored?

Some teachers prefer to keep their lessons in a book, with one book for each class they teach. In this way the plans are always kept in sequence and form an easy-to-refer-to neat record of the classes. If you do this you may like to leave alternate pages blank when you are writing your plans so that after the lesson you can write in comments on the success or otherwise of each part of the lesson. This could form the basis of a very useful teaching diary (see p7).

Another common way of storing lessons is within plastic pockets, kept in a ring binder. With this system aids such as cards and pictures can be kept together with the plan.

Instead of filing lessons together by class you can arrange them under such headings as: grammar points, topics, skills areas, coursebook, etc. Alternatively, you can file lesson plans and accompanying aids in cardboard folders and use different coloured folders for different sections. They can be stored in a filing cabinet, a plastic or even a cardboard box. If you adopt this system it is also useful to number each folder and keep a small card index with headings arranged in alphabetical order. In this way you can find plans easily and quickly. You will be surprised how quickly your materials accumulate and it's very frustrating not to be able to find something when you need it.

2   Researching the language

Before you teach any language point you should research it thoroughly. If it is a grammar or functional point look at a number of grammar reference books until you are satisfied that you understand in detail both the form and the meaning. (See also Chapter 6 Section 1: *Structures: grammar and functions.*) If it is a lexical item you can look up the word or expression in one or two good dictionaries. Pay attention to how the item collocates (or goes) with other items of language. (See also Chapter 6 Section 2: *Vocabulary.*)

Now try to view the language from the students' point of view and try to predict what they will find difficult. Think about the form – is there some irregular aspect? What about the spelling and the pronunciation? Think about the meaning – are there a number of meanings that can be confused? Can the item be confused with another item of language either in English or in the students' first language(s)?

Look at the way one or two coursebooks or skills books deal with the language. They often focus on areas of difficulty. Are there any problem areas highlighted in the teachers' books? On the other hand, there may be aspects of the language not dealt with in the coursebook which students may ask about. Try to anticipate any questions your students may have and decide how you are going to deal with these questions.

3   Getting organized

Before you start your lesson there are a number of practical things you can do to make sure that everything runs smoothly:

- Check that you have your lesson plan.
- Run through your lesson plan and make sure you have all the necessary aids and equipment listed in the plan.

- Check any equipment you are going to use: for example, that the cassette recorder or video works; that the OHP is the right distance from the screen or wall, etc.
- Lay out any visual aids and handouts (pictures, worksheets, cue cards, etc) in the order you'll need them; cue up any audio or video tape you are going to use.
- Make sure the seating is arranged the way you want it.
- Check that the board is clean.
- If there is anything you can put on the board (the date, notices, a plan of work, etc) do so in advance if possible, so you don't waste time at the beginning of the lesson.
- At the same time, be ready to chat to the students as they come into the class!

4 Follow-up

After teaching the lesson you have planned and getting feedback on it you can consider doing all or some of the following:

- Note any changes you made when teaching the lesson from what you had put in your lesson plan.
- Make a note of the students' reactions to the lesson as a whole and to the various parts: did they find some parts more useful than others, easier or more difficult than you expected? Occasionally it may be appropriate to ask them for their opinions and feelings.
- Note how you felt about the lesson and its stages: did you feel comfortable or were there times when you felt a bit unsure of what to do next?
- Make a note of any oral and/or written feedback you receive from your supervisor and any useful comments and suggestions you may receive from fellow trainees.

After evaluating the feedback from these different sources you can add pertinent points to your lesson plan or you may even like to write it out again incorporating suggested changes. In this way you should have an improved lesson plan if ever you want to use it as a basis for a lesson with a future class.

You may want to include what you have learned from planning and teaching the lesson in a TP diary and you can base your 'personal aim' for your next lesson on the lesson and the feedback received.

5 Planning a series of lessons

Linking lessons

In a TP situation you may have to plan your lessons based, to a large extent, on the information and direction you receive from your TP supervisor. Because of this there is a danger, particularly at the start of TP, of viewing each lesson as a separate unit – not linked to the other lessons that make up the students' course.

However, it is important to consider the overall learning diet that the students receive. Try to think about the balance of skills and activities, not just within a single lesson but over a series of lessons which take place on the same day or over a number of days or weeks. If you are sharing a class with others you should also make sure that your lesson fits in with what has gone before and what is to follow. This is especially important if you are sharing an integrated lesson and what you do directly affects the lesson of the person who follows you. For example, one of your aims may be to introduce a vocabulary set which the person following you is going to practise with the students. (See also Chapter 1 Section 2: *Working with others*.)

Planning a scheme of work

You may not be responsible for the students' programme of work, but it is useful to think about how you would design such a programme, and to think about how your lesson would fit in. You may be required to plan a series of lessons for the group you are teaching. This is often done in liaison with other trainee teachers and/or with the group's class teacher.

These are some of the questions you can ask when planning a scheme of work for a TP class or for any new group you teach:

How old are the students, what is their level and what are their needs?
Is the class following a particular coursebook or syllabus?
Did their course begin before your period of TP?
What language/topics/materials/activities has the class already covered?
Do you need to liaise closely with other teachers or trainees and link in your lessons with theirs?

Looking at students' needs

Normally when planning a scheme of work one of the first steps is to look at the needs of the students in the class.

The needs of particular students depend on such factors as their purpose for study: for example, will learning English help them in their job or their studies, do they have to survive in an English-speaking country, are they learning a language purely for interest, because it is an intellectual challenge, or simply because it is part of their school programme? Students may have specific short-term aims: to pass an exam, to be able to talk to a business colleague on the telephone, etc. Such needs will often change with the age of the students. Students' needs will also depend on their mother tongue(s), their overall level and strengths and weaknesses in particular areas of language knowledge and skills, their language learning and general educational background and their interests.

How do you balance what individual students in a class need with what the class as a whole needs?

At beginner level it is easier to construct a course – a series of lessons – that all students find relevant. Even in multinational groups the distinct differences of personality, culture, and educational background do matter in terms of how the group works together but the students in the main assent to a common purpose. If they are in an English-speaking country this may be to help them survive in an alien language environment. If the students are studying in their own country, in monolingual groups, you are more likely needed to help students learn the language for vocational reasons or because it forms part of their general education. At this level, too, the differences in how well the students perform in the main language skills of listening, speaking, reading and writing are perhaps less important, except in some multinational classes, where, for example, you may have some students who can write in the Roman script and some who cannot.

As they improve, so all students quickly become less satisfied with a blanket approach, particularly adults on a more intensive course, not only because their abilities become increasingly diverse but because they feel that their personal interests and the reasons they are learning the language should start to determine far more noticeably the content of the lessons.

At all levels, different students have different learning styles; some may actually need the language explained to them a bit more than others; some may like to rely on dictionaries. Don't be too dogmatic about the way they learn. Students can learn from the knowledge and skills of other individual students just as they can from a teacher working on, say, the oral problems of a single student. But it is a question of balance.

1 Avoid forming an opinion of the class, either as to its level or its interests, on the basis of one or two individuals. It is sometimes easy for your planning decisions to be influenced by the more vocal or demanding students at the expense of the others.
2 Plan your lessons to reconcile individual needs with group needs. Don't choose material or focus on points that only one or two students will find of interest.
3 During the class don't plan to focus disproportionately on individual problems, such as pronunciation difficulties in a multinational class, when you are commanding the attention of the whole group. Try to deal with them during groupwork or during breaks.
4 Try to accommodate different learning styles as much as possible within your general approach.
5 Pace your lessons so that everyone can keep up with them or add an activity to free you to help slower students.
6 Plan to set some individual and/or group tasks geared to each particular student. As well as providing you with the necessary discipline of considering individual needs, it can provide extra motivation for the students and make them realize you take an interest in them. Perhaps time will need to be set aside for individual attention while the group is getting on with something else.

Task 1

Aim
To focus on some of the ways in which individual students can be catered for within a group.

Procedure
1 Find a group of language learners to help you. It might be possible to do this with the class you are doing TP with.
2 Devise a questionnaire to help discover why they need English, how they learned it in the past and how they think they should learn it in the future. Keep it short and easy to understand. (The sort of questions you might ask are: *What things will you write in English when you have finished your course? Have you used translation in your learning of English? Do you think this is a good way of learning?* etc.)
3 Work out a ten-hour timetable for the group based on what you have discussed, taking into account the needs of the group as a whole and including some work which allows you to give individuals different tasks and different roles.
4 Make a list of activities that could be given to each individual to carry out on his or her own, either during the class if time were allocated or after the class, and some activities which students can work on together in groups.

Task 2

Aim

To discuss solutions to problem situations that might arise in class.

Procedure

1 In groups, discuss what contingency plans you could make for the following situations:

- Some students refuse to work in pairs.
- The students ask *Why are we doing this? This is silly* during a game.
- The students take a longer or shorter time to do the activities than you had planned.
- They find an activity easier or more difficult than you thought they would:
  – some students finish before the others;
  – there are some students who need extra support;
  – there are uneven numbers for a pairwork activity;
  – the students have already met the material you have based your lesson round: for example, they have already seen the video you were going to show.

2 Compare your solutions with those of another group.

Comment

This can be a more realistic activity if you have a particular lesson and group of students in mind. You can do this activity if you are planning a series of lessons together.

Task 3

Aim

To help ensure that your lesson plans work towards your stated aim.

Procedure

1 Retrieve a lesson plan from your file.
2 Make a copy of it. On the copy obliterate or cut off the statement of aims.
3 Exchange lesson plan copies with someone else in your group.
4 From what is in the lesson plan, try to write down a clear statement of both the learning outcomes and the teaching aims of the lesson.
5 Compare what you have both written with the originals.

Task 4

Aim

To highlight the different forms lesson plans can take.

Procedure

1 Discuss a particular teaching point with someone else in your group. Agree on aims and activities for a particular group of students.
2 Both of you write a plan for the lesson you discussed.
3 Compare and discuss the different layouts you have used.

Task 5

Aim

To help evaluate how far discussing one's work with colleagues can help one's own learning.

Procedure

1 Ask each member of your group to submit a lesson plan.
2 Redistribute them among the group.
3 Mark each other's work according to agreed criteria (for example: practicability, variety, logical staging, etc) on a scale of 1–5.
4 Mark your own on the same scale.
5 Discuss the marks and whether the criteria were appropriate.

Comment

This exercise may be worth doing several times on various pieces of written work. This will help reduce self-consciousness and embarrassment as well as the possibility of succumbing to group pressure.

Further reading

Nunan, D. 1988 *The Learner-Centred Curriculum* (CUP)
Nunan, D. 1988 *Syllabus Design* (OUP)
Yalden, J. 1987 *Principles of Course Design for Language Teaching* (CUP)

Chapter 9 For the new trainer

This chapter is different from the others in the book in that it will be primarily of interest to the trainer rather than the trainee. We examine the role of the TP supervisor and give suggestions for how TP classes and feedback sessions can be organized and conducted. We hope that trainers new to the role of TP supervisor will find the practical suggestions useful and 'old hands' may like to compare what they already do with the procedures described in the chapter.

1 Organizing TP

Ways of providing teaching practice

The way TP is organized depends on the particular course or training scheme of which it forms a part. The table on p189 demonstrates some of the ways in which trainees can obtain teaching practice.

TRAINEES: ACTIVITIES AND GROUPING	**SOURCE OF STUDENTS**	**OBSERVERS**	**FEEDBACK**	**COMMENTS**
1 Trainees, as whole group or in small groups, teach specific points for short periods (eg five to ten minutes).	Other trainees sometimes assuming predetermined roles (eg a quiet student, slow to participate).	Course tutors; peers.	Usually immediately after someone has 'taught'; possibly leading to the same trainee trying to teach the point again. The sessions may be videoed and analysed.	Allows everyone to concentrate closely on specific techniques (eg gesture).
2a Three to eight trainees per group. Each trainee takes part of a lesson (the students receive a whole lesson). **2b** Individual trainees teach whole lesson.	Groups of volunteer students.		From course tutor and peers, either immediately after each teacher has taught or after the whole 'lesson'. Re-teaching not normally possible unless two groups of students available.	As above but with real learners. Allows for real teaching tasks and enables one to judge the effectiveness of the teaching. 'Real' teaching points with the students' needs in mind give trainees a greater sense of a whole lesson and how learners respond and develop. A more systematic use of coursebooks is also possible.
3a Individual trainees or pairs of trainees take part of a whole lesson. **3b** Individuals teach whole lesson.	Real class taking place at usual time.	Normal class teacher; possibly course tutor(s) and peer(s).	Usually after lesson. Normally, no re-teaching is possible but interruption, demonstration and re-teaching possible provided it is acceptable to any students paying for their classes and to the institution.	Observation by an experienced teacher combined with practice and help can encourage the teaching to be more meaningful. Difficulty of trainee fitting in with problems of planning and co-ordination with class teacher. Feedback by class teacher more individual but trainees can miss the support of colleagues. Teaching an entire lesson to a real class is very close to real situation but can discourage experimentation and not be very helpful in learning specific teaching techniques.

As TP can be organized in different ways, so the terms used to refer to TP can vary from centre to centre. Here are some commonly used terms with an explanation of how they are usually employed:

Apprenticeship

A teacher at the centre who is responsible for teaching a group of students has one or two trainees as 'apprentices'. They usually observe the teacher teaching the students and then teach part or all of some of the lessons. They can be guided by and observed by the group's teacher or by another person acting as TP tutor or supervisor.

Peer teaching

When peer teaching, one trainee takes the role of the teacher and the part of the students is taken by his or her fellow trainees.

Microteaching

This term usually refers to a time when the trainees are not teaching what is normally regarded as a whole lesson, either in terms of time or content, but where the focus is on one particular teaching technique or aspect of a lesson – for example, illustrating word stress, setting up a pairwork activity, etc.

Each of the different ways of providing practice has its advantages and disadvantages. More than one way or combination of ways can be usefully employed on the same training scheme. It might be thought from the table that there is some progression from peer teaching to the teaching of whole lessons with 'real' students. However, peer teaching for the improvement of technique is usually useful at any stage in a course and the teaching of whole lessons can be useful from the earliest stages.

The aims of teaching practice

It is worth discussing the overall aims of TP with trainees. You could ask them to read Chapter 1 of this book, particularly Section 1: *The role of TP on a teacher training course*, either before or at the beginning of the course and set some time aside for questions and discussion. They should be clear about what it is they should be trying to do, how they will be assessed, the role and responsibilities of the centre, the TP tutor and any external examining body.

You should try to present some kind of progression to trainees, even if your course is non-linear in approach. The progression might be represented in the form of milestones they can tick off along the way, perhaps under such headings as *techniques* and *types of lesson*. For example, under *techniques* the list to tick off might include: using an OHP, adapting a unit from a coursebook, planning a lesson around a piece of authentic material. Under *types of lesson* might be included: presenting a new item of language, integrating reading and writing skills, focusing on pronunciation, etc. The headings in Chapters 2–8 should provide both you and the trainees with items that might usefully be included on a checklist.

Who teaches with whom?

This means forming effective groups of trainees for TP or, in some cases, making sure that the trainees are 'apprenticed' to the most appropriate teacher and class.

The formation of TP groups

It is difficult to decide on the composition of a group without meeting the people concerned. Sometimes, however, groups have to be formed quite quickly at the beginning of the course. The following factors can be borne in mind:

Sex

A balance of the sexes is worth going for if it is at all possible – if only for the sake of variety for the students. This of course assumes an overall balance on the course which is not always the case. If you have one or more groups of students which for cultural reasons cannot be taught by men or women, this would, of course, influence the grouping.

Age

Are all the trainees roughly the same age or is there a significantly older or younger person? You may have to decide whether to put the younger ones together and the older ones together – or mix them up.

Experience

Even though in this book we are more concerned with training courses where the participants have little or no experience, there are often those who have had some classroom experience, perhaps even of teaching a language other than English. They can provide useful models to non-experienced colleagues especially where aspects of classroom management and the use of resources and technology are concerned. Other trainees might have an excellent background in language learning; non-native speakers of English generally have a better formal knowledge of grammar than native speakers. Perhaps one of the trainees has studied linguistics at university and another might have a background in EFL publishing and be familiar with a wide range of materials. Usually this experience can be used to advantage and trainers generally aim to get people with a mix of backgrounds together so they can learn from one another. Occasionally a person's background can cause problems. For example, a successful teacher of another subject may try to transfer inappropriate techniques to the EFL classroom and be resistant to changing the habits of a lifetime. As long as this situation is handled firmly yet tactfully it should not cause a problem to the other trainees in the group.

Convenience

If the group is to be asked to work closely together is it physically possible for them to do so? Do they live close to one another? Do they have telephones? Is travel likely to be involved and if so can they share a car? Simple considerations like these may easily be overlooked and yet can be very important.

A well thought-out application form or a questionnaire at the beginning of the course can provide the details you need to help you group. In addition, if the trainee is interviewed, make sure there is a way for any helpful information to be noted and made available at the time of grouping. Also, there are ways of finding out how people react to one another before the groups are finalized. An informal party early on in the course will often reveal how people group themselves naturally and whether there is anyone who is likely to be out on a limb. A classroom 'icebreaking' activity can show how they react to each other in a more formal atmosphere.

It must be noted that occasionally effective groups just don't happen, despite all the care taken by those organizing TP.

Apprenticeship

The same kind of factors affect the pairing of trainees with full-time teachers, although it is sometimes better for the trainees to meet the apprentice teachers before decisions are made. The advantage here may be that those teachers are your colleagues and this makes it much easier for you to arrange a meeting to discuss any problems.

2 Preparing trainees for TP

How can you encourage co-operation among trainees?

In many situations trainees are expected to work together in the preparation of classes and in the sharing of views after the classes. In such cases, the success of TP depends to a great extent on how well the group works together. An institution in this situation therefore needs to:

- select and group trainees with a view to mutual compatibility (see *The formation of TP groups* on p191);
- explain to them the degree of co-operation necessary. Refer them to Chapter 1 Section 2: *Working with others;*
- make it clear that the trainees are directly responsible for their students' learning;
- make sure that supervisors do not take away responsibility by being too noticeable in class;
- provide facilities for preparation and feedback.

If TP is failing because of poor co-operation it is worth setting up a group co-operation exercise or 'having it out' with the group before trying to shuffle people around. There may be times when the trainer has to intervene. The problem may be resolved by making everyone aware of it – talking it through in a tutorial. Recording feedback sometimes and discussing what makes good feedback, focusing on the way the group talk about each other, can also be useful.

Teaching guidelines

The way teaching guidelines or teaching points are produced and utilized depends on such factors as the centre where training is taking place, the length of the course, the way TP is timed in relation to input, whether the students are volunteers or regular students in the institution. Your eventual aim is to get the trainees to the stage, by the end of the course, where they can plan a series of lessons based on a given syllabus – usually in the form of a coursebook – which meet the needs of their students.

There are a number of points that can be considered:

1 Should guidelines be linked with the training timetable or based on the students' needs?

If guidelines are based on the training timetable, TP can be linked to input and it can be arranged so that no trainees have to use a technique they haven't been given information about, practised and perhaps tried out on their peers. Similarly trainees would not be asked to teach language points that they hadn't considered in some depth beforehand. This arrangement is particularly suited to courses which have a block of input followed by a block of TP and has a number of advantages: trainees know exactly what they are focusing on at any one stage in the course, they are all concentrating on the same areas so can observe and help each other from an informed point of view and, most importantly of all, the thorough preparation gives the trainees confidence in the classroom.

Unfortunately, there are a number of disadvantages which make this arrangement difficult to operate in practice. Sometimes TP takes place from the beginning of the course, before the trainees have had a chance to benefit from many input sessions. If the teaching techniques are broken down into small units it may be several lessons before the trainees are beyond the stage where they can greet the students, make good eye contact, learn and use the students' names and do a simple icebreaking activity. They would need to be a very tolerant group of students to put up with that type of lesson – perhaps from four or five trainees over several days. Later on the class may have to cope with one language presentation after another or a whole series of reading texts – depending on the area of focus at that stage in the course.

Since TP is in many ways an attempt to simulate the real situation then it can be argued that it is always the students' needs that should be satisfied – that teaching points set for TP should always be aimed at the students in the class, irrespective of the stage in the training course. Often a coursebook forms the basis of the teaching programme – a coursebook that has been chosen with the students' needs in mind. In addition, in many teaching practice situations trainees have to teach classes which are already constituted and which are following a course which has been in progress for some time; they are perhaps part way through a coursebook. They may be actual classes which are part of the teaching programme offered by the institution.

The advantage of this approach is that, even if the classes are specially arranged for TP, the situation is much more like real life, the trainees' attention is drawn immediately to the students and away from their 'performance', there is an opportunity for the integration of techniques, and most importantly the goodwill of the students is more likely to be maintained if they feel they are getting 'real' lessons and are not just being used as guinea pigs.

The disadvantages are that trainees often feel they have been thrown in the deep end, there are too many things to think about at once, they are having to use techniques and teach language points and skills that may not have been covered on the course, and that any consequent negative feedback is unfair. In addition, it may mean that the trainees never have the opportunity to practise certain aspects of teaching if the syllabus is wholly directed by what the students demand. However, it must be stressed that peer teaching of specific techniques and skills throughout the course can do much to obviate this problem. Many of the tasks in this book are designed with this in mind.

In practice it is usually best to aim at some compromise between these two extremes of making the guidelines totally trainee-centred or totally student-centred. It is important to focus the trainees' attention on the students' needs, especially as regards level, past learning experiences and interests. You need to discuss the balance of language and skills work appropriate to the class and to what extent language needs to be revised rather than presented. However, it is also possible to reduce the difficulty of the trainees' task by not asking them to deal with tricky points of grammar, to set up elaborate multi-media activities or to devise their own material – particularly at the beginning of the course when some of them may be concentrating on getting the basic techniques under control. It should be possible to focus on those areas that trainees have some familiarity with and which, with some preparation and support, will be useful for them to tackle in class and at the same time provide enough variety to keep the students happy.

2 Who devises the TP guidelines?

Again there are various options:

The institution

Having a bank of guidelines to particular activities and materials saves work for the TP supervisor and for the trainees and ensures a certain standard in the guidelines set. In centres where a number of training courses take place, having TP guidelines organized in this way ensures that students get a varied and balanced diet if they are taught by more than one group of trainees. However, they are frequently unintegrated and can have a very disjointed effect. In addition, the system can be quite rigid – the guidelines may fit in with the training timetable if the timetable for all courses run by the institution is fixed, but it cannot pretend to address (except in a very broad way) the needs of the students or the individual needs of the trainees. This is especially so if the trainees are not encouraged to omit, supplement or modify points. Moreover, as neither the trainer nor the trainee 'own' the points there is less commitment to making them work and a greater tendency to blame the TP guidelines if things go wrong.

The overall teacher-training course tutor or director

This has the advantage that techniques, approaches, ideas, etc can more easily tie in with what trainees are learning on other parts of the course and it gives the trainer greater overall control. Depending on the number of trainees on the course this can be very time-consuming and it must be done in close liaison with the TP supervisors. Also, unless the points are made specific to a group of students, it has the disadvantage of making the students' needs secondary.

The regular teacher of the group

This is appropriate when the trainees are attached or 'apprenticed' to a particular group. It is likely that the trainee will start by teaching part of a lesson planned by the group's teacher and build up to taking over whole lessons. This can work well as long as the teacher liaises with the teacher-training course tutor so that what the trainee is being asked to do fits in with what is happening on other parts of the course.

The trainees' supervisors, when they know the group of language students being taught on TP

This has the advantage that teaching points can be tailored to the students on a day-to-day basis and so reflect the real teaching situation more closely. It also has the advantage that particular teaching skills can receive the amount of practice appropriate to the individual trainees in a group. Such an approach, however, demands supervisors with a great deal of experience and knowledge, and plenty of time. They also need to liaise closely with the course tutor to ensure that what is being asked is not too much out of phase with what is happening on other parts of the course.

The trainees

As they must eventually make the decisions about what to teach it is useful to involve them as early as possible. Group discussions about students' needs can precede suggestions as to what could be taught in the next series of lessons. The trainees, armed with a checklist (see *The aims of teaching practice* on p190) and with the help of their supervisor, can decide which areas they need to cover and how this would fit in with the students' needs and the lessons of the other trainees. This is particularly useful if TP points are based on a coursebook. Towards the end of the course the trainees alone can be responsible as a group for decisions concerning what to teach and the activities and materials used over a series of lessons. The advantages of such an arrangement are that the trainees are being trained to be independent, to work closely with colleagues, and to take responsibility for their own decisions. It approaches quite closely the real world of teaching they will soon be entering. On the other hand, as with most student-centred activities, it is much more time-consuming. It also carries more risks: trainees are much more likely to meet disaster occasionally. It is also important to check that a weak trainee is not sabotaging, albeit unwittingly, the efforts of the other members of the groups causing frustration and lowering morale.

The coursebook

This may be considered more a 'what' than a 'who' but don't forget that coursebooks are written by people! Basing the main points of the lessons on a syllabus set down by a coursebook has a number of advantages:

- It is what the majority of teachers do in real life.
- It provides a framework within which the trainees can plan lessons.
- It gives continuity and progression which is evident to the trainees and to the students.
- It makes it easy for trainees to see how their lessons link with those of other trainees.
- It saves the course tutor or supervisor having to spend a lot of time devising TP guidelines.
- A modern coursebook contains focused treatment of grammar, pronunciation and vocabulary and integrated skills work.
- It is a ready-made source of tried and tested activities and materials.
- It has accompanying materials – cassettes and student workbooks.
- It has a teacher's book which is usually invaluable in stating aims and objectives, outlining procedures and mentioning pitfalls to be wary of.

The main objections to using a coursebook are that it prevents trainees from exploring a wide range of materials, and possibly devising their own; it can make trainees too accepting of what is in the book and not questioning or creative enough; the coursebook may not suit the students' needs or fit in with the techniques the trainees need to practise. To some extent some of these objections can be overcome if the following steps are taken:

- Don't decide on a coursebook immediately. Let the trainees spend the first couple of lessons getting to know the students and their needs. Their supervisor can suggest or specify activities from a number of published sources, including coursebooks: 'getting to know you' activities, questionnaires, short tests, etc.

- Spend time with the trainees looking at a range of coursebooks that could be used with their group and guide them as to one that would be suitable.
- Make sure that the trainees approach the coursebook critically – that they read the teacher's book carefully but also do their own research into the language, that they examine exercises and texts for difficulties specific to their students (perhaps not highlighted by the book's authors) and think constantly of ways of lifting the contents of the book 'off the page' and bringing them to life by introducing their own realia and visuals. (See Chapter 4 Section 1: *Published materials* for guidance to the trainee on coursebooks.)
- Encourage the trainees to see the coursebook as a resource for creating a lesson. Discuss which parts could be omitted, which could be used and which need supplementing with activities and materials from other sources. Explore ways in which the book could be 'personalized' to suit the needs and interests of the students. (See also Chapter 4: *Using materials.*)
- Encourage the trainee (together with other trainees if they share a class) to devise a scheme of work for a series of lessons, based on the coursebook – in which the aims, learning outcomes and activities are clearly set out. (See Chapter 8: *Planning lessons.*)

Of course there is nothing to prevent you from combining one or more of these options, depending on the type of course and the stage it is at.

3 What should be included in TP guidelines?

There are many things one may identify but again it will depend on the level of the students, the stage of the course the trainees are at, whether they are using a coursebook with the students, the amount of time you can spend with trainees working out the details of the TP guidelines, etc. Generally the earlier in the course you are the more detail you give.

In the early stages of TP it is helpful for the aims of the lessons to be discussed and made clear to the trainees. As the course progresses the trainees should be able to identify and articulate the aims themselves. Lesson aims can be set out under headings such as:

Grammar: for example – to revise the regular form of the past simple and to introduce some irregular verbs.
Functions: for example – to present and practise ways of asking for directions.
Topic/vocabulary: for example – to revise and introduce a number of words associated with a bank.
Skills: for example – to practise listening for key words in a radio news bulletin.

It is very helpful to encourage the trainees to distinguish between teaching aims and intended learning outcomes. A teaching aim might be *To present and give controlled practice of ...* whereas an intended learning outcome might be *By the end of the lesson the students should be able to ...*

It is also important to differentiate aims from activities: for example, not *to do a roleplay* but *to practise making a complaint.*

Other things you may want to identify include:

- the steps required to achieve an aim (for example – **1** Arouse interest and elicit context by showing a picture; **2** Set some general gist questions; **3** Play the cassette);
- parts and timing of a lesson: for example – **a** icebreaker (5 mins); **b** reading (15 mins); **c** speaking (15 mins). (This is minimal guidance for later in the course);
- the materials and aids to be used and any reference to resource material, coursebooks, reference books, etc;
- the activity (for example – a gap fill, a matching exercise, a roleplay);
- things to watch out for in general or with these particular students (common problems for the nationality group, or difficulties particular students have had in the past).

4 How and when should guidelines be presented to trainees?

TP guidelines should be written down. Even when you and the trainees have worked out a programme together, make sure that you have an agreed set of points written out for you both to refer to before, during and after the lesson. Telling the trainees what they are to teach orally without having anything written down has severe disadvantages:

- Without anything to refer to trainees can feel insecure.
- It can lead to misunderstandings.
- Trainees can easily forget what they have been told, especially the subtleties.
- It can lead to recrimination if things go wrong *(But I'm sure I was supposed to ...!)*.

It should be clear how the lessons of different trainees or of trainees and regular group teachers fit together. Both trainees and students benefit from a timetable so that they all know where they are going. Trainees should have copies of each other's lesson guidelines.

Points should be given or agreed well in advance so there is plenty of time for preparation. You may want to adopt a procedure as follows:

1 the setting or agreeing of what is to be taught;
2 trainees prepare lesson plans;
3 lesson plans discussed with trainers and/or with other trainees;
4 trainers make any necessary re-adjustments;
5 trainees teach;
6 feedback.

If stage **4** is to be worthwhile, stage **3** must happen in sufficient time – trainers must be careful not to suggest sudden changes to lesson plans at such short notice that trainees are thrown. Such discussion is very rewarding in the early days and irons out radical problems inherent in the *preparation* of lessons as opposed to the *execution*. If possible and especially at the beginning of a course or when trainees are having to teach a new group, it is advisable to give over class time to preparation so that it can be done in conjunction with trainers.

As noted above, you and the trainees should work out a system to ensure that they are given the opportunity to cover a wide range of teaching skills (to avoid, for example, one trainee giving three presentations but no skills lessons). If they are sharing lessons they should have equal turns in beginning or ending a lesson.

3   The role of the TP supervisor

The role of the supervisor varies according to how TP is organized. In many situations the supervisor may be the teacher-training course tutor. With an apprenticeship scheme it may be the regular classroom teacher and in other situations the supervisor may be someone whose job on a course is primarily to supervise TP.

Often the supervisor must fulfil the dual roles of developer and evaluator. On some courses supervisors not only set TP points but may also give considerable help and support to trainees at the planning stage. On others the supervisor's function may be limited to the practical sessions themselves. While there are occasions when the trainees may teach unobserved, or be observed only by their peers, or recorded on video so that 'self-observation' is possible, the usual arrangement is for the supervisor to observe and give feedback on the lesson. The assessment of the supervisor may then be noted by the centre and used in the overall evaluation of the trainee's performance.

In general, try to observe the following guidelines:

- Regard yourself as a developer of the trainee's teaching skills rather than just a critic and evaluator of lessons.
- Don't show off your knowledge. Simplify what you have to say in direct relation to how experienced the trainees are.
- Give advice and ideas, but be careful not to overload trainees with more than they can handle.
- Try to see things from their point of view. They lack the knowledge and experience you have.
- Blame yourself first if things go wrong – not the trainee.
- Try to avoid doing or saying anything which undermines the trainee's confidence.
- Be aware of the damaging effect of negative criticism. Even the most confident trainee can only take so much. Most adults are not accustomed to being criticized. A training course, especially an intensive one, is stressful. Try to avoid adding to the stress. On the other hand, be honest – even if it is sometimes necessary to say difficult things. If done sensitively it is less harmful in the long run than letting a trainee think that everything is fine when it is not.

During the lesson(s):

- Show your support and confidence. Try to look relaxed and interested in what is going on.
- Be silent during the lesson. Don't talk to the other trainees or to the students.
- If the trainees are teaching a group of students don't interrupt, even if the trainee is in some difficulty. Trainees need to learn what it is to be responsible for a class and build up their confidence in their ability to conduct it. Class teachers to whom trainees are apprenticed might find it necessary to break in if they feel the trainee is doing damage to the class – but because it is so undermining of confidence interruption should be avoided if at all possible. (If trainees are practising on their colleagues, on the other hand, interruption could be justified.)
- If things go wrong, think about what you could have done to help prevent the situation. Don't undermine the trainee's confidence by showing despair or exasperation.

- Don't be too obvious a presence in the eyes of the students. If you are too friendly or chatty with the students, take the register, organize the classroom, answer their queries, the students will forever regard you as the real teacher and never feel 100 per cent confident when the trainees are teaching. The aim is for the trainees to take responsibility for everything that takes place in the classroom and for the language students to turn naturally to the trainee teachers for help.

4 Giving feedback on lessons observed

What are your aims?

As a TP supervisor you may have a number of responsibilities. For example, your assessment of the trainees' performance may count to a greater or lesser extent towards the decision as to whether they attain a pass grade for the course. However, you should remember that your first duty is not to judge the trainees but to make them self-critical and aware of how far they can affect what goes on in the classroom, so that on future occasions they are able to improve by themselves, even if a supervisor is not around. Make sure feedback is ongoing, that there is a logical development, that it is seen as contributing to improving the trainees' skills and that it encourages effective trainee self-criticism.

Making feedback effective – organization

When organizing TP feedback you may like to consider the following suggestions:
- Conduct feedback in privacy and comfort. The trainees can't talk freely about others' lessons or listen happily about their own in a public place.
- Leave yourself enough time. A rushed feedback session can be a waste of time.
- Consider the best time to conduct feedback. Usually feedback takes place immediately after teaching, before anything is forgotten. Often the trainees are anxious to know your opinion straight away and don't want to be left on tenterhooks. However, there are disadvantages in launching straight in: often the trainees are tired and tense; they can feel very raw and vulnerable, particularly if they feel things did not go very well; they don't have any time to put the lessons into perspective and to evaluate them other than on an emotional level. TP feedback conducted after a time interval can be a much more productive, rational and efficient process when tackled with fresh minds and after everyone has had a chance to gather their thoughts.
- It might be worth keeping the form and style of feedback consistent within the same institution if trainees see different supervisors.
- If separate supervisors have been observing lessons they should keep in close touch with the training course tutor or director, not only to provide consistency of approach and attitudes but so as to know what areas have been covered and to liaise about points that could be included in future input sessions.

Making feedback effective – your approach

Every supervisor develops his or her own style. You may like to consider the following suggestions and think about how they fit in with your approach:
- Focus on the aims of the lesson and whether they were achieved or not, before looking at individual techniques and how well they were done.

- Consider how the trainee had understood and used the language taught as much as the way in which it was taught.
- Consider the planning of the lesson separately from the execution (ie did any problems arise because of faulty planning, or was the planning fine but the teaching weak?).
- Be constructive and encouraging, concentrating on good things first. Also remember to include them in any final summary.
- Concentrate on the central issues rather than the detail.
- Remember that trainees will naturally forget to do things – try to distinguish between *their* mistakes and errors.
- Focus on a few things rather than try and cover everything. Don't go on too long. Be sensitive to just how much can be absorbed, particularly by trainees who have just finished teaching. This is particularly true at the beginning of TP when the trainees have so many new things to cope with.
- Ask the trainees why they chose to do particular things and look at *why* things have succeeded or failed.
- Describe rather than criticize. Describing what the trainee and the students did rather than whether you thought something was good or not helps the trainees draw their own conclusions. It is also more objective and less likely to be reacted to in a defensive way. For example:

  Supervisor: When you gave out the worksheet did you notice that Maria looked puzzled and asked Claudia what she had to do?

  Rather than –
  Supervisor: Your instructions were not very good.

  You can encourage any other observers to describe behaviour by giving them specific tasks. This has a number of advantages: you can make sure that an area the whole group needs to focus on is covered; you can use the observer's findings to pinpoint a particular aspect of the trainee's teaching – either a strength or a weakness; you can discourage unhelpful, evaluative remarks such as *I thought it was wonderful* (when it wasn't) or uninformed and sometimes very hurtful criticism.
- Elicit rather than tell. By asking real (not just rhetorical) questions you can usually get the trainees to reach a realistic assessment of the lesson by themselves. By carefully chosen questions you can focus on topics you feel need to be considered. It is also much less time-consuming than asking trainees to say what they thought in general about the lesson. For example:

  Which aspect of your/Simon's lesson do you feel showed most improvement over yesterday's?

- Give the trainees time to contribute to the discussion and be prepared to listen.
- Give the trainees a clear and honest idea as to their overall development after each observation.

Types of oral feedback

There are a number of different formats which can be used for feedback. Often certain types of feedback are more suitable at different stages in the course. Some can only be used where a group of trainees are working together and teaching the same class, some rely on observation tasks, some are better suited for giving individual feedback. Generally you will need to be more directive at the beginning of the course. However, it is much more interesting and motivating if you can vary the types of feedback – it is very easy for feedback to become predictable and almost formulaic. The following formats can be considered:

1 *You tell the trainees about the lesson*

Advantages
- It is economical in terms of time and focuses only on what you wish.
- Your views have authority and are listened to.
- It can be used at the beginning of a course before trainees are able to assess their own lessons very well.
- It is useful during an individual feedback session when you have to make sure a trainee who is having difficulties knows where he or she stands.

Disadvantages
- Trainees tend to be overconcerned with whether you think they did a good or a bad lesson and not listen to anything else.
- Trainees are not encouraged to discover for themselves and so are less well trained in being critical of themselves.
- There is a reduced sense of responsibility towards the students.

2 *You elicit comments from the trainees*

Advantages
- By eliciting from the trainee who has taught you can direct the trainee's attention towards an understanding of the strengths and weaknesses of a lesson without having to tell them – thus trainees are guided to be critical of themselves.
- It lets them justify/explain first, rather than being told something they are very well aware of.
- Key areas can be focused on.
- If you set observation tasks which they use as a basis for comment, the other trainees can contribute to each other's development.
- It aids motivation.
- You can assess the degree of awareness the trainees have and base any comments you wish to make on what they have already said.

Disadvantages
- It demands more skill and sensitivity on your part: you have to think carefully about the questions you ask.
- It can be difficult when trainees (especially observing trainees) make comments which you consider to be very wide of the mark.
- You may end up telling anyway.

3 *You chair, you invite each trainee to comment on his or her lesson, then any other trainees to comment. Finally, you sum up.*

Advantages
- There is less concern for the supervisor's view.
- There can be a greater sense of group responsibility and everyone has a chance to contribute.
- Trainees express a variety of opinions.
- You can assess the degree of awareness the trainees have.

Disadvantages
- It can take far longer.
- It can only be done where a group of trainees have observed the same lesson.
- The discussion can be very unfocused.

- The main issues tend to get obscured by the detail unless the summing-up is good.
- Unless observing trainees are given a strict brief – perhaps based on an observation task – misleading, unhelpful and sometimes hurtful comments can be made.
- It is difficult for you not to take over if you feel the trainees are not coming up with the points you think ought to be made.
- The trainees can see their discussion as just going through the motions until you give 'the answers' in the summing-up.

Comment
The trainees can take quite a bit of responsibility for eliciting feedback for their own lessons: they can set questions they want answered by the observers.

4 *A trainee chairs*

Advantages
- There is less concern for the supervisor's view.
- An even greater sense of independence is encouraged.
- The trainees are more prepared for 'real-life teaching' when they may have to rely on colleagues to provide feedback on their teaching.

Disadvantages
- Poor chairing can ruin feedback.
- Uncertainty about your role can cause the trainee to feel insecure.

5 *Structured discussion*

This can take a variety of forms:

- The trainees who taught can be paired up with trainees who observed. They spend some time agreeing on particular points (perhaps those based on an observation task). The trainees who taught can then report back to the group on their discussion of those points.
- Each trainee lists the three best points and the two worst points about a lesson, then pairs off with another trainee to compare lists and to thrash out the three best and two worst from both their lists. The pair then groups with another pair and performs the same task. This can be repeated until all the trainees agree.

Advantages
- It is good for the dynamics of the training group.
- A lot of important issues get discussed.
- It gives all the trainees a chance to contribute.

Disadvantages
- It can take a long time.
- It is possible for all the trainees to miss the point.
- The second version is only possible when more than one trainee has observed the same lesson.

6 *Free-wheeling discussion*

Advantages
- The informality can reduce the pressure and discourage talk about the teacher's 'performance'.
- Points of concern you never imagined can come up.

Disadvantages
- Lack of guidance can create insecurity and frustration.

7 *Self-criticism with comments from you*

After the lesson the trainee writes a criticism of his or her own lesson (perhaps based on agreed criteria or on a set of questions written by you during the course of the lesson). The criticism is handed in to you and then discussed. Alternatively, written comments can be added by you and the criticism returned.

Advantages

- It encourages self-awareness and independence.
- The criteria or your questions can focus the trainee's attention on important issues.
- It can save time if you want to see a number of trainees individually.
- It is particularly useful when you want to discuss a trainee's progress in private.

Disadvantages

- The trainee needs time in which to write the criticism – it is more useful when the feedback session is held the following day.
- Unless the trainees are given clear guidelines they may feel uncertain of what is required.
- It is probably not useful at the beginning of a course.

Comment

If you have access to video-making equipment the lesson can be videoed. The video can then be watched by the trainee before he or she writes the criticism and even referred to during the ensuing discussion.

8 *Feedback from students*

If you feel it appropriate you can get the trainees to elicit feedback from the students – perhaps in the form of a questionnaire or a structured discussion. Questions should probably not focus on whether the students like particular trainees but rather on the programme: Do they feel that they are getting enough grammar? Is the balance of skills work right? Is the work too easy, too difficult or just right? The results of the survey can then be discussed and future lessons considered in the light of students' comments.

Advantages

- Getting feedback from students is an important part of the teaching process. This is an opportunity to help trainees become skilled in this area.
- It gives them a greater feeling of responsibility for the class and their lessons.

Disadvantages

- It can seem very daunting for new and trainee teachers and it is difficult for them not to take adverse criticism personally.
- The students need to understand the purpose of such a session and be guided in their discussion if they are not to lose confidence in their 'teachers'.
- It can only be useful if the group of students is made up of people who have been attending consistently for a number of lessons.

Written feedback

With peer teaching, where the focus is on techniques, feedback is usually immediate and leads to the trainee having another go. Oral feedback is all that is necessary. On other occasions written feedback instead of, but usually in addition to, oral feedback is very useful.

One common practice is to use a book or pad which gives carbon copies so that both the supervisor and the trainees have a record of comments and both can look over a series of lessons. The lessons of each trainee can be documented in a separate book or, if the trainees are in a group, one book can be used for the group. At the end of the course the book can be taken apart and the relevant papers for each trainee filed separately. Some supervisors like to give all trainees in a group copies of written feedback for all lessons – their own and their colleagues'. In this case it is convenient to photocopy the feedback sheets.

What are the advantages of giving written feedback?

- Points can be made to individuals in writing which cannot easily be made in a group feedback session. It is often better to concentrate on matters of group interest in the oral feedback and leave individual comments to the written notes.
- Written feedback can reinforce points made in oral feedback – there is twice the chance that the trainee will take an important point on board.
- In written feedback the various points discussed in oral feedback can be put into perspective. Perhaps something that was discussed at length was not really the main point to be drawn from the lesson.
- A written record can be referred to by the trainee and used as a basis for future work. It may contain points that the trainee wasn't able to take on board in the rather stressful atmosphere of the oral feedback.
- For the trainer the written feedback can form an important part of the records kept on the trainees – to assess progress and, if necessary, as documentation that will contribute towards the awarding of a course grade.
- If the trainees change TP supervisors the written records are very useful to the trainer taking over.
- In the rare cases where a trainee is under a misapprehension about how well he or she has done on the course the written feedback forms can be used to back up the assessment of the TP tutor or course tutor.

Layout of notes

As with the formats for oral feedback you will have your own way of doing things. Below are some suggestions. They should not be viewed as totally different approaches: different methods may be best suited to certain situations or stages in the course and you may want to combine methods or use different methods on different occasions.

Running commentary

Take notes as soon as the trainee begins teaching, writing down a running commentary as the lesson goes on. This requires a considerable alertness and an ability to watch, listen and write at the same time but it has the advantage of giving both you and the trainee a fairly accurate reminder of what went on from minute to minute. You can also stage the comments according to the stages of the lesson, perhaps with the help of a copy of the trainee's lesson plan handed in beforehand. However, this approach, where comments are undistilled, sometimes prevents trainees from getting an overall balanced picture of the general strengths and weaknesses of a lesson and can lead to a lot of crossing out and apologies.

Considered comments

Take notes as the lesson progresses and either convert them into considered comments as the lesson draws to a close or, if feedback is to take place the following day, write them up after the session in preparation for the feedback session.

Focus on certain areas

Tell trainees or, after discussion, come to an agreement that the session is only going to concentrate on certain areas. This helps to focus attention, to remedy problems, and saves trainees from seeing reams of comments on every aspect of their lesson.

Two columns

Divide the page into two columns, one saying what was good, the other making suggestions for improvement, then at the bottom an overall comment. Usually you can't start writing immediately as you end up with too many comments. It is better to wait a few minutes for a few examples of a problem to occur before you commit it to writing. You can, of course, keep rough notes on a separate sheet.

Questions

Instead of (or in addition to) writing comments, you can write a number of questions for the trainee. These questions form the basis of the oral feedback session and replies are added at this time. You may wish to give the questions to the trainee for consideration before the oral feedback session. (See Point 7 under *Types of oral feedback* on p203.)

Alternatives

For each activity, don't comment but list as many alternative activities as you can think of to accomplish the same aims. Then give an overall comment. This helps the trainees to be more flexible and creative in their approach but can be rather discouraging if the trainees feel that their choice of activity was inferior.

Printed form

Some institutions prefer to have a printed form. The form is filled in by the supervisor and a copy is given to the trainee. The headings might be as follows:

---

1 Lesson plan and intended aims and learning outcomes
including reference to students' needs, anticipated problems, grading, staging

2 Aims and objectives achieved
What did the students learn in terms of linguistic knowledge, skills development, self-awareness, etc?

3 Knowledge of the language being taught
grammar, phonology, vocabulary

4 Classroom manner and management
rapport, effective organization of materials, technology and activities, instructions, timing, etc

5 Clear communication
presenting language, giving explanations, responding to students' questions, etc

6 Response to student performance
giving appropriate feedback, correction, etc

7 Suggestions and ideas

8 General comments
including overall progress on the course

If necessary, some headings may have sub-divisions (Stage 1, Stage 2, etc) to indicate which stage of the lesson the comment refers to.

It is sometimes better not to write your overall comments until you have discussed the lesson with the trainee as points may seem to be more or less important as a result of the discussion. Also, you may want to add a few notes to your copy *after* you have given the trainee his or her copy. These notes can comment on:

- the degree of self-awareness shown by the trainee in feedback;
- a grade for the lesson or a projected grade if one is required at the end of the course;
- anything a future supervisor or the course tutor might need to be aware of concerning the trainee.

Finally, it is important to note that these are just some of the ways in which feedback can take place. Other ways not detailed include the use of learner/trainee diaries or records that can provide a personal dialogue with a supervisor or tutor; the formalization of whole-group feedback from TP in such a way that input sessions on the course can be modified as trainees' needs become apparent; etc.

Some common difficulties encountered in TP feedback

Often difficulties can be predicted and forestalled. You can ask the trainees to read Chapter 1: *Approaching teaching practice*, follow up with a group discussion before TP begins, and remind trainees of particular points during the course. Even so, you may have to cope with one or more of the following problems:

- Trainees who seem to accept everything but who change nothing. It can help to set specific targets and get the trainees to write down one or two personal aims on future lesson plans. In feedback focus on these aims and leave the trainee in no doubt as to whether they have been achieved or not and that failure to achieve these aims means lack of progress. (See Chapter 8: *Planning lessons.*)
- Trainees who are very defensive and who often try to blame others for their own shortcomings – you and other teachers on the course, the other trainees, the students. Make it clear to trainees that, ultimately, they are responsible for their own lessons. Often teachers do not work under ideal conditions but they have to do their best in spite of difficulties.
- Trainees who undervalue their work. Some students lack confidence and may need reassurance, especially at the beginning of a course. Sometimes, however, trainees are falsely modest and start every evaluation of their lesson with wails of *Oh, it was awful!* Make it clear that you expect trainees to be realistic in their assessment and that the development of self-awareness is an important aspect of the course.
- Trainees who overvalue their work. Sometimes trainees are too easily satisfied with certain aspects of their lesson to the neglect of other crucial aspects. A common comment is *I think the students really enjoyed that!* about a lesson in which little or no learning took place. Take the trainee through the aims and intended learning outcomes of the lesson and make it clear to him or her whether they were achieved or not.
- Trainees who, towards or at the end of the course, claim that they were not told how badly they were doing. It is difficult, especially on a short course, to tread the fine line between encouraging and reassuring on the one hand and letting someone know that they are failing to meet the required standard on the other.

That is why it is crucial to give the trainees a clear and honest idea as to their overall development after each observation, preferably in writing. You may have to talk to the trainee in private or in a special tutorial. Problems can arise if the trainees change TP supervisors during the course. They often view their first supervisor as 'nicer' and 'more encouraging'. Liaison between supervisors is important so that trainees get a consistent view of their progress.

5   The recruitment of 'volunteer students'

Many teacher-training courses rely on recruiting students to take part in classes specially formed for teaching practice. It can be quite difficult to find and to keep enough students so that the 'class' resembles a real-life class. Here are some ideas you might like to consider.

Before the course

- Design attractive posters and leaflets, display them on local noticeboards and distribute them to information agencies (libraries, tourist offices, etc), local schools, colleges and universities, hospitals, hotels and restaurants.
- Make it easy for students to enquire about the course.
- If it is very difficult to recruit locally you may consider laying on transport.

At the beginning of the course

- Make it easy for the students to enrol.
- Make sure the trainees know how important it is to be welcoming.
- You may consider charging a small sum for the course – on the premise that people value more what they have to pay for. You may agree to refund the fee if students attend most classes (say 80 per cent).
- Tell the students that a register will be taken and regular attenders will receive an end-of-course certificate.
- You may consider offering additional facilities – use of a library or self-access centre, use of catering facilities, and even free refreshments.
- You can promise a free book (perhaps the coursebook being used for TP or the workbook) to those students who attend most of the classes.

During the course

- Obviously try to ensure that the lessons given by the trainees are as good as possible, without sacrificing their training to keeping the students at any cost!
- Keep emphasizing to trainees how important the teacher/student relationship is and how responsible they are for this relationship. Encourage them to talk to students before and after lessons, to enquire about absences; in short, to do everything they can to make the classes worthwhile for the students.

At the end of the course

- Arrange a party for the trainees and the students.
- Make sure the students have information about any future courses.

6 Trainer-training

It is clear that the 'job description' of a TP supervisor is a very exacting one which can include taking on the role of counsellor, negotiator, friend, support, organizer as well as assessor and developer. As a trainer you should expect to receive training, guidance and continuing support from the training centre where you work. You should also seek and receive feedback on your own performance.

Further reading

Parrott, M. 1993 *Tasks for Language Teachers* (CUP)
Wajnryb, R. 1992 *Classroom Observation Tasks* (CUP)
Wallace, M. 1991 *Training Foreign Language Teachers* (CUP)

Glossary of terms

accuracy
The ability to produce grammatically correct sentences.

acquisition
The process by which a person learns a language is sometimes called acquisition – especially if the language is 'picked up', as with a first language, rather than 'studied'.

authentic (text and task)
Authenticity refers to the degree to which language-teaching materials have the qualities of natural speech and writing. Texts which are taken from newspapers, magazines, etc and recordings of natural speech taken from radio and television programmes, etc are called authentic materials. An authentic task is one which would be done 'in real life'.

backchaining
A language-teaching technique in which the word, phrase or sentence is divided into parts, and then the students are taught to say it by repeating the last part, then the two last parts, etc, until the whole item is repeated. For example: *-tion, -ation, -ducation, education.*

CALL
Computer-assisted language learning. *CAL* stands for computer-assisted learning.

choral repetition (also chorus repetition)
When a teacher asks a whole group or class to repeat an example together.

communicative activity
An activity in which the student uses the language they have at their command to provide or elicit from other student(s) information or opinions hitherto unknown.

concept (checking, questions)
Methods the teacher uses to determine to what extent students have understood the language being taught.

context
The language that occurs before and/or after a word, a phrase or a sentence. The context often helps in understanding the particular meaning of the word or phrase. The general context can also provide a social setting for the language and is a guide to the appropriate use of words and phrases.

contraction, to contract
The reduction of a word and often its combination with another word. For example: *I am* into *I'm*, *should have* into *should've*.

controlled practice
Practice in which the teacher guides or limits the students' use of language – such as by providing questions to be answered, sentences to be completed, or words or pictures to follow.

creative practice (also known as *freer practice* or *the production stage*)
Practice in which the students use language (perhaps newly introduced items) more freely, with little or no control by the teacher. They can express their own ideas and opinions.

cued practice
Practice in which the students' language is produced in response to a cue given by the teacher. Cues can be words, signals, pictures, actions, etc. For example:
Cue   Response
time   What time is it?
day   What day is it?

deductive learning or approach
Learners are taught rules and given specific information about a language. They then apply these rules when they use the language. By contrast see *inductive learning or approach*.

drill
A technique commonly used in language teaching for practising sounds or sentence patterns in a language, based on guided repetition. See also *cued practice*.

echo
Teachers echo when they repeat language provided by students. For example:

Teacher:	What day is it today?
Student:	It's Tuesday.
Teacher:	Yes, it's Tuesday.

elicit
To bring out students' knowledge by asking questions and providing guidance towards answering questions.

ESP
English for special purposes: for business, medicine or law, for example.

extensive (usually extensive reading, sometimes extensive listening)
Reading (or listening) in quantity in order to gain a general understanding of what is read (or heard). Extensive reading, for example of fiction, is intended to develop good reading habits, to enable students to acquire vocabulary and structures and to develop pleasure in reading.

fluency
The features which give speech the qualities of being natural, including effective pausing, rhythm and intonation. The ability to produce written or spoken language with ease, to communicate effectively and smoothly, though not necessarily with perfect grammar or pronunciation. *Fluency* is sometimes contrasted with *accuracy* (see above).

freer practice
See *creative practice* above.

function
The purpose for which language is used. In language teaching functions are often described as categories of behaviour: eg requests, apologies, complaints, etc. The same function can often be expressed using different grammatical structures.

generative situation
A situation or context which naturally produces a number of examples of a particular language item or pattern.

gist
The general understanding. The term *gist reading* is sometimes used to refer to when a student reads through a text very quickly to get a general understanding. The teacher may then ask *gist questions* to check that understanding.

global (listening or reading)
Listening or reading for a general understanding of the whole text, as opposed to an understanding of the details.

grading
The arrangement of the content of a course or coursebook so that it is presented in a helpful way. Grading affects the order in which words, word meanings, tenses, structures, topics, functions, skills, etc are presented.

guided practice
Practice which takes place within a framework set up by the teacher. See also *cued practice*.

inductive learning or approach
Learners are not taught grammatical or other types of rules directly but are left to discover or induce rules from their experience of using the language. By contrast see *deductive learning or approach*.

information gap activity
A situation where information is known by only one or some of those present. Students use the language they have at their command to bridge the information gap – by asking questions, giving information, etc. This is sometimes also known as a *communication gap*. The students communicate to bridge the gap.

intensive (reading)
Unlike extensive reading, intensive reading is generally at a slower speed and may involve re-reading all or part of the text. The reader pays more attention to detail and seeks a more thorough understanding.

interaction
Two-way communication between language users.

metalanguage
The language used to analyse or describe language.

microteaching
A technique used in the training of teachers, in which individual teaching skills are practised under carefully controlled conditions. Often one trainee teacher teaches a part of a lesson to a small group of his or her classmates.

mingle activity
When students move around, speaking in pairs or groups which are constantly being formed and reformed, often in a random fashion, as at a party.

model sentence/structure
Used to describe any item/aspect of language given to the class as an example. This is also referred to as the *target language* or *structure*.

monitor
The teacher monitors when he or she listens to the students and compares what is being said with what is intended. Students can also monitor themselves, sometimes making instant corrections to utterances they have just made. The term *monitoring* is also used more loosely to refer to when the teacher checks that an activity is going according to plan, that the students are following instructions correctly, etc.

monolingual/multilingual group
In a *monolingual group* all the students share the same first language. In a *multilingual group* there are students with different first languages.

nominate
To call upon an individual student by name.

pairwork (open and closed)
In *open pairwork* two students exchange language across the classroom with the other students listening. In *closed pairwork* students talk privately in twos, with all the students in the class working simultaneously.

peer teaching
Classroom teaching in which one student (or trainee) teaches another, or others.

personalize
To make an example of language of interest to (an) individual student(s) or to fit an individual student's situation.

presentation

The introduction of new items, when their meanings are illustrated, explained, demonstrated, etc and other necessary information given.

process vs. product

Where the 'doing' of an activity is considered to be as important as or more important than the final result or end-product.

productive skill

Speaking and writing skills. Also sometimes referred to as *active skills*.

realia

Actual objects and items which are brought into a classroom as examples or as aids to be talked or written about. Examples may include such things as photographs, articles of clothing, kitchen utensils, items of food.

receptive skill

Listening and reading skills. Also sometimes referred to as *passive skills*.

scan

A reading technique used when the reader wants to find a particular piece of information without reading or understanding the whole text.

skim (skim-read)

A type of rapid reading when the reader wants to get the main idea(s) from a text.

staging a lesson

Organizing the different parts of a lesson so that they follow on logically and smoothly to make an effective whole.

structure (grammatical)

A sequence of linguistic units that are in a certain relationship to one another. For example, the structure called the *present perfect* is made up of *have* + past participle.

STT

Student talking time.

subskills (of reading or listening)

Those skills or techniques such as predicting, skimming, scanning, analysing which make up the general receptive skills of listening and reading.

syllabus

A description of the contents of a course and the order in which they are to be taught/learned.

target language/structure

See *model sentence/structure*.

text

A piece of written or spoken language.

TTT

Teacher talking time.

Index

crème
de
menthe